Nostalgia and the post-war Labour Party

Manchester University Press

Nostalgia and the post-war Labour Party

Prisoners of the past

Richard Jobson

Manchester University Press

Copyright © Richard Jobson 2018

The right of Richard Jobson to be identified as the author of this work has been asserted by them in accordance with the Copyright, Designs and Patents Act 1988.

Published by Manchester University Press
Oxford Road, Manchester M13 9PL
www.manchesteruniversitypress.co.uk

British Library Cataloguing-in-Publication Data
A catalogue record for this book is available from the British Library

ISBN 978 1 5261 1330 6 hardback
ISBN 978 1 5261 1331 3 paperback

First published 2018
Paperback published 2021

The publisher has no responsibility for the persistence or accuracy of URLs for any external or third-party internet websites referred to in this book, and does not guarantee that any content on such websites is, or will remain, accurate or appropriate.

Typeset in Sabon and Gill
by Deanta Global Publishing Services,
Chennai, India

Contents

Acknowledgements	vii
Introduction	1
1 Revisionism and the battle over Clause IV, 1951–63	30
2 'White heat' and the Labour Party, 1963–70	60
3 Labour's Alternative Economic Strategy, 1970–83	85
4 Reinventing the Labour Party, 1983–92	109
5 The New Labour era, 1992–2010	134
6 Back to the past? Labour's return to opposition, 2010 to the present	157
Conclusion	185
Select bibliography	194
Index	209

Acknowledgements

Firstly, my thanks go to Hugh Pemberton and Mark Wickham-Jones. Their advice and insightful comments have been invaluable. I owe them both a tremendous debt of gratitude. As well as their excellent supervisory skills, they have been immeasurably supportive and helpful throughout the researching and writing of this book. I am also very grateful to David Thackeray and Richard Toye at the University of Exeter for their encouragement and support during the final writing stages. James Cronin and James Thompson provided some very good advice that enabled me to begin reworking and extending my research into a book suitable for publication.

There are a number of people who have discussed, commented on and displayed an interest in the contents of this book and whose opinions and expertise have been extremely welcome. As I am sure is usually the case, there have been too many discussions over coffee to mention. However, I would especially like to thank Clive Abbott, Dean Blackburn, David Drew, Nora Mulready, Luke Place and Reshima Sharma. I am also very appreciative of the way in which colleagues and students at the University of Bristol and the University of Oxford have helped to shape and refine my ideas.

The team at Manchester University Press have been very helpful throughout the publication process. I would like to thank the anonymous peer reviewers who commented on both my initial book proposal and the final draft. My gratitude goes to the Arts and Humanities Research Council for their funding during my studies: their financial contribution facilitated this research. Published material and excerpts from previous journal articles on the subject of Labour and nostalgia are reproduced in this book with the kind permission of *British Politics*, *Contemporary British History*, the *Journal of Policy History* and *Renewal*. In all previous publications, the suggestions made by peer reviewers have enabled me to develop my thoughts and arguments. I also want to thank the excellent assistance and expertise provided by archivists at the Churchill Archives Centre at the University of Cambridge, the Labour History Archive in Manchester, the archive at the London School of Economics, the Modern Records Centre at the University of Warwick and The National Archives in London (where I accessed the temporarily relocated Gaitskell Papers).

The initial conceptualisation of the central idea that informs this book was made away from the academic world and, because of this, I thank my friends and former colleagues amongst the weavers, warpers, dyers and finishers who worked at the textile mill in my village for their inspiration and encouragement. I hope that this work reflects the influence that they had on me at a particularly formative stage of my life.

Finally, I would like to thank my family. This book has only been made possible by their support throughout the years.

Introduction

Having secured a decisive mandate from the party's internal electorate, Jeremy Corbyn delivered his first annual conference speech as Labour Party leader in Brighton on 29 September 2015. With its slightly tentative delivery and meandering structure, Corbyn's speech was met with a lukewarm reaction from the political commentators and journalists who were covering the event for the national media. It was received rather more rapturously by party members within the conference hall. One section of the speech seemed to resonate in particular. Keir Hardie, a former coal miner and one of the founding figures of the Labour Party, died on 26 September 1915. Speaking three days after the centenary anniversary of Hardie's death, the new leader of the Labour Party sought to pay homage to this historic figure's memory. At the climactic end of his speech, Corbyn proclaimed:

> We owe him [Hardie] and so many so much more. And he was asked once, summarise what you are about, summarise what you really mean in your life. And he thought for a moment and he said this: 'My work has consisted of trying to stir up a divine discontent with wrong.' Don't accept injustice, stand up against prejudice.[1]

Writing in *The Times*, Philip Collins, Tony Blair's former speech writer, noted the effectiveness of this specific passage of Corbyn's speech but criticised the speech for being 'almost all past and party'.[2]

When placed in the immediate context of the rise of 'Corbynism', this speech's historically orientated nature and its emphasis on the party's past were not anomalous. In many ways, Corbyn's 2015 leadership campaign had been framed around a perceived need to recapture Labour's historic principles and mission. On the campaign trail at the Durham Miners' Gala in July, Corbyn recalled the struggles and sacrifices of the Labour

Party's industrial working-class past.[3] Eight days later at the Tolpuddle Martyrs' Festival in Dorset, he urged the labour movement to 'remember where we come from. Our cultural roots, our cultural heritage, our cultural expression ... Let's lift our sights up. Lift our spirits up. Lift our hopes up for a decent, better world. That's what our forebears fought for. That is what we proudly campaigned for.'[4] Speaking on the *Andrew Marr Show* on the BBC one week after his Tolpuddle appearance, Corbyn outlined his leadership campaign's overarching strategy: 'what we are doing here is putting forward a view that the Labour Party has to offer a credible alternative that is true to the roots of the Labour Party'.[5] In policy terms, Corbyn often appeared to advocate reinstating visions of the past in the present. At one point during the campaign, Corbyn indicated that, if successful, he would seek to reinstate Clause IV of the party's 1918 constitution.[6] At another point, when speaking to the BBC, he made a verbal pledge to reopen some of Britain's closed coal mines.[7]

When located in their recent historical context, such public venerations of the party's past were, perhaps, rather surprising. During Labour's period in government between 1997 and 2010, it had widely been believed that, under 'New Labour', the party had been substantially reoriented away from the past and towards the future. Writing in 2002, Peter Mandelson proclaimed that Tony Blair and his supporters had 'turned Labour into the party of the "modern" and the "future"'.[8] In 2006, in his final annual conference speech as party leader, Blair noted that 'Values unrelated to modern reality are not just electorally hopeless, the values themselves become devalued ... Our courage in changing gave the British people the courage to change. That's how we won.'[9] Looking back on his time as party leader, Blair believed that New Labour had held 'a basic belief – recovering Labour values from outdated tradition and dogma and reconnecting the party to the modern world'.[10] In September 2015, it appeared that Labour's attachment to the past had proven itself to be rather more resilient than the leading figures within the New Labour project had hoped, foreseen and, indeed, later believed.

New Labour's critique of Old Labour

Various explanations have been given for New Labour's hostility towards the party's past. Academics have tended to stress the strategic nature of the way in which New Labour positioned itself in a temporal sense. James Cronin has argued that members of the New Labour project 'gained a rhetorical edge over their opponents within the party by portraying themselves as modern, their critics as backward-looking'.[11] Eric Shaw has suggested that attacks on 'Old Labour' played a role in the rebranding of the party: once the name 'New Labour' had been chosen, in order 'To maximise the public impact of the new name, the contrast with the old had to be as stark as possible'.[12] Yet the distinctions that New Labour made between 'Old' and 'New' Labour were not simply the product of either strategic opportunism or the need to reinvigorate an ailing brand name. They often originated from a genuinely held belief that British society had changed and Labour had not.

More specifically, New Labour argued that Old Labour had been a fundamentally nostalgic party. This idea was often ill-defined, underdeveloped and lacked any real analytical depth. To a certain extent, it offered a mechanism by which New Labour could signal to the electorate that it had made a distinct break from the party's past.[13] However, it also originated from the notion that, in the past, nostalgia had impacted on the party's development in a negative manner. From its inception, New Labour targeted and attempted to overturn the nostalgic attachment to the past that it believed existed within the party. During his first speech as leader of the Labour Party in 1994, Blair declared that 'Parties that do not change die, and this party is a living movement not an historical monument.'[14] Labour's 1996 draft manifesto proclaimed that 'There is no place in serious politics for nostalgia.'[15]

Tony Blair frequently attacked nostalgia in his speeches, interviews and articles.[16] In 1996, in an interview with *The Times*, Blair dismissed the idea of 'a lurch into nostalgia'.[17] Observers noted that Blair seemed 'refreshingly nostalgia-free'.[18] In 1995, Blair's attempt to reform Clause IV of the party's 1918 constitution was widely understood to represent an attack on Labour's nostalgia. One journalist declared that Blair and his advisors realised that the battle against Clause IV represented 'a battle against one of the most powerful forces in the party – its nostalgia'.[19] Another newspaper article described how Blair knew that 'If he wins [the battle over Clause IV], he can present his victory before the voters as evidence that Labour is no longer beholden to its own nostalgia.'[20] Jonathan Powell, who became Blair's Chief of Staff in 1994, would later describe how the rewording of Clause IV had committed Labour to a new agenda 'rather than to some shibboleth of the past'.[21]

New Labour argued that Old Labour had held a traditional industrial working-class identity that had become outdated during the postwar era. It suggested that, since the 1950s, structural changes in the British economy had rendered the traditional industrial working class less numerous, less representative of the population as a whole and less politically significant.[22] Blair acknowledged that Labour had been born out of Britain's traditional industrial trade unions but he also noted that 'As the class contours of society changed, however, this has meant that the party has struggled against a perception that it had too narrow a base in its membership, finance and decision-making.'[23] Looking back on the pre-New Labour era in his autobiography, Blair talked about how the party's traditional industrial working-class identity had contributed to the fact that 'There was something irretrievably old-fashioned about the meetings, the rules, the culture' of the Labour Party.[24] According to the New Labour pollster, Philip Gould, the party's attachment to a bygone industrial era had meant that it 'had failed to understand that the old working class was becoming a new middle class'.[25] Gould outlined how Labour had 'lost the last century because it failed to modernise, and lost connection with the people it was founded to represent. It was a party trapped by its past, even at the moment of its birth.'[26]

One of the prevailing assumptions in the historiography of the Labour Party is that the party's political development has been shaped by modernity (see the following 'Historical Approaches to the Labour Party' section for more detail). In contrast, this book represents an investigation into the impact that nostalgia has had on Labour's political development since 1951. Chapters 1 to 4 assess the validity of New Labour's claims that nostalgia shaped the trajectory of the post-war Labour Party. They examine the extent to which nostalgia for a heroic male traditional industrial working class proved problematic when coupled with the social and economic developments that took place in post-war Britain. Thereafter, by assessing the period in which Blair and his allies gained control of the party, Chapter 5 aims to provide a more critical and nuanced examination of New Labour's relationship with nostalgia than a superficial acceptance of their anti-nostalgic proclamations allows. In order to provide an analysis of the present state of the party, Chapter 6 interrogates Labour's continued relationship with nostalgia in the post-New Labour era.

What is nostalgia?

The word 'nostalgia' is derived from the Greek words 'nostos', which means 'to return home', and 'algia', which means 'a painful feeling'.[27] It was this same painful feeling or longing for a return home that led Swiss doctors in the late seventeenth century to believe that nostalgia was a mental affliction or illness that could be found amongst people displaced from their homelands.[28] Over three centuries have passed, but the negative association of the word 'nostalgia' with emotional weakness is one that still remains largely intact. Individuals who are deemed guilty of nostalgic tendencies are stereotypically portrayed as living in the past or as sentimental reactionaries fighting the inevitable tide of modernity. Academics have declared that nostalgia is a type of memory that is particularly dependent on a heightened sensitivity to the passing of time and has therefore been augmented by the increased pace of modern society.[29] In part, this belief has been reinforced by the recent growth in the number of museums, monuments and sites of perceived historical significance, combined with what almost amounts to a culture of instantaneous commemoration.[30]

Despite our growing awareness of nostalgia as a powerful cultural force with the ability to shape modern society, the degree to which nostalgia provides social, political and economic guidance for identifiable groups and, thus, political parties has largely been neglected. Memory has been installed as 'the word most commonly paired with history'.[31] Yet the concept of nostalgia itself, its role within collective memory and identity and its relationship with power and power structures all remain under-analysed within the academic fields of political science and political history.

Nostalgia, identity and 'nostalgia-identity'

Nostalgia, in its simplest sense, is idealised positive memory and nostalgic sentiments represent positively charged visions of the past. Marianne Hirsch and Leo Spitzer have argued that nostalgia, as a positive form of memory, is created in the process of 'splitting' bad memories, such as traumatic experiences, from good memories.[32] However, a negative understanding of the past can also be reformed to gain positive or nostalgic meaning. Whilst the British collectively remember the horrors of the blitz during the Second World War, such memories have also been reworked into a broader nostalgic conceptualisation of the past that celebrates national strength and unity in the face of adversity.[33] In this way, nostalgia can be formed within a wider process that serves to reform, devalue or indeed to forget, the negative memories that surround individuals or groups, a time-period, an event or a location. More broadly, a discursive emphasis on the past can generate the mnemonic climate in which nostalgia can flourish.

The process by which we imbue certain memories with positive significance is interlinked with the identity or identities that we hold in the present. An individual's identity determines the way in which that person views and interprets him or herself within society.[34] Individual identities both influence and are influenced by the other identities that exist around them. They contribute to the form that collective identities take and, in turn, are shaped by the collective identities which they inhabit. This leads to a striking level of similarity in understandings and interpretations of the past within certain groups. Whilst an English football supporter might interpret the memory of the 1966 World Cup final in an entirely positive manner, a German football supporter probably would not. Such similarities allow us to talk of collective memory. As Wulf Kansteiner has argued, 'Collective memories originate from shared communications [in the present] about the meaning of the past.'[35] To take one example, this concept allows us to understand why the British might still reflectively understand the stories of the Great War as a 'compelling part, of our own buried lives' and interpret memories that are not the product of personal experience through the lens of a national collective identity.[36]

However, the idea that collective identities shape collective memories is, in a sense, only one half of the story. As Raphael Samuel once noted, 'memory, so far from being merely a passive receptacle or storage system, an image bank of the past, is rather an active, shaping force that is dynamic.'[37] In other words, collective memories also shape collective identities. As 'our experience of the present very largely depends upon our knowledge of the past,' the memories that a specific group holds are shaped by the collective identity that is assumed in the present.[38] This means that the relationship between collective identity and collective memory is best understood as a reciprocal two-way process. As Barbara Misztal has succinctly summarised, 'memory and identity depend upon each other since not only is identity rooted in memory but also what is remembered is defined by the assumed identity.'[39] Memory and identity are symbiotically reliant and neither could exist or gather emotional coherence without the other. Thus, the concept of 'memory-identity' – the idea that the relationship between memory and identity is a symbiotic process – has been used by memory theorists to provide theoretical clarity.[40]

The idea of 'memory-identity' can be extended to incorporate the concept of 'nostalgia-identity'. Group nostalgia-identities are characterised by a dynamic two-way relationship between identity and nostalgia. Whilst positive idealised memories of Thatcher's Britain might inform the identity of many in the Conservative Party today, simultaneously, their political identity as Conservatives might imbue memories of her time in power with nostalgic meaning. In short, nostalgia matters because nostalgia-identities determine how groups understand themselves and their past. Subsequently, these understandings influence the way in which groups interact with society. This concept of the group nostalgia-identity also explains why, as Tim Strangleman has highlighted, personal experience is no prerequisite to the formation of nostalgia and individuals can hold nostalgic memories that are detached from the reality of their actual 'lived' experiences.[41]

Academics have suggested that group memories and identities are inherently unstable.[42] This particular understanding of memory has its origins in the idea that 'The past is not fixed, but is subject to change: both narratives of events and the meanings given to them are in a constant state of transformation.'[43] Notions of instability and transformation have informed the conclusions of a number of studies on nostalgia. In particular, Paul Cooke ended his work on 'Ostalgie' in the former East Germany by suggesting that nostalgia for the German Democratic Republic's way of life is in decline and seems 'to be going the way of all crazes as its impact lessens'.[44] Similarly, other academics have suggested that nostalgic sentiment has also increased in periods of rapid transformation as a pessimistic resistance to change.[45]

Yet collective memories and collective identities can also be characterised by continuity over time.[46] Kansteiner has described how 'Most groups settle temporarily on such collective memories and reproduce them for years and decades until they are questioned and perhaps overturned, often in the wake of generational turn-over.'[47] This mnemonic continuity is often the product of a relatively stable group identity. Furthermore, although a group nostalgia-identity might either express or manifest itself in different ways over time, variations in expression and manifestation do not mean that the core idealisations at the heart of the nostalgia-identity have been fundamentally altered. The long-term continuity of a group nostalgia-identity is dependent on the relative generational stability of a collective identity, the passing down of nostalgic memories from generation to generation and the ability of a nostalgia-identity to adapt to, incorporate or repel contestations.

Variants of nostalgia

Much of the concern surrounding the use of nostalgia as a tool for historical and political analysis originates from the perception that nostalgia is a highly elusive and slippery concept. This perception has been reinforced by the fact that studies of nostalgia have, on the whole, made little or no attempt to either define or isolate particular types, strands or variants of nostalgia. Nevertheless, the distinction that Svetlana Boym made between 'reflective' and 'restorative' nostalgia offers a useful theoretical starting point. On the one hand, Boym argued that 'reflective' nostalgia 'thrives in *algia*, the longing [for the past] itself, and delays the homecoming – wistfully, ironically, desperately'. More specifically, she suggested that 'reflective' nostalgia is characterised by a pragmatic understanding that the past can but never should be recreated.[48] If we apply Boym's definition of 'reflective' nostalgia to sentiments that we often hear expressed in society, then one example would be the coupling of the view that 'things were better back then' with the immediate qualification that 'but times have changed'. In order to conform to Boym's definition, this particular expression of an idealised vision of the past must also be supported by the acknowledgement that 'times have changed' irreversibly.

On the other hand, Boym argued that 'restorative' nostalgia 'attempts a transhistorical reconstruction of the lost home' or, put simply, seeks the reinstatement of a particular vision of the past in the present.[49] In this way, she suggested that restorative nostalgia is characterised by an intention to shape social, cultural, economic or political development. One example of 'restorative' cultural nostalgia that adheres to Boym's definition would be the Gothic Revival in architecture in Britain during the nineteenth and twentieth centuries.[50] Essentially, Boym's division of nostalgia into 'restorative' and 'reflective' forms allowed her to make normative judgements regarding what she believed was harmless, almost inconsequential, reflective nostalgia and naïve and foolhardy restorative nostalgia. Indeed, Boym's separation of 'reflective' and 'restorative' nostalgia was driven by her personal belief that 'The dreams of imagined homelands cannot and should not come to life.'[51] She argued that 'Sometimes it's preferable ... to leave dreams alone, let them be no more and no less than dreams, not guidelines for the future.'[52]

Boym's attempts to separate 'reflective' and 'restorative' nostalgia have been criticised by Aaron Santesso who, in a study on eighteenth-century poetry, questioned the value of differentiating between 'reflective' and 'restorative' nostalgia and declared that such distinctions complicate our understanding.[53] Santesso argued that 'idealisation' is the central and only necessary component of nostalgia. He was correct in so far as both 'reflective' and 'restorative' nostalgia require the idealisation of the past and, because of this, Boym's definition offers something of a false dichotomy between reflective and restorative nostalgia. All nostalgia is 'reflective' – though it does not always exhibit the degree of self-awareness that Boym suggested – and is characterised by the act of looking back upon an idealised vision of the past; but not all nostalgia is 'restorative'. It is possible to declare 'things were better back then' without necessarily seeking the reinstatement of that particular idealised vision of the past in the present. However, it is not possible to attempt to reinstate an idealised vision of the past without the initial idealised understanding that 'things were better back then.' As Boym also acknowledged, reflective nostalgia can still shape current actions by both informing ideals and by shaping our understanding of the present.[54] Thus it is important not to see reflective nostalgia as being merely passive. The relationship between reflective idealised visions of the past and restorative impulses is fluid and complex. To gain a better understanding of how nostalgia shapes developments in the present, we must look at its relationship with power and the way that it can be manipulated for instrumental purposes.

Power and instrumental nostalgia

Central to any discussion of how nostalgia might become 'restorative' or characterised by an intention to shape social, cultural, economic or political development is the notion of power. Power operates in any pluralist system in ways that are not always immediately apparent or visible.[55] In his study of 'invented traditions' during the period from 1870 to 1914, Eric Hobsbawm showed how power elites manipulated a popular understanding of the past in order that it could be used as the 'cement of group cohesion'.[56] Ultimately, Hobsbawm depicted a world in which, through a process of ritualisation and constant repetition, collective memories and identities were shaped and moulded by power elites, so that support could be gained for political agenda, regimes and nation-states.[57] In a similar manner, Peter Novick's work on the Holocaust argued that the collective memory and identity of Jewish Americans were reformed in the 1960s and 1970s by Jewish American leaders as a consequence of both the rise of 'identity politics' in the United States and the desire of the same Jewish Americans to assert an ethnic group identity that had a particular moral claim on society, given its experience during the Holocaust.[58] Power elites therefore contributed to shaping the way in which the Holocaust itself was actually remembered.

However, Novick perhaps undervalued the two-way process of interaction and negotiation that occurs between those with and those without power in any group or collective.[59] Whilst a collective understanding of the past might be shaped by power elites as Novick suggests, those same power elites might be unknowingly affected by the collective understanding of the past that characterises the group to which they belong. Furthermore, this collective understanding of the past might define the parameters within which power elites can operate; for example, if the Jewish American leaders that Novick talked about had suddenly begun to diminish the significance of the Holocaust, then they would have been shunned and more than likely rejected by the collective to which they belonged. It follows that collective nostalgia, as a form of collective memory, operates in a similar way within the same complex power relationships that exist within groups.

Tim Strangleman has argued that nostalgia has to be understood as a concept 'actively used at both the managerial and political levels' by those in charge of developing the British railway system in order to gain consensus for change or inaction.[60] Strangleman repeatedly emphasised his idea that power elites manipulate nostalgia to achieve political goals.[61] In his study, they do this in a way that can best be described as instrumental. In this way, nostalgia can be used instrumentally to persuade, placate or influence an audience. The success of instrumental nostalgia is dependent on the degree to which the nostalgia being deployed by the actor resonates within the collective or group that the actor is trying to communicate with. Power elites can also shape and nurture group nostalgia-identities through an instrumental use of nostalgia and this might provide fertile ground for the implementation of policies that can be defined in nostalgic terms at a later date. In such a manner, instrumental nostalgia can serve to bind people together by strengthening the bonds of the collective nostalgia-identity that unites them.

Strangleman also touched upon, though did not develop, the notion that politicians like John Major actually felt genuine personal nostalgia for the railways and that this shaped their political discourse.[62] In a sense, by highlighting examples of instrumental nostalgic manipulation, his study undervalued the role of the spontaneous nostalgic impulse, or the heartfelt expression of a group nostalgia-identity. Power elites and non-power elites alike can spontaneously express nostalgic sentiments publicly that are characteristic of the nostalgia-identity of the group to which they belong. Primarily, this occurs because these power elites have often grown up and existed under the influence of the same nostalgia-identity that shapes both them and their followers; for example, a leader in the trade union movement is likely to have a fairly similar nostalgic understanding of the past as he did when he was a rank-and-file trade unionist.[63] Thus, the leader remains, at least at a basic level, conditioned by the same group nostalgia-identity as his or her followers.

Indeed, there is a danger that we assume that the relationship between power and collective nostalgia is entirely top-down and that we assign spontaneous nostalgia to the masses and the use of instrumental nostalgia to power elites. Stuart Tannock has suggested that the 'return to the past to read a historical continuity of struggle, identity and community, [and] this determination to comb the past for every sense of possibility and destiny it might contain ... is a resource and strategy central to the struggles of all subaltern cultural and social groups.'[64] Tannock believed that subaltern groups interpret their own collective memory and identity in a manner that gives rise to a desire to pursue actively their own restorative nostalgic impulses. Yet, even within subaltern cultural and social groups, power relations may impact on the form that the articulation of a nostalgia-identity might take. One only has to look at the way in which white male skilled industrial workers have determined the discourse of the British labour movement during the twentieth century to see that certain groups can develop power over others within their subaltern collective groups.⁶⁵

Furthermore, it is not only power elites who deploy nostalgia instrumentally. A delegate at a conference might use nostalgia to persuade, placate or influence an audience or legitimise an argument in just the same way as a member of the executive committee might do so. Nevertheless, because of the top-down nature of politics, the activation of the impulse to restore the past in the present within any collective group relies, at some point, on its acceptance by those with influence. In this way, the process by which reflective nostalgia becomes restorative can be intrinsically linked with the notion of power.

Manifestations of nostalgia

Group nostalgia-identities manifest themselves in a number of forms. Nostalgia can present itself in discourse and rhetoric, visual representations and symbols, traditions and rituals, and rules and norms. It is often at its most apparent when it is used in popular political discourse in either a rhetorical or an oratorical form. In order to gain consensus from collective groups and to obtain political legitimacy, political discourse and rhetoric need to resonate with the nostalgia-identity of the group that the speaker is seeking to influence. As Hobsbawm's study showed, 'the most successful examples of manipulation are those which exploit practices which clearly meet a felt – not necessarily a clearly understood – need among particular bodies of people.'⁶⁶

Politicians will often knowingly speak to the nostalgia-identity of the group that they wish to persuade. The ability of a politician to elicit a positive reaction is not so much dependent on individual rhetorical or linguistic style as it is on touching the emotional historically orientated identity of the particular group that is being addressed.⁶⁷ Strangleman has shown that rhetoric that has centred on a perceived 'golden age' of the railways in Britain has been a particularly effective tool for nostalgic manipulation.⁶⁸ Nostalgia can also be deployed by a politician in the classic rhetorical form of 'us' against them when 'us' is used in a historical sense to generate, nurture or manipulate a positive emotional response to the past that plays to the collective nostalgia-identity.⁶⁹ Of equal importance to the manipulation of nostalgia for political purposes is the way that nostalgia-identities can subconsciously shape discourse and rhetoric. Due to the pervasiveness of his or her nostalgia-identity, a speaker might casually talk nostalgically about the past in a spontaneous and expressive manner without recognising that they are doing so. It is also worth stating at this point that, as 'political struggles have always been partly struggles over the dominant language', so too the discursive nature of a nostalgia-identity can be contested by opposing discourses.[70]

Visual representations and symbols can be nostalgic if they elicit a positively charged emotional response to the past. Their ability to produce such a response depends largely upon the collective group to which the viewer belongs. In such a manner, visual representations or symbols are only nostalgic if they are interpreted in an overtly sentimentalised manner by the viewer. In a similar manner to discourse, visual representations can simultaneously be the product and the manipulator of a collective nostalgia-identity. One only has to look at the continued reinvention of the image of Lord Kitchener and the slogan 'Your Country Needs You' to see how a collective British nostalgia-identity has been manipulated to gain popular support for events, brands and advertising campaigns.[71] Yet the continued success of this particular image relies, for the most part, on a nostalgic attachment to historic national strength in the face of adversity and past military victories. Its resilience as a visual tool for nostalgic manipulation is therefore dependent upon its popular acceptance within the British nostalgia-identity.

Hobsbawm defines 'invented traditions' as 'responses to novel situations which take the form of reference to old situations, or which establish their own past by quasi-obligatory repetition.'[72] However, the ability of a collective group or institution to accept this 'form of reference to old situations' is often dependent on these 'old situations' being interpreted in a nostalgic manner. Nostalgia can be built into norms and patterns of behaviour. Traditions and 'quasi-obligatory' rituals can be intertwined with collective nostalgia-identities. Thus the repeated ritualistic singing of a national anthem before a sporting event might be aided by the nostalgic nature of the national anthem itself. The Scottish national anthem 'Flower of Scotland' nostalgically recalls a past military victory against the English that is integral to the Scottish nostalgia-identity today.[73] Yet, if we take the example of 'Flower of Scotland', we can see how nostalgia that is expressed in its verses gathers greater sentimental meaning when Scotland play England at sport compared to matches against other nations. Thus, when we talk about nostalgic traditions and rituals, we must not make the assumption that the emotional significance of these 'quasi-obligatory repetitions' always remains static and unchanged.[74]

When compared to its manifestation within discourse, visual representations and traditions, nostalgia's relationship to established rules or norms is not always immediately obvious. Nevertheless, they are equally vital to our understanding of collective nostalgia-identities. Nostalgia-identities can both influence and be influenced by 'rules' and 'norms'. The trade union movement's tacitly accepted rule 'never cross a picket line' might partially be the product of a sentimental nostalgic attachment to past examples of industrial solidarity that have been passed down from generation to generation.[75] Group nostalgia-identities simultaneously affect the implied form of the rules, condition normative behavioural responses to events in the present and perpetuate a nostalgic understanding of the past. In this way, rules and norms both define and are defined by collective nostalgia-identities.

Historical approaches to the Labour Party

There has been a dominant strand in the historiography of the Labour Party that has been shaped by a teleological understanding of the party's development.[76] This understanding has been characterised by the idea that Labour has tended to act in a logical and functional manner. It has explained the party's development by the purpose that it has served rather than by underlying factors and causes. In this manner, it has often been implied that Labour's political development has been purpose-driven and that it has responded to historical developments in an instrumental, rational and calculated way. This strand of historical interpretation has tended to emphasise the roles that power, policy, theory and strategic goals and objectives have played in determining the party's trajectory.

At the same time, there has been a less dominant but increasingly influential strand in the literature that has suggested that the party's political development has been shaped by factors that have not always been immediately obvious to onlookers.[77] This strand has emphasised the role of tradition, rules, norms and ethos. This interpretation of Labour's political history has often depicted the party as lacking a well-defined, coherent and logical purpose. In this strand of thought, Labour's trajectory has been shaped less by a purpose-driven desire to obtain political goals and more by the often illogical and irrational nature of its own unique identity, beliefs and attachments.

A traditional party

Writing in the late 1920s, Egon Wertheimer, a German journalist and political scientist, believed that the Labour Party's British identity set it apart from its continental counterparts.[78] For Wertheimer, the British trade unions, in which Labour had its origins, typified the conservative nature of the party. They remained resistant to Marxist ideology, suspicious of change and attached to a form of apolitical craft-unionism.[79] According to Wertheimer, this lack of ideology meant that an intense sense of 'Britishness' was able to permeate the labour movement and determine its political direction.[80] When he compared Labour to its continental counterparts, he found it to be a conservative party that lacked a well-defined theoretical and ideological basis.[81] Thus, in Wertheimer's analysis, it was the party's innate conservatism rather than a purpose-driven desire to achieve political and ideological goals that shaped Labour's political trajectory.

Wertheimer believed that Labour's lack of a distinct political ideology afforded a great deal of inclusivity and meant that the party was 'more able to absorb people who are outside the immediate framework of the working class'.[82] He suggested that, when compared to other socialist groups and parties abroad, its conservative national identity enabled the type of group coherence that held the party's membership together. Moreover, Wertheimer outlined how this shared identity allowed the party to accommodate intraparty divisions and disputes. He noted that the 'composition of the Labour Party was of such heterogeneous character that an unusual measure of personal liberty was both offered to and exercised by its members.'[83] Wertheimer also implied that this identity was informed by an attachment to the past. In particular, he described the belief held by party members that 'the political genius of the British nation, which has been proved in innumerable past emergencies, will again find the right improvisation at the right moment.'[84]

Wertheimer did not elaborate on this idea in any more detail. Nevertheless, the belief in the supremacy of British tradition and history that he depicted was seemingly influenced by an overtly sentimental attachment to a bygone era.[85] The identity that he described was one that was acutely informed by a specific historical understanding of itself and one that largely prioritised positive memories (particularly of the British Empire) over negative memories. Therefore, according to Wertheimer, the Labour Party was from the outset a collective body whose identity was determined as much by a positively charged sentimental attachment to the past as by an ideological commitment to the present. In many ways, his study was a forerunner of the strand within the historiography of the Labour Party that would downplay the significance of power, policy and theory and would emphasise the role that emotional and less logical factors have played in shaping the party's identity and, in turn, its political trajectory.

Purpose and power

Writing over thirty years after Wertheimer, Robert McKenzie offered a distinctly teleological interpretation of Labour's historical development.

He argued that the party's central purpose had been to obtain parliamentary power and he described how the desire to achieve this goal had shaped both the party's political form and its commitments. McKenzie believed that the 'primary function' of the Labour Party's membership was 'to try to secure an electoral majority for its parliamentary party'.[86] He declared that the parliamentary system necessitated that, when in government, power must operate in a top-down manner and he described how Labour's membership would invariably accept this whenever the party was elected to govern.[87] McKenzie stated that, in this situation, political power rested with the Labour Party's leadership and he suggested that 'the PLP's [Parliamentary Labour Party's] "democratic" practices are jettisoned when Labour assumes office because the party considers them to be incompatible with the cabinet system as it has evolved in this country.'[88]

Similarly, the Marxist historian Ralph Miliband focused on the party's perceived attachment to the obtainment of parliamentary power and he described Labour as 'a party of modest social reform in a capitalist system within whose confines it is ever more firmly and by now irrevocably rooted'.[89] He declared that 'the leaders of the Labour Party have always rejected any kind of political action (such as industrial action for political purposes) which fell, or which appeared to them to fall, outside the framework and conventions of the parliamentary system.'[90] Above all, Miliband argued that 'The Labour Party has not only been a parliamentary party; it has been a party deeply imbued by parliamentarianism.'[91] In this way, in both McKenzie and Miliband's analyses, Labour's form and trajectory had been shaped by the purpose it had served as a parliamentary party. Their descriptions of Labour were overtly teleological: both McKenzie and Miliband believed that the party's political development had been profoundly influenced by its role in the British political system. Unlike in Wertheimer's account, there was little sense that Labour might have been either in thrall of an emotional historically orientated identity or shaped by a collective understanding of the past.

In the same way, more recently, Leo Panitch and Colin Leys have argued that Labour's leadership 'were more committed to the centralised and elitist state than to socialism' and they suggested that this commitment meant that the party's political elites were able to repel the advance of the radical New Left in the 1970s and early 1980s.[92] They discussed 'the frustrations and the costs associated with advancing radical democratic socialist goals while parliamentary paternalism remained dominant in the party'.[93] Panitch and Leys concluded their study by suggesting that Labour's attachment to its own parliamentary purpose was resilient, that it had ultimately led to the 'parliamentary capitalism' of New Labour and that socialists should try to find other ways to achieve their aims and objectives.[94]

Class and ideology

In his book *Modern British Politics*, Samuel Beer stated that Labour's political development had been shaped increasingly both by its identity as a working class party and by its distinct collectivist ideology. He suggested that 'Labour's class image of politics, as well as its Collectivist view of policy, made it a distinctive type of political formation.'[95] Beer argued that from the outset it was acknowledged that 'If the party was to pursue power independently, it needed a set of beliefs and values distinguishing it from other parties.'[96] When compared to its British political counterparts, he noted that Labour had historically held a distinct class identity and had, after its break with Liberalism, pursued different ideological goals.[97] Specifically, Beer argued that the Labour Party, after the First World War, had adopted this 'class image' and the political creed of socialism in order to differentiate itself from liberalism.[98]

Beer presented the history of Labour's political development as having been shaped largely by logical class self-interest. The nationalistic impulses, traditions and understanding of the past that were presented as being so integral to Labour's political identity in Wertheimer's study were therefore, for Beer, of limited importance when compared to its 'class image' and its socialist ideology. Although Beer noted that Labour's trajectory had been shaped by the desire to gain political power through parliamentary representation, in contrast to the work of McKenzie and Miliband, he suggested that, after 1918, there had been a genuine socialist ideological commitment that had underpinned Labour's attachment to parliamentary democracy.[99] Effectively, Beer suggested that the form that Labour took as a parliamentary party determined the ideology and identity that the party assumed. Yet, in turn, the ideology and identity that emerged from this teleological process went on to shape the party's development in non-teleological ways as important underlying causal factors in their own right.

Significantly, Beer argued that the changing social and economic nature of post-1945 Britain had forced Labour to re-evaluate its socialist ideology and class identity and that this had led to an increase in intraparty disputes and divisions.[100] He portrayed the battle over the modernisation of the Labour Party in the 1950s and 1960s as 'a crisis in the party [that] was, in the first place, the product of the confrontation of old Socialist commitments with new social and political realities.'[101] However, by focusing on ideological disputes and not the party's emotional response to the underlying structural shifts in the demographic base of the country that were fuelling this crisis, he undervalued the role played by Labour's collective attachment to its working-class past. As Beer himself acknowledged, 'The "ghost" haunted the party of the 1950's because it had been the soul of the party in the 1920's and 1930's.'[102] More generally, Beer's study raised questions about how Labour's class identity might have been reinforced and sustained. Undoubtedly, 'Labour's supporters identified it [The Labour Party] as the party that was supported by the working class and which stood for the working class.'[103] Yet, at the very least, this collective class identity would have relied upon the creation and subsequent preservation of a shared understanding of the past.

Ethos

Henry Drucker's study *Doctrine and Ethos in the Labour Party* was published in 1979. This book pioneered new ways of thinking about Labour's political development. In contrast to teleological descriptions of Labour's history, Drucker emphasised the way in which less visible underlying factors had shaped the party's identity and, thus, its political trajectory. His work used a broad understanding of ideology that incorporated the twin concepts of 'doctrine' and 'ethos'. He believed that there was more to the 'party's ideology than socialist doctrines' and he presented the case for a broad and coherent ethos that he suggested had affected the party's orientation.[104] In this way, he extended his definition of ideology to incorporate 'the traditions, beliefs, characteristic procedures and feelings which help to animate members of the party'.[105]

Drucker argued that Labour's ethos was primarily 'defensive' and characterised by 'solidarity' and group unity.[106] Central to this particular understanding of the party's collective identity was the belief that 'The Labour Party has and needs a strong sense of its own past and of the past of the Labour movement which produced and sustains it.' Drucker stated that this sense of the past was 'an expression of the past experience of the various parts of the British working class'.[107] Thus, for Drucker, Labour's political identity was, at least partially, the product of traditional industrial working-class memories. He noted the influence that memories of the heroic struggles of the past had exerted on the party's behavioural orientation in the present and he described how 'People brought up in such [traditional industrial working-class] traditions, such as Jennie Lee and Aneurin Bevan, often feel a very strong obligation to those who have struggled before them.'[108] Elsewhere in his book, he suggested that Labour's understanding of the past determined 'what kind of future policies it will tolerate.'[109]

For Drucker, the 'positive content' of a party's traditions and history determined whether or not it was either backward or forward-looking. As he viewed Labour's past as having impacted upon its identity in an exceptionally positive manner, the party was portrayed primarily as progressive rather than regressive.[110] He saw Labour's unique understanding of the past to be conducive to a commitment to progressive policies rather than to nostalgic stagnation or regression. Furthermore, he depicted a level of detachment and objectivity that meant that, rather than seeking the reinstatement of visions of the past in the present, party members were able to learn positive lessons from the past.[111] Essentially, he implied that this level of self-aware detachment offered a mechanism by which nostalgia could be easily separated from shared positive historical understanding.

Rules, norms and traditions

In both *The Labour Party Conference* and *The Contentious Alliance*, Lewis Minkin argued that, during the post-war period, the Labour leadership's power had been constrained by subtle structural and procedural factors. The conceptual underpinnings of Minkin's studies constituted a rejection of teleological descriptions of the party's history. Indeed, Minkin attacked McKenzie's suggestion that power had been concentrated solely in the hands of the party leadership and that its development had been predominantly determined by a parliamentary elite.[112] He highlighted the extent to which the relationship between the Trades Union Congress (TUC) and the Labour Party was governed by a number of 'rules' which 'acted as boundaries producing inhibitors and constraints' and 'which [in turn] prevented the absolute supremacy of leadership groups in either wing in the relationship'.[113] These 'rules' included the separation of industrial and political issues and increased trade union restraint when the party was in government.[114]

Minkin also outlined the role that tradition had played in Labour politics. In particular, he showed how it had constrained the power that could be wielded by the party's leaders and parliamentarians. In this sense, like Wertheimer, he placed a degree of emphasis on Labour's attachment to the past. The attachment to the past that Minkin described was predominantly male and traditional industrial working class in origin. When discussing Labour's historical commitment to intraparty democracy, he declared that

> The tradition affirms a belief deeply rooted in the Party's genesis as the creation of predominantly manual workers, that each has an equal capacity in policy making. It therefore stands in contradiction to the belief that the

requisite understanding to make wise decisions on principle springs from some special educated facility or even from direct proximity to the point where decisions are implemented.[115]

He suggested that, in the past, the restraints that the party's traditions had placed on Labour's leadership had been at their most acute when it had been believed that party leaders were acting against the symbols of the labour movement: 'They were tight where there were deeply entrenched union traditions involved – the symbolic goal of public ownership and the principle of free collective bargaining both fell into this category.'[116]

Minkin's role in broadening the historical debate has been considerable. He moved the discussion further away from the idea that Labour had merely been a political vehicle for a parliamentary elite, socialist ideology or instrumental class self-interest. In a similar manner to Drucker's emphasis on 'ethos', Minkin's argument that rules, norms and traditions had informed the party's development paved the way for new interpretations of the party's post-war trajectory that stressed the critical nature of the role that had been played by less visible underlying factors.

Recent developments in the literature

Jeremy Nuttall's suggestion that 'Labour Party history was thus shaped by a complex range of psychological, ideological, social, economic and physical factors' is indicative of the degree to which the scope of research into Labour's history has expanded in recent years.[117] Academics working on Labour's politics and history are now thinking in greater detail about how the party's political form and trajectory might have been shaped by factors that do not always seem to have been instrumentally orientated, logical and purposive. In his insightful study of the post-war Labour Party, James Cronin described how

> Labour was never just a political party. It was a movement, a way of thinking and feeling, and an intense set of loyalties and antipathies. Its evolution therefore refused to obey the logic of a mere political party and the party acted, at least on occasion, as if the winning and holding of office was a distinctly secondary, perhaps even unworthy, objective.[118]

Jon Lawrence has outlined how 'shared stories about the past – stories which, *regardless of their veracity*, have helped to shape political identities within the twentieth-century Labour Party.' He noted that 'there is little doubt that Labour activists have always had an especially strong sense of their party as a historic "movement", which must know its past in order to envisage its future.'[119] In this way, he opened the door for future studies on the way in which memory has shaped Labour's political identity and, in turn, impacted upon its development. More recently, Emily Robinson's important book *History, Heritage, and Tradition in Contemporary British Politics* has argued that 'particular interpretations of the past are used to provide legitimacy for particular courses of action, to orient identity and to supply lessons for the present.'[120] She has also shown how memory becomes institutionalised within party practices.[121] Elsewhere, Alastair Bonnett has described the manner in which a 'radical' nostalgia has shaped the British left's political thought and imagination.[122] Yet, whilst recent studies have examined the relationship between memories of the past and the British political arena, there has been no systematic exploration of the important role that nostalgia has played in Labour's political development.

Labour in 1951

This book's analysis of Labour's relationship with nostalgia begins in 1951. Having enacted a radical programme of reform, Labour exited from power after six years in government.[123] As we shall see, the 1945–51 Attlee Governments would play a prominent role in the party's post-war nostalgia. Significantly, the period after Labour's return to opposition represented something akin to a watershed moment for political thought within the party. Whilst Aneurin Bevan's *In Place of Fear* was a restatement of the traditionalist aims of the Labour Left, Anthony Crosland's chapter in *New Fabian Essays* paved the way for what has been perceived as the revisionist ascendancy of the 1950s.[124] The 1950s were dominated by bitter conflict between these traditionalist/fundamentalist and revisionist groups. Moreover, this intraparty conflict was often the product of a direct contestation of Labour's attachment to the past and its male traditional industrial working-class identity.[125]

In 1951, the major social and economic structural changes that have continued to shape Britain to the present day were about to accelerate.[126] Yet, as James Cronin has stated, 'the occupational structure of Britain was not markedly different from two decades before.'[127] The British traditional industrial working class was still numerically significant and relatively culturally, socially and economically homogenous. As Cronin has suggested, 'The relative backwardness in the industrial underpinnings of the working class was matched by the persistence of styles of life inherited from before the war, and together these made for a certain hardening of class identities and allegiances.'[128]

Labour remained dominated by men, both numerically and in terms of those who held political power. In 1933, the first year that women and men were recorded separately in the party's internal statistics, Labour had 211,223 male members and 154,790 female members. Women represented around 42.3 per cent of the party's total membership.[129] By 1951, the Labour Party had 512,751 male members and 363,524 female members. Women constituted approximately 41.5 per cent of the party's total membership.[130] Thus, between 1933 and 1951, the relative proportion of female members actually declined slightly.[131] In 1951, apart from the five women who were elected to Section IV (women members), there was only one woman (Barbara Castle) who sat on the Labour Party's National Executive Committee (NEC).[132] This meant that women only represented one-fifth (six out of thirty) of the party's NEC members.[133] The same year, only 17 of the 572 delegates who the trade unions sent to the Labour Party Conference were women.[134] Even unions from traditional industries that employed a high proportion of women, such as the textile industry, sent predominantly male delegations: only one of the ten delegates sent by the National Union of Dyers, Bleachers and Textile Workers was a woman.[135]

Furthermore, women made up only 96 of the 611 delegates who attended the conference from the various Constituency Labour Parties (CLPs).[136] When socialist societies, co-operative societies and federations are also factored into the equation, we can see that men constituted the overwhelming majority of the total number of delegates.[137] Women represented roughly 10 per cent of the total 1,210 delegates who attended the 1951 Labour Party Conference.[138] These statistics seem to call into question Alice Bacon's statement at this conference that 'It is in the Labour Party that the woman's viewpoint gets its fullest expression today.'[139] They are also indicative of the 'male' identity of the party at this stage in its development and the relative political power, both representative and actual, that men held over their female counterparts within the party at this time. Alice Bacon was referred to in the 1951 conference report as the conference's 'Chairman'. This title was, in itself, indicative of the heavily gendered notion of power that existed in the Labour Party in 1951.[140]

Both Labour's political identity and the internal politics of the party were shaped by the numerical supremacy and substantial influence of party members from the nation's traditional industries. In 1951, because of the union block vote, trade unions held 80.5 per cent (4,987,000 out of 6,192,000 votes) of the total voting power at the party's conference.[141] Within the trade union delegates' section, unions representing the nation's traditional industries (coal-mining, iron and steel, textiles, shipbuilding and railways) made up approximately 46 per cent of the total delegates.[142] When the unions representing other manual workers are added, the percentage is much higher. Coal miners were particularly well-represented and the National Union of Mineworkers sent 127 delegates, more than any other union, to conference and cast 646,465 votes.[143]

Many of the traditional industrial unions also had a lower member to delegate ratio at the 1951 conference than their white-collar counterparts. The British Iron, Steel and Kindred Trades Association sent one delegate per 5,156 members, the National Union of Mineworkers sent one delegate per 5,090 members, the Textile Factory Workers' Association sent one delegate per 5,136 members and the National Union of Dyers, Bleachers and Textile Workers sent one delegate per 6,400 members. In contrast, the Clerical and Administrative Workers' Union sent one delegate per 9,187 members, the National Union of Public Employees sent one delegate per 9,000 members and the Union of Shop, Distributive and Allied Workers sent one delegate per 9,057 members.[144] The numerical representative bias towards delegates from Britain's traditional industries at the 1951 Labour Party Conference is clear. Away from its annual conference, Labour recruited many of its members from the traditional industrial working class and its support base was 'heavily concentrated in distinct parts of the country' where the nation's traditional manual industries had developed.[145] Perhaps interlinked with the decline that occurred in Britain's traditional industries from the late 1950s onwards, the party's individual membership (excluding affiliates) peaked in 1952.[146]

In the early 1950s, Labour had a distinct working-class identity. Labour understood itself to be the party of the working class. As Geoffrey Foote has suggested, a large proportion of the Labour Party's membership adhered to Aneurin Bevan's belief that

> the working class had created the Labour Party and looked to it for a transformation of society in its own interests. It was their only real alternative, as the individual strivings of personal ambition characteristic of the middle class were absurd to those who worked in the steel mills, the foundries and the mines.[147]

Indeed, Mark Jenkins has claimed that, between 1947 and 1952, the party's membership increased in response to this particular understanding of the party's political role.[148]

Certainly, Labour's electoral support base was predominantly working class. At the 1951 General Election, 63 per cent of the party's support came from voters from manual backgrounds and only 22 per cent came from non-manual groups.[149] One study of voting behaviour in the Bristol North East constituency at this election noted how 'the voting behaviour of the British elector appears to be more a product of his social background, whether viewed objectively or subjectively, than that of the American elector'.[150] At this stage in its development, Labour's electoral fortunes were intrinsically linked to its ability to mobilise its working-class support base.

As Patrick Seyd and Paul Whiteley noted in 1992, data on the social background of Labour Party members is scarce: 'Since the creation of an individual membership in 1918 almost nothing has been known about its social composition.'[151] However, it can be reasonably argued that, in 1951, the majority of its members, despite significant numbers of middle-class activists,[152] were from working-class backgrounds.[153] Conducted in the early 1950s, Anthony Birch's study of Glossop, Derbyshire found that 'industrial workers' constituted 76 per cent of the local Labour Party's membership.[154] Likewise, a survey of the Labour Party's membership in Newcastle-under-Lyme in 1960 noted that 77 per cent of party members belonged to either 'skilled manual' or 'less skilled' working-class groupings.[155]

The British working class was comparatively underrepresented amongst those who held power within the party.[156] Barry Hindess has shown how 'Ministers from working-class backgrounds provided about half the membership of the Attlee cabinets in the 1940s.'[157] In 1951, only 37 per cent of Labour's MPs were from manual backgrounds (19 per cent were deemed to be from 'miscellaneous' backgrounds).[158] However, in almost every other sense, the Labour Party retained a male traditional industrial working-class identity in 1951.

Notes

1. J. Corbyn, 'Jeremy Corbyn's Labour Party Conference Speech 2015: Full Text', *New Statesman: The Staggers Blog*, 29 September 2015, www.newstatesman.com/politics/staggers/2015/09/jeremy-corbyns-labour-party-conference-speech-2015-full-text.
2. P. Collins, 'Speech Unspun', *The Times*, 30 September 2015, 9.
3. J. Corbyn, 'Speech to the Durham Miners' Gala 2015', 11 July 2015, www.durhamminers.org/videos.
4. J. Corbyn, 'Speech to the Tolpuddle Martyrs' Festival', 19 July 2015, https://www.youtube.com/watch?v=yQ8nO1n1YVg.
5. J. Corbyn, 'I want to convert Labour into a "more social movement"', *The Andrew Marr Show*, 26 July 2015, www.bbc.co.uk/programmes/p02y2ffn.
6. J. Merrick, 'Jeremy Corbyn to Bring Back "Clause IV"', *The Independent*, 9 August 2015.
7. See R. Wearmouth, 'Labour Leadership contender Jeremy Corbyn vows to reopen coal mines', *Chronicle Live*, 8 August 2015, www.chroniclelive.co.uk/news/north-east-news/labour-leadership-contender-jeremy-corbyn-9817411.
8. P. Mandelson, *The Blair Revolution Revisited* (London: Politicos, 2002), xvii.
9. T. Blair, 'In Full: Tony Blair's Speech', *BBC*, 26 September 2006, http://news.bbc.co.uk/1/hi/uk_politics/5382590.stm.
10. T. Blair, *A Journey* (London: Arrow Books, 2011), 95.
11. J. Cronin, *New Labour's Pasts: The Labour Party and its Discontents* (Harlow: Pearson, Longman, 2004), 4.

12 E. Shaw, *The Labour Party since 1945: Old Labour – New Labour* (Oxford: Blackwell, 1996), 217. For a detailed analysis of New Labour's language and discourse, see N. Fairclough, *New Labour, New Language?* (London: Routledge, 2000).
13 For an analysis of the ways that New Labour attacked the party's past in order to signal that it had changed, see J. Lawrence, 'Labour – The Myths it has Lived By' in D. Tanner, P. Thane and N. Tiratsoo (eds), *Labour's First Century* (Cambridge: Cambridge University Press, 2000), 341–366; S. Fielding, 'New Labour and the Past' in Tanner, Thane and Tiratsoo, *Labour's First Century*, 367–392; C. Hay, *The Political Economy of New Labour: Labouring Under False Pretences* (Manchester: Manchester University Press, 1999).
14 T. Blair, quoted in The Labour Party, *Report of Conference: Annual Conference 1994/Special Conference 1995* (London: The Labour Party, 1995), 105.
15 The Labour Party, *New Labour, New Life for Britain* (London: The Labour Party, 1996), 18.
16 For example, see M. White, 'Blair Defines British Dream', *The Guardian*, 11 May 1996, 1.
17 T. Blair, 'Towards a Decent, Responsible Society', *The Times*, 4 November 1996.
18 A. Marr, 'Blair Dares where Gaitskell Failed', *The Independent*, 5 October 1994, 15.
19 A. McElvoy, 'The Killing of Clause 4', *The Times*, 22 April 1995.
20 Editorial, 'Due Clause', *The Scotsman*, 28 January 1995, 11.
21 J. Powell, *The New Machiavelli: How to Wield Power in the Modern World* (London: Vintage Books, 2010), 34.
22 See P. Gould, *The Unfinished Revolution: How Modernisation Saved the Labour Party* (London: Little, Brown, 1998), 22.
23 T. Blair, *New Britain: My Vision of a Young Country* (Boulder, CO: Westview Press, 1997), 16.
24 Blair, *A Journey*, 40.
25 Gould, *Unfinished Revolution*, 4.
26 Ibid., 394.
27 M. Hirsch and L. Spitzer, '"We Would Not Have Come Without You": Generations of Nostalgia' in K. Hodgkin and S. Radstone (eds), *Contested Pasts: The Politics of Memory* (London: Routledge, 2003), 82.
28 Hirsch and Spitzer, '"We Would Not Have Come Without You"', 82; R. Rosaldo, 'Imperialist Nostalgia', *Representations*, 26 (Spring, 1989), 108–109.
29 For example, see S. Boym, *The Future of Nostalgia* (New York: Basic Books, 2001), xiv.
30 R. Samuel, *Theatres of Memory. Volume 1: Past and Present in Contemporary Culture* (London: Verso, 1994), 356.
31 K. L. Klein, 'On the Emergence of Memory in Historical Discourse', *Representations*, 69, Special Issue: Grounds for Remembering (Winter, 2000), 128.
32 Hirsch and Spitzer, '"We Would Not Have Come Without You"', 84.
33 For more on this, see A. Calder, *The Myth of the Blitz* (London: Pimlico, 1992).

34. B. A. Misztal, *Theories of Social Remembering* (Maidenhead: Open University Press, 2003), 132.
35. W. Kansteiner, 'Finding Meaning in Memory: A Methodological Critique of Collective Memory Studies', *History and Theory*, 41:2 (May, 2002), 188.
36. P. Fussell, *The Great War and Modern Memory* (London: Oxford University Press, 1975), 335; Santesso argues that nostalgia is commonly nationalised in A. Santesso, *A Careful Longing: The Poetics and Problems of Nostalgia* (Newark: University of Delaware Press, 2006), 15.
37. Samuel, *Theatres of Memory*, x.
38. P. Connerton, *How Societies Remember* (Cambridge: Cambridge University Press, 1989), 2.
39. Misztal, *Theories of Social Remembering*, 133.
40. W. J. Booth, *Communities of Memory: On Witness, Identity, and Justice* (New York: Cornell University Press, 2006), xiii.
41. T. Strangleman, 'The Nostalgia of Organisations and the Organisation of Nostalgia: Past and Present in the Contemporary Railway Industry', *Sociology*, 33:4 (November, 1999), 742–743.
42. See Samuel, *Theatres of Memory. Volume 1*, x.
43. K. Hodgkin and S. Radstone, 'Introduction: Contested Pasts' in Hodgkin and Radstone (eds), *Contested Pasts*, 23.
44. P. Cooke, *Representing East Germany since Unification: From Colonization to Nostalgia* (Oxford: Berg, 2005), 202.
45. Boym, *Future of Nostalgia*, xiv.
46. See Booth, *Communities of Memory*, 180.
47. Kansteiner, 'Finding Meaning in Memory', 190.
48. Boym, *Future of Nostalgia*, xviii.
49. *Ibid*.
50. See Samuel, *Theatres of Memory: Volume 1*, 119.
51. Boym, *Future of Nostalgia*, 354.
52. *Ibid.*, 355.
53. Santesso, *Careful Longing*, 16.
54. Boym, *Future of Nostalgia*, 355.
55. S. Lukes, *Power: A Radical View* (London: Macmillan, 1974), 37.
56. E. Hobsbawm, 'Mass-Producing Traditions: Europe, 1870–1914' in E. Hobsbawm and T. Ranger (eds), *The Invention of Tradition* (Cambridge: Cambridge University Press, 1983), 306.
57. *Ibid.*, 283.
58. P. Novick, *The Holocaust and Collective Memory: The American Experience* (London: Bloomsbury, 2000), 170.
59. *Ibid.*, 176.
60. Strangleman, 'Nostalgia of Organisations', 725.
61. *Ibid.*, 743.
62. *Ibid.*, 734.
63. For example, see J. Jones, *Union Man: The Autobiography of Jack Jones* (London: Collins, 1986); J. Gormley, *Battered Cherub* (London: Hamish Hamilton, 1982).

64 S. Tannock, 'Nostalgia Critique', *Cultural Studies*, 9:3 (1995), 458–459.
65 R. Johnson, G. McLennan, B. Schwarz and D. Sutton (eds), *Making Histories: Studies in History-Writing and Politics* (London: Hutchinson in association with the Centre for Contemporary Cultural Studies, 1982), 214.
66 Hobsbawm, 'Mass-Producing Traditions', 307.
67 For more on how individual rhetorical styles can be effective, see M. Atkinson, *Our Master's Voices: The Language and Body Language of Politics* (London: Methuen, 1984), 180.
68 Strangleman, 'Nostalgia of Organisations', 725, 729.
69 For the dominant discursive constructs of 'us' and 'them', see Atkinson, *Our Master's Voices*, 37.
70 Fairclough, *New Labour, New Language?*, 3.
71 See also C. Ginzburg, '"Your Country Needs You": A Case Study in Political Iconography', *History Workshop Journal*, 52 (Autumn, 2001), 1–22.
72 E. Hobsbawm, 'Introduction: Inventing Traditions' in Hobsbawm and Ranger (eds), *Invention of Tradition*, 2.
73 See M. Lynch, *Scotland: A New History* (London: Pimlico, 1997), xiii; B. Majumdar, 'Series Editor's Foreword', *The International Journal of the History of Sport*, 22:4 (July, 2005), 495; L. Allison, 'Sport and Nationalism' in J. Coakley and E. Dunning (eds), *Handbook of Sports Studies* (London: SAGE, 2000), 344.
74 Hobsbawm, 'Introduction: Inventing Traditions', 2.
75 Alastair Reid has described how picketing's origins were actually in violence and intimidation. See A. J. Reid, *United We Stand: A History of Britain's Trade Unions* (London: Penguin, 2004), 21.
76 For example, see R. T. McKenzie, *British Political Parties: The Distribution of Power within the Conservative and Labour Parties* (London: Heinemann, 1963); R. Miliband, *Parliamentary Socialism: A Study in the Politics of Labour* (London: Merlin Press, 1972); L. Panitch and C. Leys, *The End of Parliamentary Socialism: From New Left to New Labour* (London: Verso, 1997).
77 For example, see H. M. Drucker, *Doctrine and Ethos in the Labour Party* (London: Allen and Unwin, 1979); L. Minkin, *The Contentious Alliance: Trade Unions and the Labour Party* (Edinburgh: Edinburgh University Press, 1991).
78 E. Wertheimer, *A Portrait of the Labour Party* (London: G. P. Putnam and Sons, 1930), xv.
79 Wertheimer, *Portrait of the Labour Party*, 7–8.
80 *Ibid.*
81 *Ibid.*, 94.
82 *Ibid.*, xvi.
83 *Ibid.*, 261.
84 *Ibid.*, 306–307.
85 *Ibid.*, 115.
86 McKenzie, *British Political Parties*, 558.
87 *Ibid.*, 603.
88 *Ibid.*, 412.
89 *Ibid.*, 376.

90 *Ibid.*, 13.
91 *Ibid.*
92 Panitch and Leys, *End of Parliamentary Socialism*, 264.
93 *Ibid.*, 65.
94 *Ibid.*, 262–271.
95 S. Beer, *Modern British Politics: Parties and Pressure Groups in the Collectivist Age* (London: Faber, 1982), 86.
96 Beer, *Modern British Politics*, 149.
97 *Ibid.*, 140.
98 *Ibid.*, 145.
99 *Ibid.*, 156.
100 *Ibid.*, 238.
101 *Ibid.*, 235.
102 *Ibid.*, 135.
103 *Ibid.*, 241.
104 Drucker, *Doctrine and Ethos*, vii.
105 *Ibid.*, 1.
106 *Ibid.*, 21–22.
107 *Ibid.*, 25.
108 *Ibid.*, 34.
109 *Ibid.*, 25.
110 *Ibid.*, 40.
111 *Ibid.*, 25.
112 Minkin, *Contentious Alliance*, 395.
113 *Ibid.*, xiv.
114 Minkin, *Contentious Alliance*, 30; L. Minkin, *The Labour Party Conference: A Study in the Politics of Intra-Party Democracy* (Manchester: Manchester University Press, 1980), xiii.
115 Minkin, *Labour Party Conference*, 332–333.
116 *Ibid.*, 120.
117 J. Nuttall, *Psychological Socialism: The Labour Party and Qualities of Mind and Character, 1931 to the Present* (Manchester: Manchester University Press, 2006), 23.
118 Cronin, *New Labour's Pasts*, 19.
119 Lawrence, 'Labour – The Myths it has Lived By', 342.
120 E. Robinson, *History, Heritage, and Tradition in Contemporary British Politics: Past Politics and Present Histories* (Manchester: Manchester University Press, 2012), 181.
121 Robinson, *History, Heritage, and Tradition*, 79–82.
122 See A. Bonnett, *Left in the Past: Radicalism and the Politics of Nostalgia* (London: Bloomsbury, 2010).
123 See P. Hennessy, *Never Again: Britain 1945–51* (London: Penguin, 2006); S. Fielding, P. Thompson and N. Tiratsoo, *'England Arise!' The Labour Party and Popular Politics in 1940s Britain* (Manchester: Manchester University Press, 1995); K. Jefferys, *The Attlee Governments, 1945–1951* (Harlow: Longman, 1992); K. O. Morgan, *Labour in Power, 1945–1951* (Oxford: Clarendon Press,

1984); R. Pearce, *Attlee's Labour Governments, 1945–51* (London: Routledge, 1994); N. Tiratsoo (ed.), *The Attlee Years* (London: Pinter Publishers, 1991).

124 See A. Bevan, *In Place of Fear* (London: Heinemann, 1952) and C. A. R. Crosland, 'The Transition from Capitalism' in R. H. S. Crossman (ed.), *New Fabian Essays* (London: Turnstile Press, 1952), 33–68.

125 In particular, see M. Abrams, R. Hinden and R. Rose, *Must Labour Lose?* (Harmondsworth: Penguin, 1960).

126 For example, although already in decline, the numbers of British workers employed in 'mining and quarrying' fell from 841,000 in 1951 to 336,000 in 1981. In contrast, the number of those employed in 'professional, scientific' occupations rose from 1,536,000 to 3,649,000 in the same period. Source: D. Butler and G. Butler, *Twentieth Century British Political Facts 1900–2000* (Basingstoke: Macmillan, 2000), 386. More generally, economic historians have noted the 'decline of the Victorian staples' during these years, see N. F. R. Crafts, 'The British Economy' in F. Carnevali and J. M. Strange (eds), *Twentieth-Century Britain, Economic, Cultural and Social Change* (Harlow: Pearson Longman, 2007), 12. For an analysis of the broader changes, see S. Bazen and T. Thirlwall, *UK Industrialisation and Deindustrialisation* (Oxford: Heinemann, 1997).

127 J. E. Cronin, *Labour and Society in Britain, 1918–1979* (London: Batsford, 1984), 136.

128 Cronin, *Labour and Society*, 137.

129 Recorded in The Labour Party, *Report of the 50th Annual Conference held in Spa, Grand Hall, Scarborough October 1st to October 3rd, 1951* (London: The Labour Party, 1951), 36.

130 Recorded in The Labour Party, *Report of the 51st Annual Conference held in Winter Gardens, Morecambe September 29th to October 3rd, 1952* (London: The Labour Party, 1952), 34.

131 1971 is the final year that male and female membership is recorded separately in the Labour Party's conference reports. It shows that, in 1970, 42 per cent of the party's individual members were women. The Labour Party, *Report of the Seventieth Annual Conference of the Labour Party, Brighton, 1971, October 4th to 8th* (London: The Labour Party, 1971), 62. After the 1971 conference, the party's conference reports only give a combined total.

132 For a brief overview of this section's post-war history, see Minkin, *Contentious Alliance*, 332–333.

133 Labour Party, *LPACR 1951*, 2.

134 *Ibid.*, 147–152. These figures are calculated on the basis that all of the women who attended this conference were attributed a suffix (e.g. Mrs) in the report. Male delegates (except those who held a title other than Mr) were attributed no suffix.

135 *Ibid.*, 148.

136 *Ibid.*, 157–173.

137 *Ibid.*, 153–154.

138 *Ibid.*, 73.

139 *Ibid.*, 75.
140 In the Labour Party conference reports, the men and women who held this role were referred to as the 'chairman' until 1982. At the 1982 Labour Party Conference, Judith Hart was elected as 'chair' and the 'chairman's address' became the (more gender neutral) 'chair's address'. The Labour Party, *Report of the Annual Conference of the Labour Party 1982* (London: The Labour Party, 1982), 3.
141 Labour Party, *LPACR 1951*, 73; for the block vote procedure, see Minkin, *Labour Party Conference*, 234–235.
142 Labour Party, *LPACR 1951*, 147–152.
143 *Ibid.*, 149; They were also particularly well-represented in Parliament. See J. Singleton, 'Labour, the Conservatives and Nationalisation' in R. Millward and J. Singleton (eds), *The Political Economy of Nationalisation in Britain, 1920–50* (Cambridge: Cambridge University Press, 1995), 27.
144 *Ibid.*, 148–150.
145 H. Pelling and A. J. Reid, *A Short History of the Labour Party* (Basingstoke: Macmillan, 1996), 193.
146 Butler and Butler, *Twentieth Century British Political Facts*, 159.
147 G. Foote, *The Labour Party's Political Thought: A History* (Basingstoke: Macmillan, 1997), 267.
148 M. Jenkins, *Bevanism: Labour's High Tide. The Cold War and the Democratic Mass Movement* (Nottingham: Spokesman, 1979), 120.
149 A. Heath, R. Jowell and J. Curtice, *How Britain Votes* (Oxford: Pergamon, 1985), 32.
150 R. S. Milne and H. C. Mackenzie, *Straight Fight: A Study of Voting Behaviour in the Constituency of Bristol North-East at the General Election of 1951* (London: The Hansard Society, 1954), 43.
151 P. Seyd and P. Whiteley, *Labour's Grass Roots: The Politics of Party Membership* (Oxford: Clarendon Press, 1992), 23.
152 See B. Hindess, *The Decline of Working-Class Politics* (London: Granada, 1971).
153 A survey conducted in Greenwich in 1950 indicated that 89 per cent of local Labour Party members broadly belonged to 'working class' socioeconomic groupings. See M. Benney, A. P. Gray and R. H. Pear, *How People Vote: A Study of Electoral Behaviour in Greenwich* (London: Routledge and Kegan Paul, 1956), 47.
154 It should be noted that Birch's figures on the background of local party members were 'based on rather small samples'. See A. H. Birch, *Small-Town Politics* (Oxford: Oxford University Press, 1959), 81.
155 F. Bealey, J. Blondel and W. McCann, *Constituency Politics: A Study of Newcastle-under-Lyme* (London: Faber and Faber, 1965), 250.
156 Ross McKibbin has highlighted the shift from working-class to middle-class leadership in Labour during the period 1914–1951. See R. McKibbin, *Parties and People: England 1914–1951* (Oxford: Oxford University Press, 2010), 200.
157 Hindess, *Decline of Working-Class Politics*, 9.
158 D. Butler, *British General Elections since 1945* (Oxford: Blackwell, 1995), 82.

1

Revisionism and the battle over Clause IV, 1951–63

Within the party, the 1950s were characterised by conflict between Labour's fundamentalist and revisionist wings. Labour's fundamentalists were led by the charismatic and oratorically brilliant, but politically volatile, figure of Aneurin Bevan. Throughout his political career, Bevan argued that public ownership remained integral to the implementation of socialism.[1] Hugh Gaitskell, who became Labour leader in 1955, was the political figurehead of Labour's revisionists.[2] As Stephen Haseler has detailed, the party's revisionists stated that British capitalism had changed in fundamental ways since the 1920s and 1930s.[3] They argued that such changes meant that the implementation of widespread public ownership was no longer a necessary prerequisite to the obtainment of socialist goals.[4]

On 8 October 1959, Labour suffered its third successive defeat at a General Election. In the aftermath of this defeat, Hugh Gaitskell declared that the party needed to revise Clause IV of its 1918 constitution. Clause IV committed Labour to securing 'the workers by hand or by brain the full fruits of their industry, and the most equitable distribution thereof that may be possible, upon the basis of the common ownership of the means of production and the best obtainable system of popular administration and control of each industry or service.'[5]

Historians have noted the emotional nature of the party's response to the proposed revision of Clause IV.[6] It has been suggested that, within the party, Clause IV represented something akin to an irrational 'myth'.[7] There has also been a sense that Labour's attachment to the past shaped the dispute's outcome. Lawrence Black has declared that 'The ghosts of the past were an everyday presence' for Labour in the 1950s and that 'This was never more evident than during Gaitskell's attempts to annul Clause IV.'[8] Yet, in general, there has been a tendency to see the battle over the party's commitment to public ownership as ideological.[9] In contrast, this chapter explores the role played by nostalgia in the revisionist versus fundamentalist debates of the 1950s and, more specifically, during the 1959–60 battle over Clause IV.[10]

The fundamentalist appeal

Aneurin Bevan's book *In Place of Fear* was published in 1952. In this text, Bevan stated that socialism could not be achieved without public ownership.[11] He stressed the role that state intervention had played previously in the development of the British economy.[12] The vision of the present that Bevan outlined was acutely informed by the past. In order to support his analysis, he described how Britain's industrial workers 'had a long tradition of class action behind us stretching back to the Chartists'.[13] He also mobilised memories of the heroic struggles that had taken place at Peterloo in 1819, Tolpuddle in 1834 and during the 1926 Miners' Strike.[14] In this manner, he justified his beliefs through an overtly nostalgic discourse.

More broadly, Bevan emphasised the similarities between British society in the late nineteenth and early twentieth centuries and in the early 1950s.[15] There was little acknowledgement of the social and economic changes that were taking place in Britain. Instead, in terms of the substantive examples that he used to develop his arguments, Bevan deployed memories of a time when 'Idle looms, deserted pits and silent steelworks mocked at the claims of capitalist economics.'[16] Journalists seized upon this historical orientation. *The Economist* described Bevan as 'the [Labour] party's emotional conservative … He insists that the world is pretty much as he always thought it was' and suggested that his ideas 'reflect the common experience on which the growth of the Labour movement was based.'[17] *The Times* argued that Bevan's 'autobiographical passages are, however, even less revealing than the political language which Mr. Bevan uses. It is out-of-date language.'[18]

Yet Bevan's ideas were popular amongst Labour's rank-and-file. As the *Manchester Guardian* noted in 1955, Bevanism was 'a throw-back to the Socialist Fundamentalism of forty years ago' and its 'attraction to the constituency Labour parties (who put pressure on their MPs) lies in its beautiful sentimental vagueness'.[19] Bevan's frequent references to 'the philosophies that the pioneers of this Movement laid down' resonated with party members.[20] Indeed, when presenting the case for public ownership, members on the Left of the party often echoed his language and they made statements like 'The pioneers of our Movement, led by Keir Hardie, had no doubts as to what means should be used to achieve that end. The means were the nationalisation of the basic industries and on that policy the Party was built.'[21] Furthermore, there was often an explicitly restorative dimension to this nostalgia. Writing in the Fabian Society's journal in 1952, Barbara Castle, a leading Bevanite and future Cabinet Minister, declared that 'Labour must turn the clock back.'[22]

The rise of revisionism

Contributing to *New Fabian Essays* in 1952, Anthony Crosland outlined many of the ideas that would become associated with revisionism. He argued that capitalism had been fundamentally altered by 'statism' and that the relationship between capitalism and the means of production had changed. He believed that the collapse of capitalism, as envisaged by Marxists, would not take place.[23] Moreover, Crosland stated that 'it is now clear that capitalism is undergoing a metamorphosis into a quite different system, and that this is rendering academic most of the traditional socialist analysis' and he declared that Labour's political thought was in danger of becoming outdated.[24] Specifically, he suggested that the effects of public ownership 'in an economy already ruled by government controls and high taxation, are not enormous, and although the long-run case for it remains extremely strong it cannot … be the main line of advance.'[25]

Crosland described how living standards had risen amongst the working class in a way that had not been envisaged by socialists in the early to mid-twentieth century.[26] He argued that British society had become less defined by the class divisions that had characterised the 1920s and 1930s and he highlighted the importance of the 'rise of the technical and professional middle class'.[27] Above all, he emphasised the need for Labour to move on from its past: 'Most of the unbearable social tensions which have afflicted capitalism will have disappeared; there will be no repetition of Jarrow and Ebbw Vale, dole queues and hunger-marches, to inspire violent feelings and actions in the working class, whose relative gains are, indeed, significantly large.'[28]

In this way, Crosland's analysis represented a rejection of the contemporary applicability of the memories of male traditional industrial working-class struggle that were central to Bevan's analysis. He challenged the idea that these struggles would be recreated in the future: 'There will be no revival of the angry dynamic of revolt against the obvious miseries and injustices of capitalism. The temper of the people will be more contented and therefore more conservative.'[29] This rejection of the past was significant. *The Times* proclaimed that there were now revisionists within Labour who 'recognize in their own writings, they cannot expect – *pace* Mr. Bevan – to find the authority for these principles in past Socialist thought or, still less, in past Labour deeds'.[30]

Crosland's ideas were by no means unique. Written by Allan Flanders and Rita Hinden under the moniker of 'Socialist Union' (a revisionist group associated with the monthly *Socialist Commentary* journal), *Twentieth Century Socialism* was published in 1956.[31] Although historians have tended not to recognise this book to be as significant as Crosland's *The Future of Socialism* (published the same year), an analysis of its content can give us an insight into the manner in which nostalgia operated in Labour during the mid-1950s. Like Crosland's work, it exhibited anti-nostalgic characteristics. It described how the party's fundamentalists 'tilt at the old windmills and take refuge in the easy slogan that all that is still wrong would be righted if only we had a socialist system cut to the pattern of traditional belief.'[32] Attacking the Left's attachment to widespread public ownership, it condemned those 'who cling to what they imagine to be the dogmas of the established church and condemn any attempt to revise them as heresy'.[33]

Twentieth Century Socialism engaged directly with the changing nature of Britain. It outlined how, in the industrial society of the past, 'Society and industry both accepted these same inhuman values [of capitalism] and reinforced each other. But society has now begun to move away from industry and to destroy the compulsions on which industry relied.'[34] The book's authors declared that socialism 'cannot live on old loyalties or on the record of past achievements. It must arouse devotion among the present generation, and prove its relevance by showing them too how to act.'[35] This modern emphasis was met with hostility. One article in *Tribune* (the paper of the party's fundamentalist wing) condemned the text unequivocally. The author stated that 'It's probably too much to hope that Socialist Union will heed Aneurin Bevan's advice that what is wanted is not so much new thinking as old courage' and he attacked the book's rejection of Labour's historic identity.[36] Similarly, the Transport and General Workers' Union's *Record* magazine emphasised the way that Socialist Union's conceptualisation of socialism was alien to the party's traditions and it stated that 'Behind their theory of Socialism lies the shadow, no longer of Marx or even of Keir Hardy [sic], but of John Locke, the father of English liberalism.'[37]

Interestingly, *Twentieth Century Socialism* was not completely devoid of nostalgia. In the book's foreword, the authors stressed that 'We share Keir Hardie's view that socialism is "at bottom a question of ethics or morals. It has mainly to do with the relationships which should exist between a man and his fellows."'[38] The book both started and ended with quotes from Keir Hardie.[39] It also quoted Robert Blatchford, William Morris and the Hammonds.[40] In a text concerned with modern developments, these references felt out of place. The notion that Flanders and Hinden deployed the past instrumentally cannot be discounted. Both authors were clearly aware of the grip that nostalgia had on the party. Nostalgia represented a source of political capital: the centenary anniversary of Keir Hardie's birth was in 1956 and there were numerous references to him at that year's Labour Party Conference.[41]

However, as we have seen from the nature of some of the book's reviews, it appears that these instrumental deployments had limited success. Primarily, they served to focus the debate on the past. Writing in *Plebs*, one reviewer responded at great length to Socialist Unions' references to Hardie and Blatchford. He proclaimed that 'These great men helped to rouse the workers. They taught them that they would get nothing out of the hard-faced men who had done so well out of the 19th century industrial revolution unless they organised and fought to get it.'[42] His hostility towards Socialist Union was framed by a broader nostalgia for an industrial past that attacked both affluence and the rise of the service sector. In particular, the author expressed anger at *Twentieth Century Socialism*'s 'conclusion that we can live by taking in each other's washing.'[43]

The Future of Socialism

Crosland's influential 1956 book *The Future of Socialism* declared that Labour's historic commitment to widespread nationalisation was outdated and should be re-evaluated.[44] He argued that 'there is no reason why means that are suitable in one generation should be equally suitable in the next' and he derided the fact that 'the appeal to tradition is so appealing a catchphrase.'[45] He criticised the way that 'conservative or indolent-minded people on the left, finding the contemporary scene too puzzling and unable to mould into the old familiar categories, are inclined to seek refuge in the slogans and ideas of 50 years ago.'[46] Furthermore, Crosland declared that 'Keir Hardie cannot provide, any more than the Gracchi [redistributionist brothers in Ancient Rome], the right focus with which to capture the reality of the mid-twentieth-century world.'[47] He decried those who might mobilise the past against his arguments: 'it is too late to settle these matters now by evocations of the spirit of Keir Hardie.'[48]

Contemporary commentators highlighted *The Future of Socialism*'s anti-nostalgic orientation. *The Times* suggested that Crosland 'shows in detail the present irrelevance of doctrines and policies that were forged to combat the consequences of a capitalism that no longer exists'.[49] One reviewer in the *Financial Times* was impressed by 'the fairness of Mr Crosland's analysis of contemporary society and his refusal to be bound by irrational loyalty to old party slogans'.[50] *The Economist* noted that 'This book is an attempt to re-think Labour policy, not in order to placate the shade of Keir Hardie, but to accord with a Britain in which ... national output can double in a generation.'[51] In a similar manner, the *Daily Telegraph* described how, unlike Bevan, Crosland was 'disillusioned with nationalisation and impatient of going back to the past'.[52]

In Labour circles, Crosland was attacked for disowning the party's past. Writing in *Co-operative News*, Alan Thompson (a lecturer in political economy at the University of Edinburgh) dismissed Crosland's 'negative arguments – the clearing away of all the dead wood of the past to make way for his new proposals.'[53] Comments on one draft of *The Future of Socialism* criticised the book for questioning the party's attachment to its socialist pioneers. The commenter bemoaned Crosland's attacks on the Webbs and described how

> The well-fed howling down Hardie and saying 'Of course, I can say at once that the Government does sympathise with these poor people' [the victims of a mining disaster] and passing on to next business, burnt a picture right into the minds of those who can go back to 1913.[54]

Elsewhere, the *Catholic Herald* noted that Crosland's book was unlikely to inspire party members and it declared that 'this is dehydrated stuff by comparison with what Hardy [sic] called Socialism. I doubt whether it will put the fire of the pioneers into Labour's latter day supporters. But without that, where do they go from here?'[55]

Industry and Society

During the mid to late 1950s, Labour's internal memoranda and policy documents generated the misleading impression that the party was coalescing around an approach to public ownership that responded to modern developments. In 1955, one sub-committee document suggested that 'state intervention has developed in a backward-looking rather than a forward-looking fashion' and it noted that 'Whatever expansion of public ownership may take place, in the foreseeable future the private sector is unlikely to dwindle in significance.'[56] In 1957, an attempt to clarify Labour's position on public ownership entitled *Industry and Society* was endorsed at the party's annual conference by 5,309,600 votes to 1,276,000 votes.[57] It concluded that 'major changes during recent decades have taken place in the structure of industry and in the degree of state influence over the economy. These have modified the approach but not lessened the importance of the case for public ownership.'[58] However, *Industry and Society* also described how, 'if public ownership is to play the same major role in the future of Party policy as it has done in the past, its relevance to contemporary problems and to long-term economic and social objectives must again be demonstrated.'[59]

By procedurally manipulating Labour's annual conference, Gaitskell and his allies were able to get the document accepted with minimal opposition.[60] Academics have stressed *Industry and Society*'s adherence to Croslandite revisionism.[61] Yet, due to its ambiguous wording, Labour's adoption of this document did not resolve the issue of the party's commitment to public ownership. Speaking at the 1957 Labour Party Conference as a MP and former Deputy Prime Minister, Herbert Morrison's response to the document was fairly typical: 'I find this document in some respects positively unsatisfactory, in some respects exceedingly difficult to understand, and in some other respects satisfactory.'[62] Above all, the document's acceptance by Labour's annual conference served to disguise the extent to which the party's approach to public ownership remained characterised by tensions and divisions. These divisions were to come to the fore in late 1959.

Douglas Jay's *Forward* article

Labour's 1959 General Election defeat led to much political soul-searching amongst the party's revisionists. Douglas Jay, a Labour MP and a leading revisionist thinker, expressed the fear that 'We had been appealing too late to a generation which had gone with the 1930s and 1940s.'[63] His article in *Forward* eight days after Labour's electoral defeat served to reignite the intraparty debate over public ownership. Jay argued that Labour's emotional ties to a declining traditional industrial working class had left it out of touch with an increasingly affluent and white-collar electorate. He believed that significant structural changes in the economy were changing British society and that Labour was 'in danger of fighting under the label of a class that no longer exists'.[64]

Jay noted that 'too many average wage-earning families, with TV and second-hand car, did not see (unless they were a coal miner) so much wrong with Tory Britain.'[65] His aside 'unless they were a coal miner' represented a calculated attack on Labour's emotional ties to a declining traditional industrial working class. In this respect, he was echoing the sentiments of other committed revisionists, including Hugh Gaitskell, that one long-term problem for the party was 'that the kind of emotions and behaviours which held the Party together in the past were all based on class' and that the younger generations 'are actually repelled by what they feel to be the fusty, old-fashioned, working-class attitudes of the people who run the Labour Party'.⁶⁶ As George Brown (who became Labour's Deputy Leader in 1960) later put it, Gaitskell 'saw his task as to lead Labour away from the cloth capped image of the past'.⁶⁷

In his article, Jay linked Labour's dated class 'image' with the belief that the 'word nationalisation has become damaging to the Labour Party … we must destroy this myth decisively or we will never win again'. He declared that the party's class image and its commitment to nationalisation had contributed to the electorate's perception that Labour was out of date and backward-looking: 'we must remove the first two fatal handicaps: the class "image" and the myth of nationalisation. We must modernise ourselves quickly into a vigorous, radical, open-minded Party.'⁶⁸ He concluded his article by asking '*How do we exorcise the popular feeling that we are tied to a dying class?*' His answer was clear: Labour needed to begin 'accepting the actual society in which we live – and ourselves largely created – instead of pretending it is still the society of 40 years ago.'⁶⁹ He even mooted the idea of changing the party's name to 'Labour and Radical' or 'Labour and Reform' in order to mark a significant break with Labour's past.⁷⁰ Jay was not alone. Another article in the same publication of *Forward* argued: 'let's change the name. Fifty years ago when most men's lives were spent in brutalising toil, it was suitable; to-day, on the threshold of the electronic age, the world of leisure and pleasure dreamed of by William Morris, it is ludicrous.'⁷¹

Party members responded furiously to Jay's article. On 23 October 1959, *Tribune* ran the headline 'Who says Public Ownership is out of date?' and faced revisionist accusations of nostalgia head-on: 'To judge by some commentators, one would think that we were concerned solely to preserve the doctrines of Keir Hardie.'⁷² This statement was somewhat hindered by the fact that it was placed next to the picture of a quintessential image of the party's historic identification with heroic working-class industrial labour – a miner covered in coal.⁷³ Readers wrote into *Tribune* to express their anger at Jay's attack on Labour's commitment to nationalisation. In doing so, they often played into the hands of Labour's revisionists by making references to the past. One letter from an unsuccessful parliamentary candidate proudly declared: 'I stood for the socialism of Keir Hardie, George Lansbury and Dr Alfred Salter.'⁷⁴ Whilst presenting his case for nationalisation, another party member stated the continued relevance of Robert Blatchford – a late nineteenth- and early twentieth-century socialist journalist – and he recited Blatchford's quote that '"Socialism is not a thief, it is a policeman. It is not a plot whereby the poor may rob the rich but a plan to stop the rich robbing the poor."'' He then proclaimed that 'Some of Blatchford's old pamphlets would well repay reprinting.'[75] Other correspondents argued that the revisionists should 'take time to look at the vision of Keir Hardie and his fellows who today they dismiss as out-of-date.'[76] Significantly, these letter writers rarely indicated that they had a strong sense of what nationalisation would actually achieve in modern Britain.

Interestingly, amid the furore of the response to Jay's article, many notable revisionists seemed cautious. In another article in *Forward*, Jay suggested that he held common ground with his opponents. However, his notion that 'It is agreed that our appeal is based too much on the past and that the slogans of the 1920s and 1930s do not enthuse the young today' was optimistic, bearing in mind the attachment to the past that was being exhibited by his party.[77] After Jay had delivered a speech in Oxford clarifying the ideas that were contained within his initial article, Gaitskell wrote him a letter stating that '"I was glad that you were able to stress ... that you were not opposed to further public ownership."'[78] Yet Gaitskell was also protective of Jay's article. When Hugh Dalton stated to Gaitskell that he thought Jay's article to be 'rather badly timed', Gaitskell 'replied that we couldn't accept that Left (*Tribune*) could continually attack, and Right never reply.'[79] Furthermore, when talking to the *Guardian*'s Alastair Hetherington, Gaitskell made it clear that he believed that the party's attachment to Clause IV was emotional rather than ideological or theoretical: 'He [Gaitskell] said that the majority of members had little capacity for real thinking. To them Nationalisation was an emotional issue. This had proved to be the case even more than he had expected. There was depressingly little readiness to think hard about ends and means.'[80]

The 1959 Labour Party Conference

At the 1959 Labour Party Conference, Gaitskell restated many of the ideas that had been expressed in Jay's *Forward* article. He emphasised the 'changing character of the labour force. There are fewer miners, more engineers; fewer farm workers, more shop assistants; fewer manual workers, more clerical workers. Everywhere the balance is shifting away from heavy physical work.'[81] The image that he constructed of the new workforce was intentionally unromantic and he described how 'the typical worker of the future is more likely to be a skilled man in a white overall, watching dials.'[82] Indeed, the central theme that ran throughout Gaitskell's 1959 Conference speech was that Britain had changed – 'taking the country as a whole, the contrast with 1939 and still more with 1932 is staggering' – and that Labour needed to change with it.[83]

It was in this context that Gaitskell attacked Clause IV of the party's Constitution. He declared that Labour's aims and principles needed to be restated because 'the only official document which embodies such an attempt is the party Constitution written over 40 years ago. It seems to me that this needs to be brought up to date.'[84] He targeted Labour's nostalgia for the words of the party's 'pioneers': 'I am sure that the Webbs and Arthur Henderson who drafted this Constitution would have been amazed and horrified had they thought their words would be treated as sacrosanct 40 years later in utterly changed conditions.'[85] In full anti-nostalgic flow, he continued: 'Let us remember that we are a Party of the future, not of the past; that we must appeal to the young as well as the old – young people who have very little reverence for the past. It is no use waving the banners of a bygone age.'[86] By the end of his speech, he had left his audience with no doubt as to where he believed the emphasis currently lay within the party: 'I hope that the Executive in doing this [reconsidering Clause IV] will tilt the balance to the future rather than the past.'[87]

Gaitskell's speech contrasted greatly with many of those that preceded and followed it. Opening the conference, Barbara Castle hit out at the revisionists who wanted to change the party's 'old' direction and she pre-empted Gaitskell's argument with a reference to the past. She declared 'let us remind them [the revisionists] that it was the working people of this country, through their self-created political industrial organisations, who stumbled on the truth, while polished statesmen and economic experts were as blind as bats.' She talked emphatically about the 'lesson of the 1930's' and recalled a time in the early twentieth century when 'the working class of this country knew instinctively in their blood and bones that poverty and unemployment were unnecessary crimes; that unemployment could only be cured if the State stepped in and put a stop to it and that the only way to expand wealth was to share it more equally.'[88] Frank Cousins (General Secretary of the Transport and General Workers' Union) noted in his diary that 'Barbara Castle made a very good speech on an old time Socialist basis to open the conference.'[89]

The intense emotional anger that was felt amongst party members towards Gaitskell's proposal to change Clause IV was highlighted by the speech of one delegate who proclaimed that 'It has been suggested by some of the Jay-walkers that we should go away from nationalisation. This is almost as sacrilegious to me as to say, as someone said during the election, we ought to drop the singing of the *Red Flag*.'[90] Another delegate, despite noting that the public was not interested in the past, suggested that 'we might look to our beginnings because to some extent we feel that we have lost our own ideals.'[91] Such responses supported the revisionist argument that Labour's attachment to public ownership was neither ideological nor doctrinal but nostalgic.

At the conference, a number of party members agreed with Gaitskell's modernising agenda. The ex-parliamentary candidate for Harrow acknowledged that, as the son, grandson and great-grandson of a coalminer, 'At my home the singing of the Red Flag, the Co-op, the trade union are things that get an answer in the tingling of my blood. They get no answer in tingling blood in the suburbs of London.'[92] Thus, he suggested that, as a party member, his emotional attachment to Labour's traditions and historical identity was not shared with the wider electorate. Similarly, another delegate argued that Labour was exhibiting 'the image of an ageing Party which was basing itself on economic doctrine and an economic view of society which was 40 years out of date.'[93]

There was a mixed reaction to Gaitskell's conference speech amongst Labour-supporting papers and journals. On the one hand, the revisionist monthly *Socialist Commentary* backed Gaitskell and was critical of Clause IV and its supporters. It emphasised the emotional irrationality of those who opposed Clause IV's revision and it noted that whenever public ownership was mentioned, 'passions are aroused, the sides line up, the air is thick with battle-cries, reasoned argument goes out of the window.'[94] On the other hand, Michael Foot, writing for *Tribune* under the name 'John Marullus', defensively noted that 'Since Blackpool we have been told on all hands that what's wrong with the Labour Party is the influence of "the fundamentalists"; the old-time, old-fashioned, doctrinaire socialists.'[95]

Conflict

The intraparty conflict that defined the 1959 Labour Party Conference showed no signs of abating in the early months of 1960. In terms of both its tone and content, Gaitskell's New Year message to the party was very similar to his conference speech: 'We need to understand the social and economic changes which are going on all around us and adapt ourselves to them ... We need, in a word, to modernise ourselves.'[96] Elsewhere, Gaitskell emphasised that Labour had lost in 1959 because the Conservatives had been able to present the party as 'too much rooted in the past' and that 'we must correct this false image and present ourselves to the public to suit the circumstances of 1960 instead of 1930.'[97]

At the same time, Labour's revisionists intensified their attacks on Clause IV's supporters. They suggested that party members clung to Clause IV because of an emotional attachment that placed them out of touch with reality. Robin Marris argued that the words contained in Clause IV were 'words which have acquired emotional significance far beyond their logical meaning'.[98] Jay Blumler declared that 'the left adheres to the belief that public ownership points the way to a good society as a *tenet of faith*. It cannot draw upon empirical evidence to buttress its claim.'[99] Gaitskell told Hetherington that 'The opposition to revising Clause 4 and modernising the party's aims and appearance had grown. Most members, anyway, were simply not prepared to think about it; they were too emotional in their approach.'[100] Moreover, this emotion was understood to be informed by an attachment to the past. Rita Hinden's editorial in the February issue of *Socialist Commentary* argued that 'it is utterly impossible to tackle the world of today and the tasks of tomorrow with an intellectual instrument of yesterday.'[101]

The nostalgic dimensions of the Clause IV debate became a battleground upon which revisionists attempted to take the fight to their political opponents. Frequently, Labour's nostalgia-identity was contested: one letter in *Socialist Commentary* described how 'the nineteenth century socialists tended to be against state control with the possible exception of Lenin and Webb, and as a movement our links are with liberalism and individual freedom and not with the extended state.'[102] However, other writers explicitly characterised the dominant understanding of the past within the party as nostalgic. In one article, John Corina, an economist at Oxford University, wrote 'The image of cloth capped workers reading Blatchford's fine prose in the *Clarion* never was an accurate generalisation' and he concluded that if Labour wanted to win over the electorate in 1960s Britain, 'Nostalgia for the working class of the past will not be enough.'[103]

In 1960, the pamphlet *This is the Labour Party* highlighted the party's historical orientation. Even though it was written by Morgan Phillips, a supporter of Gaitskell, this pamphlet was fundamentally nostalgic. Beginning with a reproduced poster of the parliamentary candidature of Keir Hardie in 1896, it reminisced that 'Throughout the ages there have always been men and women who struggled against tyrannies and injustices, visionaries who saw that life could only be really worthwhile if people worked together and not against one another.'[104] It described how 'It was the evil conditions of the industrial revolution, drawing to a head in the nineteenth century, that brought people like this together, inspired them to join in common causes, and eventually to bring them together in the Labour Party.'[105] The pamphlet used a nostalgic understanding of the past – the dominant narrative being one of heroic strength in adversity – to frame Labour's political identity.

A similar type of narrative was often deployed by party members from traditional industrial working-class backgrounds in support of

Clause IV. Dick Beamish, the South Wales NUM executive member who had spoken at the party conference, talked in a letter to *Tribune* about the miners' struggle for socialism in the face of the economic and political hardships of 1931 (when Ramsay MacDonald, Philip Snowden and James Henry Thomas had been ejected from the Labour Party after they had backed public spending cuts and formed a National Government with the Conservatives and Liberals). Beamish proclaimed that 'In 1931 we lived in poverty through the betrayal of the Ramsay MacDonalds, Snowdens and Thomases – but with unflinching faith in our cause we remained true.'[106] It was in this context that Beamish proceeded to attack revisionism: 'in the spirit of the old pioneers we must infuse into our propaganda policy much more of the rich blood of Socialist thinking. Our heritage is not to manage or reform the capitalist order of society, our task is to build Socialism.'[107] This understanding of the present through the lens of the past was common amongst the party's membership. Coventry North Constituency Labour Party passed a resolution that declared that 'we deplore the proposal to amend Clause 4 of the constitution since to do so would betray the sacrifices of generations of pioneers.'[108]

Published in early 1960, one illuminating and, at the time, widely discussed text in party circles was Dennis Potter's *The Glittering Coffin*. Potter had been the chairman of Oxford University's Labour Party. He was also the son of a Forest of Dean coal miner. His book addressed the issue that 'the "image" of the Party is unattractive and out of date' and it noted that 'this is no longer the England that many on the traditional left persist in talking about where the troops marched to South Wales [during the 1926 Miners' Strike].'[109] However, his book displayed both nostalgic and anti-nostalgic characteristics. Potter argued that 'There is no going back; we have to start again' and that 'we can never be back in the thirties again.'[110] Yet, at the same time, he seemed to long for the past: 'One valuable characteristic of the thirties was that agitation on any great issue was a doorway opening out to agitation for a great many others.'[111]

Potter talked nostalgically about working men's clubs and the pictures on their walls of trade unionists 'side-by-side with prominently placed but long forgotten poems about lock-outs, pit disasters or other local variants on the harshness of work' and he asked 'What is happening to the hopes of *that England* now that the scarlet banners which led the marches have been put away in tattered remnants like the regimental honours in a country cathedral and the annual May Day demonstrations are reduced to a self-conscious and slightly apologetic shuffle.'[112] Elsewhere, Potter proclaimed that he was overtly hostile to sentimentality. In February 1960, when discussing Clause IV, he expressed his distain towards 'the nostalgia and arrogance that squirts in a continual joyless stream from so many on the old Left'.[113] Yet, he also noted in *The Glittering Coffin* that, because of the grip that nostalgia had on him, he found 'it incredibly difficult to be completely honest in my answers'.[114] As an example of the level of internal turmoil and conflict that a nostalgic understanding of the past could exact on a party member in early 1960, *The Glittering Coffin* was unrivalled in its honesty.

Within the party, there were others who displayed a similarly conflicted response to the proposed modernisation of Clause IV. *Tribune* argued that it was Gaitskell who wanted to take the party back to a pre-1918 past and that 'Those who stand by Clause 4 and what it means are not mere traditionalists wedded to an old formula.'[115] However, it then went on to declare contradictorily that 'the principle enunciated in Clause 4 of the Labour Party is as much part of our Socialist heritage as the memory of Keir Hardie and all the other Socialist pioneers.'[116] Undoubtedly, such emotional references to the past proved to be highly effective in mobilising support for Clause IV amongst the party's membership. As *The Times* noted, 'The clause represents feelings rather than ideas and many moderates cling to it as they cling to the choruses of Red Flag at party conference.'[117]

Five days previously, *The Times* had suggested that there were

> signs that Mr. Gaitskell recognizes that within the Labour Party there are many valued members for whom the old Clause 4 is virtually sacrosanct, even though they realise that it is out of date, and no doubt he is ready to accept a compromise to set their emotions and minds at rest.[118]

Faced with an imminent defeat, George Brown's idea that Clause IV should be added to (rather than altered or removed) provided Gaitskell with a potential compromise position. Gaitskell maintained to journalists that he had not been forced to retreat on the issue.[119] Nevertheless, it was difficult to see how, after his provocative conference speech, he could have become reconciled to Brown's suggestion that 'Let us accept, on the one hand, that the present constitution and statement of objects adapted so long ago has a place in our hearts and our traditions that makes it quite impossible to delete.'[120] Gaitskell had clearly underestimated the strength of feeling in the party and the hold that a shared nostalgic understanding of the past had on the party's membership. He was a pragmatist and he realised that he was now at a point where he had either to compromise or to admit defeat. He chose the former. This meant that, as *The Economist* rather morbidly put it, it was looking increasingly likely 'that clause 4, undefiled, will be "entombed" or "embalmed" within the sarcophagus of Mr Gaitskell's prose.'[121]

Towards defeat

On 16 March 1960, the Labour Party's National Executive Committee met to discuss Hugh Gaitskell's new statement of aims. Gaitskell had already sent copies of this document to his colleagues on the NEC and it had mysteriously appeared on the front page of *Tribune* five days before their meeting under the headline 'Here it is! Tribune's exclusive revelation: Mr Gaitskell's New Testament.'[122] The document began by declaring, in terms that would have been acceptable to most party members, that 'The British Labour Party is a democratic socialist party. Its central ideal is the brotherhood of man.'[123] When discussing the critical issue of public ownership, it stated that the party 'is convinced that these social and economic objectives can be achieved only on the basis of a substantial measure of common ownership in varying forms'.[124] In line with Gaitskell's thinking at the time, the document neither dismissed the need for a degree of public ownership in the British economy nor felt the need to define what 'a substantial measure of common ownership' actually constituted. Indeed, it declared that 'Recognising that both public and private enterprise have a proper place in the economy, it believes that further extension of common ownership should be decided from time to time.'[125] In this way, Gaitskell's document was fairly ambiguous in its approach to the issue of whether or not public ownership would need to be extended in the future.

At the NEC meeting, Gaitskell argued that 'Clause IV as it stood had given the Tories and their big business supporters an opportunity ... of using a vast amount of propaganda which created a misleading impression of the Party's aims in the public mind and of its attitude to public ownership and nationalisation.'[126] Diplomatically, he seems to have made no reference to the party's attachment to the past. However, Morgan Phillips suggested that the link between the old Clause IV and Gaitskell's statement should read 'the following is the restatement and amplification of Party Objects in 1960 and in the light of post-war developments and the historic achievements of the first majority Labour Government.'[127] The wording of this link was significant because it implied that things had changed since 1918.

Immediately, Phillips's link was contested and Harold Wilson said that, rather than using the words 'restatement and amplification', it should say that Gaitskell's statement 'reaffirms, amplifies and clarifies Party Objects'.[128] The addition of the word 'reaffirms' was important because it suggested that the new aims were directly supporting those that were contained in the original Clause IV. This alteration was passed by twenty-two votes to one. Furthermore, Jennie Lee moved that Gaitskell's statement should include the phrase 'an expansion of common ownership substantial enough to give the community power of the commanding heights of the economy'.[129] This alteration was approved and it shifted the tone of Gaitskell's original document away from ambiguity and towards a more overt endorsement of the need for future public ownership.

Significantly, no vote was taken to accept Gaitskell's proposed addition to Clause IV at this meeting. One reason for this hesitancy might have been the fact that the NEC had received sixty-three resolutions from various CLPs and trade unions 'on Clause IV of the Constitution and Standing Orders protesting at any amendments which would alter the principle of Common Ownership'.[130] These resolutions were indicative of the widespread opposition to Gaitskell's proposals and the strength of support for the original Clause IV within the party. As the *New Statesman* noted, 'It was the sharpness of rank-and-file reaction to the assault on Clause Four, in the trade unions as well as the constituency parties which forced Mr Gaitskell to withdraw from the position he took up at Blackpool.'[131]

It was these same groups that now attacked Gaitskell's new statement of aims with a similar level of ferocity. Primarily, this continued resistance was due to the fact that, as *Socialist Commentary* noted, the 'familiar slogans and established traditions in which two generations of socialists have been reared, are under fire' and this meant that there was the need 'to sort this out – emotionally as well as intellectually'.[132] The revision of Clause IV proved to be problematic because the clause was deeply engrained in the collective identity and memory of the party. This meant that it was difficult to resolve the situation with either reasoned intellectual debate or political compromises.

At their annual conferences in the summer of 1960, the trade unions reacted aggressively and with striking uniformity to Gaitskell's proposed addition to Clause IV. They often responded to it in much the same class terms that the revisionists suggested were out of date. They either ignored or dismissed the ideas that appeared in papers like the *Guardian* which highlighted the fact that 'the traditional working class is becoming extinct. Unless it can win votes from other sections of society, the Labour Party may become as much a quaint relic of the past as Andy Capp.'[133] One delegate at the Electrical Trades Union Annual Conference mocked the revisionists for their belief that the idea of class was outdated and he joked that 'Mr Gaitskell and company had revised the old socialist hymn to read: – Backward socialist soldiers. We've ended the class war. And just to prove it's finished. Let's chuck away Clause 4.'[134]

Frank Cousins's speech at the Transport and General Workers' Union's Conference provided an example of the emotional anger that was directed at Gaitskell. Cousins proclaimed that 'If some of the elite of the party can define it as saying that it will be kept in to satisfy the fuddy-duddies and sentimentalists of the unions, we in our union will be proud to join the ranks of the sentimentalists and fuddy-duddies because we are proud of our belief in clause 4.'[135] In effect, Cousins was embracing the revisionist accusation that the party's attachment to Clause IV was rooted in nostalgia and sentiment. It was in this climate that the Labour NEC met, once again, to make a final decision on what to do with Gaitskell's proposed statement of aims.

'A valuable expression of the aims of the Labour Party'

A special meeting of the party's NEC took place on 13 July 1960. At this meeting, Gaitskell's plans to revise Clause IV were all but defeated. The outcome was that

> The National Executive Committee resolves not to proceed with any amendment or addition to Clause IV of the Constitution, but declares that the statement which it adopted on 16 March is a valuable expression of the aims of the Labour Party in the second half of the 20th Century and commends it to Conference accordingly.[136]

In reality, the decision to endorse Gaitskell's statement as a 'valuable expression of the aims of the Labour Party' contained no constitutional implications. Yet, the statement was still contested and an 'amendment to leave out all after "Constitution" ... was moved by Barbara Castle and seconded by Arthur Greenwood.'[137] Furthermore, the decision to back Gaitskell's statement was far from unanimous and was only carried by eighteen votes to five.[138] Above all, the outcome of this meeting highlighted the strength of feeling that existed in the NEC against any alteration of Clause IV. Barbara Castle later recorded that 'No one on the National Executive wanted to know.'[139]

The decision that was reached seemed strangely divorced from an NEC report by the revisionist pollster Mark Abrams that was circulated the same day. It is likely that Gaitskell encouraged the circulation of this report. Certainly, he had already engaged with Abrams' conclusions: in a letter to Hinden on 7 July 1960, Gaitskell had described how he had 'read Mark's survey with intense interest'.[140] The NEC report described how Abrams' 'findings indicate how closely, in the public mind, we are associated with the traditional working class and how little with the new and expanding occupations.'[141] Abrams' study had also discovered that, outside of the party, '"nationalization" nowadays not only offends non-Labour electors, but it also apparently banes loyal Labour supporters.'[142]

Also contained in the memorandum for the NEC meeting on 13 July, the document *The State of the Party*, an early draft of what was to become *The Future of the Party* and then *Labour in the Sixties*, noted that 'the morale of the Labour Party ... is at an all time low' and that one reason for this was that 'The debate on Clause IV touched on the most sensitive tenet of Labour's faith.'[143] It suggested that it 'would be a widely appreciated gesture that might alter the whole tone of the Conference' if the NEC withdrew Gaitskell's statement and spent a longer period of time thinking about the issue.[144] In other words, the party's emotional attachment to Clause IV dictated that the issue should be approached with greater sensitivity and hesitancy by the NEC.

Undoubtedly, the outcome of the NEC meeting on 13 July represented a defeat for Labour's revisionists. *The Economist* noted that 'This week Mr Gaitskell's retreat on the revision of Clause 4 was carried through to another humiliation.'[145] Gaitskell met Hetherington the day after the NEC meeting and he

> said rather sadly that if he had foreseen the kind of opposition he would encounter on Clause 4 – and the obscurantist unwillingness to think – he would never have raised the Clause 4 issue at all. He admitted that he had erred very much on this. He emphasised, however, that the best thing now was simply to cut his losses.[146]

In this way, Gaitskell believed that the party's 'unwillingness to think' and its emotional rather than ideological or theoretical attachment to Clause IV had defeated his attempts to revise the party's commitment to public ownership.

Rejuvenated by their success, Clause IV's supporters increased their attacks on the party's revisionists. Speaking at the National Union of Mineworkers' Annual Conference, Sir James Bowman (a former NUM trade union official and the retiring head of the National Coal Board) talked about how

> The pioneers of the union, men of intelligence and humanity and courage, who fought against the poverty and oppression of their day, knew these things were not inevitable conditions of work in the mines. They fought for the dignity of the worker, and they expressed faith and hope in nationalization.[147]

In this way, he used the imagery of past heroic industrial working-class struggles to gain support from his audience and to present his case for Clause IV. Support from his audience was forthcoming because he deployed an understanding of the past that they both recognised and shared.

In a similar manner, at the Trades Union Congress Annual Congress in September, Walter Padley MP began his case for a pro-public ownership motion by stating that 'At the 1893 Congress, the year in which Keir Hardie founded the I.L.P. [Independent Labour Party], Will Thorne of the Gas Workers' Union moved a motion in favour of the public ownership and democratic control of the means of production, distribution and exchange.'[148] He went on to state that 'Congress carried that notion, and 25 years later, under the influence of the British trade unions, Clause 4 was inserted in the Labour Party Constitution.'[149] Padley implied that any delegates who opposed the motion would be opposing Labour's historic identity.

Labour Party Conference 1960

The discussion of *Labour in the Sixties* at Labour's annual conference at Scarborough in September 1960 was characterised by attacks on the party's nostalgic orientation. Ray Gunter opened the debate:

> Our requirement at the present time, I humbly submit, is to realise that we face the world of the 60s and not the world of the 20s and 30s. It is a different world from the world in those years when we fought our historic battles in the 20s and 30s.[150]

Indeed, during this debate and the debate on Labour's principles, a number of people spoke from the floor about the party's need to modernise itself. Roy Jenkins, one of the party's leading revisionist figures, declared that 'parties all over Europe, all over the world have been modernising themselves and bringing themselves up to date' and he demanded that Labour follow them.[151] In the same way, Eirene White from the NEC stated that 'it is no good bashing away at nationalisation like a dinosaur.'[152]

There were also a number of rank-and-file delegates who made a stand against the party's reliance on the past: one delegate from Hereford CLP talked of the need to 'interpret our principles in the '60s in a way which will be realistic and applicable in the world situation today.'[153] A CLP delegate from East Huddersfield, who was also a branch secretary in the newly formed Young Socialists, talked of how other young people frequently told him that 'the Labour Party does not seem to have anything to do with the 20th Century and the 60s, that it is still stuck back in the 30s and the past.'[154] Similarly, Tom Clarke, from Coatbridge and Airdrie CLP, stated that 'One of the principle reasons why we are not getting the younger generation is because some of us have a great nostalgia for the 20s and 30s' and he then went on to proclaim that 'We are not going to get the young people either now or in 1964 by repeating the slogans that were used then, and which even then did not bring a Labour Government with a full majority.'[155]

In contrast to this discourse of modernity, Gaitskell seemed to adopt a concessionary stance on public ownership at the 1960 Labour Party Conference. Nowhere was this more apparent than when he discussed his revised expression of aims. Even *New Left Review*,[156] an ardent advocate of the continued relevance of public ownership noticed that 'He yielded to the "sentimental" attachment of the Party to the Constitution, in a moderate and apologetic speech on Clause 4.'[157] At the conference, Gaitskell asked his audience 'Did you know that the words "brotherhood of man" [that were in Gaitskell's expression of aims] were not in the 1918 constitution, though they were the words of Keir Hardie?'[158] Clearly, Gaitskell hoped to gain legitimacy for his statement from the conference audience by instrumentally playing on the party's nostalgia for Hardie. This example indicated just how far Gaitskell, over the course of a year, had been forced to retreat from his desire to attack the party's reliance on the past and the thoughts of the party's pioneers.

The 1960 conference also witnessed a significant defeat for Gaitskell on the issue of nuclear disarmament. Aided by the voting power of the Transport and General Workers' Union, delegates were able to overturn – in so far as the conference voted for unilateral nuclear disarmament – the leadership's policies on nuclear weapons.[159] After the conference, the party's revisionists, having lost their battles on the issues of both Clause IV and nuclear disarmament, argued that the debates had sharpened 'the crisis [within the party] to the point where it must be solved in measurable time, if the patient is ever to rise from its sick-bed. The danger is not of an amputation but of paralysis.'[160] In typical revisionist fashion, the same article then went on to target 'the fundamentalists in the Party, the people who refuse to come to terms with contemporary society and fight, every inch of the way, against the modernization of the Party for which Gaitskell stands.'[161] On the other hand, *Tribune* triumphantly declared that 'On Tuesday, with scant ceremony, Conference formally buried revisionism.'[162] The following week, to celebrate their victory, *Tribune*, without a hint of irony, quoted the words contained in a party tradition that very much had its roots in nostalgia – the singing of the *Red Flag*. It concluded that 'Though cowards had flinched and traitors sneered, Labour at Scarborough had kept the red flag flying there.'[163]

Aftermath

The Clause IV controversy rumbled on well after the 1960 Labour Party Conference. However, the debates that occurred rarely reached the same levels of ferocity as they did in 1959 and 1960. This was mainly due to the fact that, after their defeat in the summer of 1960, Gaitskell and his revisionist allies were forced to all but abandon the idea of reforming Clause IV. When discussing its future plans for public ownership, Labour regressed to its pre-1959 General Election state, whereby ambiguous language was deployed to disguise what was an unpopular issue with the British electorate. Indeed, Labour's Home Policy Sub-Committee, in its outline for the party's 1961 policy statement, proposed that 'The surest and most efficient way of ensuring that resources are harnessed to public needs is the extension of public ownership in appropriate forms and sectors.'[164] Significantly, in a similar manner to the 1957 statement *Industry and Society*, the level of 'extension' that was required was never discussed in definite terms. As the 1961 document *Signposts for the Sixties* showed, the intraparty cracks concerning the issue of Clause IV were increasingly covered up by those with power with the new buzzwords of 'planning', 'control' and 'scientific revolution'.[165]

Hugh Gaitskell died in January 1963. Five years later, the journalist Geoffrey Goodman questioned Dora Gaitskell about the Clause IV episode. He was surprised to hear her suggest that her husband had 'made a mistake about that. It was not worth bringing up at that time. The timing was certainly a mistake from his point of view. It made him less popular in the movement.'[166] Furthermore, Dora Gaitskell declared that 'I think that in the end he realised it too. Although he never doubted he was right in principle.'[167] Hugh Gaitskell was correct to recognise that, by raising the issue of Clause IV, he had made himself less popular in the movement. He had challenged Labour's historic identity and its nostalgic attachment to the past: this had decreased his popularity within the party. Indeed, Dick Crossman noted that, by the end of 1960, the Labour Party and trade union personnel at Transport House had turned decisively against Gaitskell and that 'Three years ago it was 90 per cent Gaitskellite. Now he has lost every friend he had there.'[168] Similarly, Ian Mikardo, who was a leading advocate of Clause IV, stated that the idea of reforming Clause IV 'alienated not merely and predictably the Left but also many in the Centre and the Right, including the trade-union leaders who had provided the shoulders on which he climbed to power'.[169]

One article that appeared in the *Guardian*, a newspaper that had supported Gaitskell throughout the Clause IV controversies of 1959 and 1960, the day after Gaitskell's death, offered a particularly pertinent summary of his tenure as the party's leader. The article argued that Gaitskell 'did not allow sufficiently for the emotional background of large elements in the Labour Party' and that 'He was surprised and vexed that changes which appeared to him reasonable for a modern Labour Party to make struck so many of the rank and file as an attack on Labour's basic position.'[170] There can be little doubt that Gaitskell underestimated the strength of the party's emotional attachment to the past and the sacred symbol of Clause IV. However, he was also clearly aware of Clause IV's nostalgic significance and the necessity of overturning it. It was this emotional attachment to the past that Gaitskell deliberately attacked during the 1959 and 1960 Clause IV debates. Unfortunately for Gaitskell, it was also this same emotional attachment to the past that, ultimately, strengthened Clause IV's supporters and defeated the modernising agenda of the party's revisionists.

Conclusion

Historians have talked about Labour's 'emotional' attachment to Clause IV.[171] They have described how, in 1959 and 1960, party members clung to it as a 'tenet of their socialist faith' and how they did so out of 'almost religious conviction'.[172] However, they have undervalued the extent to which this emotional attachment was the product of nostalgia. Nostalgia determined the ferocity of the party's response to Gaitskell's attempts to alter Clause IV. The battle over Clause IV was more than a conflict over policy or ideology: it was a battle over the party's nostalgic orientation. The debate was framed around the party's attachment to the past. Accusations of nostalgia were levelled at the clause's supporters by revisionists. These accusations contained significant merit. Rather than expressing the continued relevance of public ownership in the modern world, party members tended to deploy nostalgia in defence of Clause IV. Such responses were indicative of a party that was fundamentally in thrall to nostalgia.

For party members, Clause IV was a representative symbol that was nostalgically linked to memories of both Labour's 'heroic' pioneers and the traditional industrial working class of the past. The sensitivity of these memories and the way that they were interwoven into the fabric of the party's understanding of itself meant that the Clause IV episode became an emotionally charged and highly destructive dispute. During this period of intraparty conflict, both Clause IV's supporters and Labour's revisionists used nostalgia for political purposes. On the one hand, the clause's supporters deployed nostalgia in order to further their case for widespread public ownership. On the other hand, when not directly attacking the party's nostalgic impetus, revisionists occasionally deployed nostalgia instrumentally in order to display their sensitivity to the party's past and to persuade and placate political opponents. To this extent, Black is right that 'Even in its desire to modify Labour, revisionism wrapped itself in tradition. The authority placed in the past remained a firm presence in its mind.'[173] Nevertheless, Labour's revisionists were generally influenced by a sense of modernity: they incorporated their attacks on Clause IV into their broader argument that Labour needed to modernise itself, primarily for electoral reasons, in line with societal changes. They declared that Clause IV's approach to public ownership needed to be confined to a bygone era.

Gaitskell underestimated the strength of the Labour's sentimental attachment to Clause IV and he was unable to reform the party's commitment to widespread public ownership. Yet this did not represent an ideological, doctrinal or theoretical defeat. Defeat occurred because the party's revisionists failed to overturn Labour's nostalgic attachment to the past. Whilst the counter-nostalgic discourse of Gaitskell and other revisionist modernisers could contest this understanding of the past and extract discursive concessions from Labour's members, it could not fundamentally alter either the party's nostalgia-identity or its mnemonic attachment to Clause IV. Gaitskell and his small group of revisionist allies were vastly outnumbered in every area of the party. Their defeat was confirmed by the NEC on 13 July 1960. Defeat occurred because, as Cronin has suggested, 'Gaitskell's colleagues at the top of the party made clear their collective unwillingness to move the party away from its anchorage in the political philosophy and programme they had inherited from an earlier era.'[174] The argument that I have presented in this chapter challenges the notion that the late 1950s and early 1960s were a period of unrelenting revisionist ascendancy.[175] Ralph Miliband's belief that the outcome of the Clause IV controversy meant that 'For all practical purposes, Labour's "revisionists" had had their way', requires a high level of qualification, if not outright dismissal.[176] The battle over Clause IV was neither simply a power struggle nor a policy disagreement. Primarily, it was a battle over Labour's historic identity and thus one which was shaped decisively by nostalgia.

Notes

1 See M. Foot, *Aneurin Bevan: A Biography, Volume 2, 1945–1960* (London: Davis-Poynter, 1973), 615.
2 During the early 1950s, Bevan and Gaitskell frequently clashed. See A. Thorpe, *A History of the British Labour Party* (Basingstoke: Macmillan, 1997), 139.
3 S. Haseler, *The Gaitskellites: Revisionism in the British Labour Party, 1951–64* (London: Macmillan, 1969), 83.
4 They did not, however, rule out the need for future public ownership. Michael Kenny and Martin Smith have argued that Gaitskell was thus 'operating within a value set familiar to most party members' in M. Kenny and M. J. Smith,

'Discourses of Modernization: Gaitskell, Blair and the Reform of Clause IV', *British Elections and Parties Review*, 7:1 (1997), 117.

5 The Labour Party, *Constitution: Adopted at the London Conference, February 26, 1918, and Amended at Subsequent Conferences to October 1924* (London: The Labour Party, 1925), 4.
6 See P. M. Williams, *Hugh Gaitskell: A Political Biography* (London: Cape, 1979), 570; Cronin, *New Labour's Pasts*, 42.
7 T. Jones, '"Taking Genesis out of the Bible": Hugh Gaitskell, Clause IV and Labour's Socialist Myth', *Contemporary British History*, 11:2 (1997), 19.
8 L. Black, *The Political Culture of the Left in Affluent Britain, 1951–64: Old Labour, New Britain* (Basingstoke: Palgrave, 2003), 16.
9 See Haseler, *Gaitskellites*, 168–177; D. Howell, *British Social Democracy* (London: Croom Helm, 1976), 222–224; Foote, *Labour Party's Political Thought*, 220–221.
10 This chapter reproduces material from R. Jobson, '"Waving the Banners of a Bygone Age", Nostalgia and Labour's Clause IV Controversy, 1959-60', *Contemporary British History*, 27:2 (2013), 123–144.
11 Bevan, *In Place of Fear*, 102–103.
12 *Ibid.*, 72.
13 *Ibid.*, 2.
14 *Ibid.*, 4–5, 22.
15 *Ibid.*, 171.
16 *Ibid.*, 23.
17 'The Siege State', *The Economist*, 5 April 1952, 3.
18 Editorial, 'Recent Books: Mr Bevan's Beliefs: Argument and Rhetoric', *The Times*, 4 April 1952, 2.
19 'Bevanism', *Manchester Guardian*, 17 March 1955, 6.
20 A. Bevan, quoted in Labour Party, *LPACR 1952*, 83.
21 H. Selby, quoted in The Labour Party, *Report of the 54th Annual Conference held in Winter Gardens, Margate, October 10th to October 14th, 1955* (London: The Labour Party, 1955), 111.
22 B. Castle, 'The Socialist Alternative' in The Fabian Society, *Fabian Journal*, 6 (London: The Fabian Society, 1952), 15.
23 Crosland, 'Transition from Capitalism', 33–68.
24 *Ibid.*, 35.
25 *Ibid.*, 64.
26 *Ibid.*, 33.
27 *Ibid.*, 42.
28 *Ibid.*, 44.
29 *Ibid.*, 68.
30 Editorial, 'Labour Thinking', *The Times*, 27 June 1952, 7.
31 For more on Socialist Union and Allan Flanders, see J. Kelly, *Ethical Socialism and the Trade Unions: Allan Flanders and British Industrial Relations Reform* (London: Routledge, 2010). For a discussion of the ideational relationship between Socialist Union and revisionism, see B. Jackson, *Equality and the*

British Left: A Study in Progressive Political Thought, 1900–64 (Manchester: Manchester University Press, 2007), 186–188.
32 Socialist Union, *Twentieth Century Socialism: The Economy of Tomorrow* (Harmondsworth: Penguin, 1956), 16.
33 Socialist Union, *Twentieth Century Socialism*, 62.
34 *Ibid.*, 59.
35 *Ibid.*, 143.
36 W. Camp, 'Is This Really 20th Century Socialism?', *Tribune*, 29 June 1956, 10.
37 The Transport and General Workers' Union, 'Review of 20th Century Socialism', *Record*, August 1956, MSS.173/7/7, Socialist Vanguard/Socialist Commentary: Correspondence and Papers, Modern Records Centre, University of Warwick.
38 Socialist Union, *Twentieth Century Socialism*, 7.
39 *Ibid.*, 9, 152.
40 *Ibid.*, 11, 53, 57.
41 For example, see E. Gooch's chairman's address quoted in The Labour Party, *Report of the 55th Annual Conference held in the Empress Ballroom, Winter Gardens, Blackpool, October 1st to October 5th, 1956* (London: The Labour Party, 1956), 69.
42 J. Bright, 'Socialism and Survival', *Plebs*, August 1956, MSS.173/8/2, Socialist Vanguard/Socialist Commentary: Correspondence and Papers, Modern Records Centre, 169.
43 Bright, 'Socialism and Survival', 171.
44 C. A. R. Crosland, *The Future of Socialism* (London: Cape, 1956), 496.
45 Crosland, *Future of Socialism*, 79–81.
46 *Ibid.*, 96.
47 *Ibid.*.
48 *Ibid.*, 496.
49 Editorial, 'Eyes Left', *The Times*, 1 November 1956, 13.
50 'Reshaping Socialist Doctrine', *The Financial Times*, 1 October 1956, CROSLAND/9, Charles Anthony Raven Crosland Papers, London School of Economics.
51 'New Jerusalem or Old Adam?', *The Economist*, 27 October 1956, 320.
52 Editorial, 'Curtain Raiser to Blackpool', *The Daily Telegraph*, 1 October 1956, CROSLAND/9, Crosland Papers, LSE.
53 A. Thompson, 'Twentieth-Century J. S. Mill says "Let's Live a Little Better"', *Co-operative News*, 10 November 1956, CROSLAND/9, Crosland Papers, LSE.
54 Unnamed writer (possibly Hugh Dalton) commenting on a draft of *The Future of Socialism*, CROSLAND/13/10, LSE Archive, 1.
55 D. Hyde, 'The Modern Way', *Catholic Herald*, 8 February 1957, CROSLAND/9, LSE Archive.
56 The Labour Party Finance and Economic Policy Sub Committee, 'The Technique of Government Economic Planning', R. 478, February 1955, Labour History Archive and Study Centre, Manchester, 1.
57 The Labour Party, *Report of the 56th Annual Conference held in the Sports Stadium, West Street, Brighton, September 30th to October 4th, 1957* (London: The Labour Party, 1957), 161.

58 The Labour Party, *Industry and Society: Labour's Policy on Future Public Ownership* (London: The Labour Party, 1957), 59.
59 Labour Party, *Industry and Society*, 10.
60 See Minkin, *Labour Party Conference*, 77–78.
61 See M. Wickham-Jones, *Economic Strategy and the Labour Party: Politics and Policy-Making, 1970–83* (Basingstoke: Macmillan, 1996), 36; Shaw, *Labour Party since 1945*, 51–52.
62 H. Morrison, quoted in *LPACR 1957*, 135.
63 D. Jay, *Change and Fortune: A Political Record* (London: Hutchinson, 1980), 271.
64 D. Jay, 'Should it Be No More "Nationalisation"?', *Forward*, 16 October 1959, 12.
65 *Ibid*.
66 R. H. S. Crossman, diary entry for 19 March 1959, in R.H.S. Crossman (J. Morgan ed.), *The Backbench Diaries of Richard Crossman* (London: H. Hamilton, 1981), 742.
67 Brown was a Labour MP who became Deputy Leader of the Labour Party in 1960. G. Brown, *In My Way: The Political Memoirs of Lord George Brown* (London: Gollancz, 1971), 80–81.
68 Jay, 'Should it Be No More "Nationalisation"?', 12.
69 *Ibid*.
70 *Ibid*.
71 J. A. Sears, 'How to Win in 1964', *Forward*, 16 October 1959, 9.
72 Editorial, 'Who says Public Ownership is Out of Date?', *Tribune*, 23 October 1959, 6.
73 *Ibid*.
74 R. S. Mallone, 'Anti-war', letter to *Tribune*, 30 October 1959, 9.
75 J. V. Saunders, 'True Meaning', letter to *Tribune*, 30 October 1959, 8.
76 G. Douglas, 'Follow the Post Office Lead', letter to *Tribune*, 27 November 1959, 3.
77 D. Jay, 'Too Smug', *Forward*, 20 November 1959, 7.
78 Jay, *Change and Fortune*, 276.
79 H. Dalton, diary entry for 16 October 1960 in H. Dalton (B. Pimlott ed.), *The Political Diaries of Hugh Dalton, 1914–18, 1945–60* (London: Cape, 1986), 696.
80 H. A. Hetherington, 'Meeting with Mr Gaitskell', 12 November 1959, HETHERINGTON/1, Alastair Hetherington Papers, London School of Economics, 1.
81 H. Gaitskell, quoted in The Labour Party, *Report of the 58th Annual Conference held in the Opera House, Winter Gardens, Blackpool, November 28th and November 29th, 1959* (London: The Labour Party, 1959), 107.
82 Gaitskell, quoted in Labour Party, *LPACR 1959*, 107.
83 *Ibid*., 109.
84 *Ibid*., 112.
85 *Ibid*., 113.
86 *Ibid*..
87 *Ibid*..
88 B. Castle, quoted in Labour Party, *LPACR 1959*, 84.
89 F. Cousins, diary entry for 6 December 1959, MSS.282/8/1/1, Frank Cousins Papers, Modern Records Centre.

90 W. Maddocks, quoted in Labour Party, *LPACR 1959*, 133.
91 W. H. Peacey, quoted in Labour Party, *LPACR 1959*, 139.
92 M. Rees, quoted in Labour Party, *LPACR 1959*, 123.
93 I. Richard, quoted in Labour Party, *LPACR 1959*, 125.
94 Editorial, 'Ends and Means', *Socialist Commentary*, January 1960, 2.
95 J. Marullus, 'Gaitskell and Co. (While they Rethink) Try to Rewrite History', *Tribune*, 11 December 1959, 4.
96 H. Gaitskell, ' New Year Message to the Labour Party', Thursday 31 December 1959, 1959/40, in The Labour Party, *The Archives of the British Labour Party, Series 2, Pamphlets and Leaflets of the Labour Representation Committee 1900–06 and the Labour Party since 1906, 1900–1969* (Brighton: Harvester Press, 1976–83).
97 'Press Release of a Speech by HG [Hugh Gaitskell] at Nottingham 13/2/60', GAITSKELL/C/212, Hugh Gaitskell Papers, University College London, 2–3.
98 R. Marris, 'A Way Out', *Socialist Commentary*, January 1960, 4.
99 J. Blumler, 'A Look at the Left', *Socialist Commentary*, February 1960, 6.
100 H. A. Hetherington, 'Note of a Meeting with Mr. Gaitskell on February 11th 1960', HETHERINGTON/2, Hetherington Papers, LSE, 1.
101 Editorial, 'German Socialists Abandon Marx', *Socialist Commentary*, February 1960, 15.
102 R. W. Parker 'Ends and Means', letter to *Socialist Commentary*, February 1960, 26.
103 J. Corina, 'Theory and Practice', *Socialist Commentary*, March 1960, 18.
104 M. Phillips, 'This is the Labour Party' (London: The Labour Party, 1960), 1960/64, in Labour Party, *Archives of the British Labour Party, Series 2*, 1.
105 Phillips, 'This is the Labour Party', 1.
106 D. Beamish, 'Miners', letter to *Tribune*, 15 January 1960, 8.
107 Beamish, 'Miners', 8.
108 Coventry North Constituency Labour Party, 'Resolution on Clause 4 of the Party', March 1960, MSS.11/3/24/109, The Records of the Coventry Borough Labour Party, Modern Records Centre.
109 D. Potter, *The Glittering Coffin* (London: Gollancz, 1960), iii, 37.
110 Potter, *Glittering Coffin*, 105.
111 *Ibid.*, 108.
112 *Ibid.*, 39–40.
113 D. Potter, 'Stop Talking such Heart Warming Bilge', *Tribune*, 11 March 1960, 6.
114 Potter, *Glittering Coffin*, 40.
115 Editorial, 'Hands up for Socialism', *Tribune*, 8 January 1960, 5.
116 Editorial, 'Hands up for Socialism', 5.
117 'Day of Decision for Mr Gaitskell', *The Times*, 16 March 1960, 6.
118 'Compromise Likely on Clause IV', *The Times*, 11 March 1960, 12.
119 G. Goodman, 'Notes on a Meeting with Hugh Gaitskell', 19 February 1960, MSS.169/64, Geoffrey Goodman Papers, Modern Records Centre, 1.
120 G. Brown speech at Belper, Derbyshire, quoted in 'Labour Urged to Finish the Argument', *The Times*, 7 March 1960, 6.

121 'After the Glossy, the Gloss', *The Economist*, 12 March 1960, 974.
122 Editorial, 'Mr Gaitskell's New Testament', *Tribune*, 11 March 1960, 1.
123 H. Gaitskell, 'Letter to NEC Colleagues', 16 March 1960, in The Labour Party, *The Archives of the British Labour Party, Series 1, National Executive Committee minutes of the Labour Representation Committee 1900–06 and the Labour Party since 1906, 1900–1967* (Brighton: Harvester Press, 1974–79), 1.
124 Gaitskell, 'Letter to NEC Colleagues', 10.
125 *Ibid.*
126 The National Executive Committee, 'Special Meeting of the National Executive Committee', 16 March 1960, E.C.5.1960/61 in Labour Party, *Archives of the British Labour Party, Series 1*, 1.
127 NEC, 'Special Meeting of the NEC', 16 March 1960, 21.
128 *Ibid.*
129 *Ibid.*, 22.
130 The National Executive Committee, 'Resolutions Received', 16 March 1960, SEC.NO.85 in Labour Party, *Archives of the British Labour Party, Series 1*.
131 Editorial, 'Silencing the Watchdogs', *New Statesman*, 26 March 1960, 438.
132 Editorial, 'The State of the Party', *Socialist Commentary*, April 1960, 3.
133 'Clarification', *The Guardian*, 17 March 1960, 12.
134 'Anti-Communist Delegate Complains of Threats – Police Called to ETU Conference', *The Times*, 2 June 1960, 8.
135 'Mr. Cousins Attacks Leadership on Defence and Clause IV', *The Times*, 30 June 1960, 8.
136 The National Executive Committee, 'Special Meeting of the National Executive Committee', 13 July 1960, E.C.10.1960/61, in Labour Party, *Archives of the British Labour Party, Series 1*, 51.
137 NEC, 'Special Meeting of the NEC', 13 July 1960, 51.
138 *Ibid.*
139 B. Castle, *Fighting all the Way* (London: Macmillan, 1993), 325.
140 H. Gaitskell, letter to R. Hinden dated 7 July 1960, MSS.173/8/3, Socialist Vanguard/Socialist Commentary: Correspondence and Papers, Modern Records Centre.
141 The Labour Party, 'Socialist Commentary Survey', Special National Executive Committee Report, 13 July 1960, RD. 80, in Labour Party, *Archives of the British Labour Party, Series 1*, 2.
142 M. Abrams, 'Why Labour has Lost Elections – Part Three: Public Ownership', *Socialist Commentary*, June 1960, 11. The full study appeared in Abrams, Hinden and Rose *Must Labour Lose?*, 11–58.
143 M. Phillips, 'The State of the Party', Special National Executive Committee Report, 13 July 1960, MSS.154/3/P/2/49, Richard Crossman Papers, Modern Records Centre, 1. For the final document, see M. Phillips, *Labour in the Sixties* (London: Labour Party, 1960).
144 Phillips, 'State of the Party', 3.
145 'One Down', *The Economist*, 16 July 1960, 252.

146 H. A. Hetherington, 'Meeting with Mr. Gaitskell: Postscript', 14 July 1960, HETHERINGTON/2, Hetherington Papers, LSE.
147 J. Bowman, 'Bowman Slaps Down the Nationalisation Critics', *Tribune*, 15 July 1960, 3.
148 W. E. Padley, quoted in The Trades Union Congress, *Report of Proceedings at the 92nd Annual Trades Union Congress held at the Villa Marina, Douglas, September 5th to 9th 1960* (London: TUC, 1960), 442. Interestingly, USDAW had voted to support Gaitskell's proposed change to Labour's Constitution at their annual meeting on 25 April 1960. See Haseler, *Gaitskellites*, 170.
149 Padley, quoted in Trades Union Congress, *TUCACR 1960*, 442.
150 R. Gunter, quoted in The Labour Party, *Report of the 59th Annual Conference held in the SPA Grand Hall, Scarborough, October 3rd to October 7th, 1960* (London: The Labour Party, 1960), 133.
151 R. Jenkins, quoted in Labour Party, *LPACR 1960*, 212. Most notably, the Social Democratic Party of Germany had rejected Marxism at Bad Godesberg on 15 November 1959.
152 E. White, quoted in Labour Party, *LPACR 1960*, 231.
153 A. R. Reynolds, quoted in Labour Party, *LPACR 1960*, 142.
154 M. Connelley, quoted in Labour Party, *LPACR 1960*, 146.
155 T. Clarke, quoted in Labour Party, *LPACR 1960*, 145–146.
156 The 'New Left' were a group of intellectuals who attempted to revise Marxism in a way that was applicable and relevant in the 1950s and 1960s. See M. Kenny, *The First New Left: British Intellectuals after Stalin* (London: Lawrence and Wishart, 1995).
157 Editorial, 'The Conference and its Consequences', *New Left Review*, November/December 1960, 3.
158 H. Gaitskell, quoted in Labour Party, *LPACR 1960*, 219.
159 For the debate, see Labour Party, *LPACR*, 178–202.
160 Editorial, 'Fight and Fight Again', *Socialist Commentary*, November 1960, 2.
161 'Fight and Fight Again', *Socialist Commentary*, 4.
162 Editorial, 'Revisionism: It Gets a Formal Burial', *Tribune*, 7 October 1960, 6.
163 'The Red Flag still Flies', *Tribune*, 14 October 1960, 7.
164 Labour Party Home Policy Sub-Committee, 'Outline for 1961 Policy Statement', November 1960, RD. 96, in The Labour Party, *British Labour Party Research Department Memoranda and Information Papers, Series 1, 1941–1979* (Marlborough: Adam Matthew, 1993), 8.
165 The Labour Party, *Signposts for the Sixties* (London: Labour Party, 1961), 12.
166 G. Goodman, 'Talk with Baroness Gaitskell (Dora), Sunday 23 June 1968', MSS.169/64, Goodman Papers, Modern Records Centre, 10.
167 Goodman, 'Talk with Baroness Gaitskell', 10.
168 R. H. S. Crossman, diary entry for 13 October 1960 in Crossman, *Backbench Diaries*, 883.
169 I. Mikardo, *Back-Bencher* (London: Weidenfeld and Nicolson, 1988), 162.
170 F. Boyd, 'A Man of Reason and Feeling', *The Guardian*, 19 January 1963, 6.

171 Cronin, *New Labour's Pasts*, 42.
172 McKenzie, *British Political Parties*, 607; Thorpe, *History of the British Labour Party*, 150.
173 Black, *Political Culture of the Left*, 136–137.
174 Cronin, *New Labour's Pasts*, 43.
175 See Shaw, *The Labour Party since 1945*, 50–67.
176 Miliband, *Parliamentary Socialism*, 352.

2

'White heat' and the Labour Party, 1963–70

The 1964 to 1970 Labour Governments have traditionally been associated with modernisation and the idea of scientific and technological revolution. Looking back on the General Election of 1964, David Butler and Anthony King noted that 'The party sought to be regarded as efficient, energetic and up-to-date.'[1] Harold Wilson's 1963 'white heat' speech at the Labour Party Conference in Scarborough has been understood to reflect his overarching commitment to modernity. Kenneth Morgan has described how Wilson's 'remarkable speech at the Scarborough party conference in October 1963 linked socialism with technological advance, with automation and the computer, instead of the sterile world of class conflict and Clause Four.'[2] In his biography of Wilson, Ben Pimlott stated that 'Wilson's speech, delivered that morning, was a commitment to science as the agent of social change. The Party Leader argued that the planning of science was the essence of modern socialism.'[3] Writing just four years after the speech, Paul Foot declared that 'It was all entirely new – no Labour leader had ever said it before. It was unquestionably modern.'[4] More broadly, it has been argued that Wilson's approach to economic planning stemmed from a 'desire' to be perceived as 'forward-thinking'.[5]

Yet, when discussing Labour's political development between 1963 and 1970, historians have tended to highlight the party's failure to deliver its modernising goals. Morgan has argued that 'On balance, Wilson's proclaimed "white heat" of a new technological revolution remained tepid.'[6] Reflecting on Wilson's record during the 1960s, Eric Shaw has written that 'placed against the aims that Labour had set itself – in terms of planning, modernization and growth – the record was less comforting.'[7] In recent years, this narrative of underachievement has been challenged.[8] Glenn O'Hara and Helen Parr have suggested that Wilson was indeed a modernising figure and that 'Perhaps, rather than being a "failure" or a "success," Wilson was simply ahead of his time.'[9] Similarly, James Cronin has declared that 'Whatever his intention, Wilson managed to redefine issues so that the left was no longer backward-looking but rather the standard-bearer for progress.'[10]

Generally, academics and commentators have emphasised the ways in which economic considerations shaped Labour's trajectory during these years.[11] In contrast, this chapter assesses the extent to which Labour's nostalgia dictated the parameters within which any forward-looking strategies could operate. By focusing on the manner in which party members responded to Labour's policies, I examine the degree to which, within the party, opposition to Wilson's programme for modernisation was informed by a nostalgic attachment to the past.

Labour in 1963

Following Hugh Gaitskell's sudden and unexpected death, Harold Wilson was elected Labour Leader on 14 February 1963. Wilson, a former Bevanite, had 'emerged as the candidate of the left and centre.'[12] The internal politics of the party that he inherited continued to operate along the same factional battle lines that had defined Gaitskell's tenure as leader. Anthony Crosland argued in his book *The Conservative Enemy* (published at the end of 1962) that the 'steady upgrading of the working class … renders Labour's one-class image increasingly inappropriate' and he linked this 'one-class image' to the idea that a number 'of the Party's old-style policies are thought (rightly) to be irrelevant to present-day conditions.'[13] In response to this text, figures on the left of the party like Michael Barratt-Brown declared that 'We have more than ever to remember the lesson of the 1930s.'[14]

Elsewhere, revisionists suggested that Britain should 'switch *quickly* from producing and selling "traditional" goods in declining markets to producing and selling "newer" goods in the expanding markets.'[15] They believed that this transition would require Labour to lose its sentimental attachment to the industries of the past. On July 1963, George Brown (Deputy Leader of the Labour Party) delivered a speech in Manchester on the subject of Britain's declining textile industry. Brown outlined how Labour would support British textile manufacturing and 'create the essential conditions for Lancashire's survival'.[16] Responding to this speech in the revisionist journal *Socialist Commentary*, Geoffrey Parker declared that 'One might lament the Bolton Clogs, the songs of Welsh miners but all this is sentiment.' He mocked the idea of protecting Britain's traditional industries and the notion of 'making Lancashire into an economic game reserve to keep alive the old working-class virtues'.[17]

In 1963, Labour and its supporters within the wider labour movement frequently articulated their demands within a historically orientated discourse. At the Trades Union Congress's annual conference, there were numerous references to the heroic struggles of the 1930s.[18] At this gathering, middle-class revisionist intellectuals were repeatedly attacked for wanting to reform Clause IV. One delegate proclaimed 'That may be old-fashioned thinking – people keep telling me so – but I suggest to this Congress that real power still lies with ownership, even if the new intellectuals tell us it does not.'[19] When presenting a motion against wage restraint, another delegate referred to the 1926 General Strike and the 1930s. He talked about how his union was now in its '130th year of existence, born in the year of the Tolpuddle Martyrs. During that 130 years we have seen slumps and booms, national crises and international crises, born by our forebears and the present generation.'[20]

The 'white heat' speech

When presenting the policy document 'Labour and the Scientific Revolution' at Labour's annual conference in October 1963, Wilson talked an anti-nostalgic discourse of modernity and change. Previously, in a meeting with Alastair Hetherington, he had outlined how this speech would represent 'an admirable opportunity for him to bring in all sorts of things on the modernisation of Britain that he wanted to speak about'.[21] When the moment arrived in Scarborough, Wilson argued that

> the strength, the solvency, the influence of Britain, which some still think depends upon nostalgic illusion or upon nuclear posturings – these things are going to depend in the remainder of the century to a unique extent on the speed to which we come to terms with the world of change.[22]

Wilson made it clear that there was 'no room for Luddites in the Socialist Party.'[23] He was equally critical of those living in the past in the upper echelons of industry and on the shop floor: 'The Britain that is going to be forged in the white heat of this revolution will be no place for restrictive practices on either side of industry.'[24] Britain's traditional industries were no longer to be propped up on an inefficient sentimental basis. Instead, they were to be reinvigorated through a (decidedly vague) process of modernisation and remobilisation.[25] Wilson's vision of modernity was bound up in the idea that economic planning would enable Labour to develop a new economy along socialistic lines. He talked about how the 'planned, purposive use of scientific progress' could be used 'to provide undreamed of living standards and the possibility of leisure ultimately on an unbelievable scale'.[26]

Certainly, there were those present, including the MP Arthur Woodburn, who enthused that the speech represented a decisive break with Labour's past and that 'This morning the movement has been given a new vision. For 50 years we have been carrying out, developing and fulfilling programmes conceived by those working men who 50 or 60 years ago formed the Labour Party.'[27] However, the speech was not embraced unquestioningly by conference attendees. Concerns about Wilson's 'new' direction clearly existed.[28] Furthermore, the 1963 conference was not a uniformly forward-looking event. In particular, the debate that took place later in the week on the textile industry contrasted greatly with the notions of scientific and technological progress, modernisation and change that Wilson had put forward in his speech. Throughout this debate, references to the past underpinned the arguments that were presented. One delegate noted that he had been handed a leaflet that said '"The Hungry Thirties: never again." Do not let us be too sure about that' and he suggested that, upon the party's ascension to power, Labour should move quickly to protect Britain's cotton industry.[29] Another speaker expressed the idea 'if we follow in the way of the Labour Party we shall be saving the textile industry, which, in the past, has played a great part in the economic life of this country.'[30]

Away from the party's annual conference, some of the reaction to the 'white heat' speech indicated that Wilson's rhetoric had been viewed through the lens of the party's historically informed identity. *Tribune* interpreted the speech to represent a commitment to Labour's traditions of planning and public ownership. It declared that 'What Harold Wilson said splendidly when introducing *Labour and the Scientific Revolution* was a reaffirmation of old principles in a new context.'[31] Another article by Raymond Fletcher proclaimed that 'the spirit of 1945 is in the air.'[32] Media commentators noted the manner in which Wilson's words had resonated. Reflecting on the speech the following year, *The Times* suggested that certain sections of Wilson's speech were 'more in the tradition of Keir Hardie than of scientific judgement'.[33]

Yet, on the whole, Labour's members were sceptical about Wilson's scientific and technological revolution. In contrast to the vision of the future that their leader had outlined in Scarborough, they argued that Labour needed to return to its historic values. One letter to *Tribune* argued that 'The Labour Party was formed to check and end the exploitation of the labourer. To stop the robbing of the poor by the rich' and it went on to ask the question 'Cannot we get back to first principles?'[34] At the

TUC's annual conference in 1964, Danny McGarvey, a trade unionist on Labour's NEC, declared

> Let me say this to the faint-hearts. We are told that we have left the thirties behind us, and we must modernise ourselves and modernise our thinking. I say very seriously that we do not need to modernise our thinking: what we must do is have a look at ourselves and do a little bit of re-thinking as to why this great Movement was formed.[35]

This suspicion of modernisation was reflected in the hostility towards the new technological and managerial classes that Wilson was trying to attract to the party. One Labour supporter declared that when technologists like himself were 'looking to the Labour Party it is ironic to read the statements by socialists who are still obsessed with all the old anachronistic attitudes towards profits and the man who makes them.'[36] This anger towards the 'new' occupational groups was fuelled by an attachment to Britain's industrial past. Articles that stated the continued relevance of declining traditional industries such as coal were commonplace.[37] Poetry, which referred to the daily travails of the British industrial worker, adorned the pages of left-wing publications.[38] This attachment contrasted with the forward-looking nature of the outputs that were originating from Labour's sub-committees. One policy document indicated that 'Technological change will inevitably outdate many job skills, but will itself create the need for many workers trained in new skills.'[39] Moreover, within the upper echelons of the party, there were politicians who firmly believed that 'Technological change is becoming faster all the time. The Labour Party is committed to speeding it up.'[40]

The New Britain

During the period before the 1964 General Election, senior Labour figures routinely deployed an anti-nostalgic discourse. In contrast to his more backward-looking speech in Lancashire in July 1963, George Brown wrote about the need to modernise Britain's declining industrial towns: 'too many of which are only relics of the industrial revolution. If you travel across the North of England on a wet Sunday afternoon they resemble coffins in an undertaker's yard.'[41] Electoral considerations and the desire for Labour to be seen as the party of the future influenced this rhetoric in no small measure. Frequently, Labour targeted accusations of nostalgia at the Conservative Party. In turn, the Conservatives responded with similar counter-accusations. Writing about the electoral battle between Wilson and Alec Douglas-Home (leader of the Conservative Party), the *New Statesman* described how 'Each is anxious to prove that the other is old-fashioned, clinging nostalgically to ancient party and class shibboleths. Mr Wilson wants to fence Sir Alec within his grouse moor; Sir Alec strives to smother Wilson's scientific eggheads in Keir Hardie's cloth cap.'[42] To this extent, the zeitgeist of the 1964 General Election was powerfully modern. Throughout Labour's General Election campaign, Wilson made virtually the same speech, stressing the need for modernisation and change.[43]

The party's election material exhibited a slightly more contradictory relationship with the past. Labour's manifesto *The New Britain* condemned the 'outdated philosophy' of the Conservatives and attacked 'their nostalgic belief that it is possible in the second half of the 20th century to hark back to a 19th century free enterprise economy and a 19th century unplanned society'.[44] Yet, simultaneously, *The New Britain* also recalled Labour's historic formation and it stated that 'Until 60 years ago when the Labour Party was founded, the ending of economic privilege, the abolition of poverty in the midst of plenty, and the creation of real equality of opportunity were inspiring but remote ideals.'[45] In the same way, one campaign leaflet from 1964 described at length how 'In the early days the struggle against appalling industrial conditions and an almost total lack of social security was hard. People learnt that one man's fight was everyone's fight. A political ideal was born ... That ideal remains the driving force behind Labour's thinking.'[46] Almost identical sentiments were contained in the literature that welcomed new members to the party.[47]

The 1964 General Election victory

Labour won the General Election of October 1964. After thirteen years in opposition, the party was returned to government with a small majority of four MPs. Within the party, Labour's electoral success was initially interpreted as a 'victory for socialism'.[48] Wilson continued to stress the need to modernise the British economy. In a television broadcast to the nation on 26 October, he argued that 'Old-fashioned restrictionist ideas have no place in our expansionist Britain, whether it is monopoly practices or insistence on overmanning a job, or some costly demarcation argument, or the temptation to indulge in wild-cat strikes.'[49]

At the party's annual Labour Party Conference in December 1964, Wilson delivered another speech that exalted the virtues of change and modernisation. However, Wilson's rhetoric also exhibited some notably nostalgic characteristics. A reference to the 'spirit of Dunkirk' (a passage of his speech that Wilson later regretted) attempted to tie in Labour's economic policies, which included planning and state-led innovation, with a more nationalistic nostalgia-identity.[50] Wilson summoned up memories of Labour's contribution to Britain's victory over Nazi Germany during the Second World War.[51] His subsequent lengthy recollection of the way that

> the founders of our Movement, men of courage, men of infinite faith, were prepared to face persecution and even death that a generation still to come might realise their ideals, might be permitted to create that new and just society which their vision could see gleaming above the squalor and exploitation and ugliness of Victorian industrialism

was more congruent with the traditional contours of Labour's nostalgia-identity.[52]

At the same conference, George Brown, who had been given the task of planning the British economy at the newly established Department of Economic Affairs (DEA), talked about how

> As every one of our pioneers, from Kingsley and Owen to Morris and Shaw, from Hyndman and Hardie to Blatchford and Bevin have repeatedly emphasised, our great aim, our great justification as a movement is that we shall arouse in a man a taste for something wider and greater than bread, whatever its modern form.[53]

Above all, there was a sense that both Wilson and Brown were mobilising recognisably nostalgic tropes in order to unite the party behind its new programmatic commitments. Without a doubt, nostalgia represented a potentially powerful political resource that could be used to secure goals and objectives. Around this point in the party's development, *Tribune* regularly ran a 'Voices of Socialism' feature that looked at the work of significant figures from the Labour movement's past and stressed their relevance to the present. One of these articles stressed that William Morris's idea that men should not be slaves to machines – 'a dream that is relevant at a hundred' – was directly applicable to the present and 'points to the 1960s'.[54] Another article argued that John Ruskin's critique of industry meant that he was 'coming into his own at last'.[55]

The 1964 General Election witnessed an influx of Labour MPs and members from the nation's new and expanding white-collar sectors. Whilst some commentators welcomed these people into the party and believed that they could help to alter Labour's '"cloth cap" image', others worried that the 'backbone of the old party' would come into conflict with the 'new groups of scientists and technocrats'.[56] When Bryan Magee argued in the *New Statesman* that Labour needed to extend its demographic support base even further, nostalgia was mobilised against him.[57] Attacks were made on the new 'bright boys' who were deemed to be 'out of touch with rank and file opinion'.[58] One MP declared that Magee 'fails to discern that what he calls dead-wood is really solid oak, whose strong beams have sustained the Parliamentary Labour Party in and out of office for over 50 years.'[59] Subsequently, another letter written to the *New Statesman* noted that the MPs who had led the backlash against Magee's article 'illustrate very adequately the reason for 13 years of Tory rule. The attitudes they have in common are nostalgia, anti-intellectualism, parochialism and complacency.'[60]

Elsewhere, activists suggested that the party should refocus its efforts away from developing new scientific and technological jobs and towards preserving traditional industrial occupations. One Labour member, who was also a coal miner, described how 'The miners have always supported the Labour Party. We have never panicked. Lies, scares, Red Letters, MacDonald's National Government the lot – when practically all of Britain fell for this we kept our faith in the movement' and he declared that this shared history merited greater support for the coal industry from the Labour Government. His analysis also exhibited a thinly veiled contempt for the expanding occupational groups of the era: 'I make so bold as to say that the party can survive demonstrations by aircraft workers, doctors, schoolmasters etc. ... but if the miners lose faith, then I can think of nothing that could save the Government.'[61]

The National Plan

Throughout 1965, Labour members continued to refer to the heroism of the party's pioneers and the need to adhere to the party's socialist 'fundamentals'. At the National Conference of Labour Women in March 1965, Gladys Langham, who was chairing the conference, described how, on the year of the fiftieth anniversary of Keir Hardie's death,

> We honour his memory and acknowledge the great debt which we owe him and those of his generation who fought and sacrificed for the Socialist ideals which we share with them ... however much programmes have been adjusted and developed to meet the needs of present day society, the fundamental ideals remain.[62]

Observers noted that Labour's attachment to the past continued to inform the party's trajectory and, in particular, its commitment to public ownership. The renationalisation of steel was seen, by the majority of party members, to represent the 'Ark of the Covenant'.[63] *The Times* scathingly reported that 'The Government's plans for the steel industry show how depressingly little the Labour Party has learnt since the war. It talks about a new dynamism in industry and acts as if nothing had changed since Keir Hardie.' The editorial went on to conclude that 'Britain's Labour Party sticks to its old dogmas with pathetic insistence.'[64] Similarly, Peter Jenkins wrote in *Socialist Commentary* that the Government's perceived failure to adopt socialist policies had led to a 'reviving interest in public ownership' within the Labour movement. Jenkins believed there was evidence to suggest that the party was, once again, 'reaching out for the old medicine bottle'.[65] The steel industry was eventually renationalised in 1967.

Labour's *National Plan* was published in September 1965.[66] In retrospect, *The National Plan* appears somewhat vague and non-committal. Sections of *The National Plan* were characterised by the same combination of modernity and nationalism that Wilson had previously utilised in his 'white heat' speech. A version of the document argued that economic success 'will take the combined efforts of the Government, managers, technicians and the workers themselves'.[67] It discussed how Britain's traditional industries would continue to decline over the coming years and how the new science-based industries would expand.[68] However, Edward Short, Labour's Chief Whip at the time, believed that *The National Plan* delighted Labour MPs because of its historic resonance and the fact that 'Economic planning had for long been the theoretical quintessence of socialism.'[69]

This delight did not extend very far outside of the Parliamentary Labour Party. *Tribune* was furious about *The National Plan*'s lukewarm commitments to the preservation of Britain's traditional industries and it questioned 'whether *The National Plan* really deserves its name'.[70] Whilst one of its regular letter writers suggested that *The National Plan* would hasten the closing of the nation's coal mines and begged readers not to 'forget' the way that the miners supported the party in '1931', *Tribune* focused on the fact that 'you will search the Plan in vain for a reference to the ending of the private monopoly in steel.'[71] For all of the seemingly forward-looking proposals that were contained within Labour's plan, journalists continued to note that the party still exhibited a tendency to 'call on the ghost of Keir Hardie' despite the fact that 'the old certainties have gone'.[72]

At the TUC's annual conference in September, there was a great deal of opposition to the centralised planned incomes policy upon which, it had long been argued, the success of *The National Plan* would depend.[73] Memories of the industrial struggles of a bygone era were mobilised by trade unionists. One delegate stated that

> Listening to some of the advocates of the prices and incomes policy, Congress should be reminded that almost 100 years ago the Government of the day was pleading that it was essential to the national economy that children should continue to work in mines. I think we are in danger of accepting a similar philosophy.[74]

Such sentiments were fuelled by the nostalgic atmosphere which surrounded the conference and manifested themselves in the belief that the TUC should and would 'live up to the traditions which we have inherited'.[75] The debate at the annual Labour Party Conference proceeded along similar lines. One trade unionist angrily described how 'This movement, since its inception, has been built up by the loyalty, the confidence and the willingness of the trade union movement to support the Labour Party. We have never veered from that. The belief that now it is necessary to bring in legislation is totally wrong.'[76] Stan Orme (MP for Salford West) argued that George Brown would not achieve his economic goals 'by trying to legislate and force people to do things which, as a democratic movement, we have opposed for over 50 years.'[77]

The 1966 July measures

In March 1966, Labour was returned to government with an increased majority of ninety-seven. Thereafter, the Labour leadership's approach to the British economy was dominated by balance of payments considerations.[78] The prioritisation of economic growth – Wilson's lynchpin for modernisation – was abandoned. [79] Labour's commitment to 'planning' was deemed to conflict with the deflationary measures that were deemed to be necessary to solve Britain's problems. As Jim Tomlinson has shown, 'If "planning" was the key term in Labour's modernisation rhetoric in the run-up to the 1964 election and through to 1965, it quickly lost its lustre in the deflationary period that followed.'[80]

Within the party, the Government's deflationary measures of July 1966 were likened to Ramsay MacDonald's 'betrayal' in 1931. One article in *Tribune* asked 'How close are we to another 1931?' and it noted that 'In 1931 the Labour Government deflated in an attempt to save the pound. The result was defeat, followed by devaluation.'[81] Another article posed the question 'Could we be back to 1929?' and, referring to the events of 1931, it went on to declare that 'We cannot afford this time to have a third world war before the Labour movement recovers again.'[82] This type of interpretation of the Government's economic approach through the lens of the past was particularly common amongst Labour's rank-and file members. One letter to the editor of *New Statesman* simply stated, '*Sir*, the ghost of Ramsay MacDonald must be laughing its bloody head off.'[83]

Part IV of the Government's Prices and Incomes Policy was understood to infringe upon trade union traditions of free collective bargaining. Frank Cousins (General Secretary of the Transport and General Workers Union) had been given the role of Minister of Technology in 1964. In his resignation letter on 3 July 1966, Cousins fervently attacked the Government's Prices and Incomes Bill.[84] One article in *Socialist Commentary* noted that the views that Cousins expressed on the Government's prices and incomes policy 'showed an old-fashioned nostalgia for the past glories of trade union battles'.[85] It went on to argue that if the left of the party were willing to view Cousins as something of a political martyr, then 'one must assume that they still prefer to fight nostalgic battles of the past rather than apply their intellects and abilities to the much harder battles of the present.'[86] Interviewed almost ten years later, one of Cousins' contemporaries in the trade union movement in the late 1950s reflected that he 'was a very emotional man: sincere mind you but very emotional'.[87] In a similar manner, Dick Marsh, who was Cousins' Parliamentary Private Secretary at the Ministry of Technology, declared that Cousins' 'decision [to resign] was not very logical – it was an emotional reaction.'[88] In this way, it was suggested that emotion and nostalgia rather than logic, theory or ideology had led to Cousins' resignation.

Held in September 1966, the TUC's annual conference was characterised by hostility towards the Government's policies. Joe O'Hagan, the TUC's President, delivered a speech that set the conference's nostalgic tone. He talked about how

> the inscription on the first membership card my union issued 80 years ago holds good in the circumstances of today:- 'Let us onward then for right, nothing more/ Let justice be the might we adore/ Build no hopes upon the sand/ For a people hand in hand/ Can make this a better land than before.'[89]

In the immediate aftermath of this speech, delegates seemed eager to draw comparisons between the current economic situation and that of the 1920s and the 1930s.[90] These references to the past created an emotionally charged environment that worked against the presentation of any vision of modernity.

At the conference, Wilson pleaded with trade unionists to support the Government's prices and incomes policy. The Labour leader displayed a level of sensitivity towards the labour movement's historic identity, but he declared that 'I know what we are asking. I know the loyalties as well as the pressures, the deeply ingrained traditions inherited from the defensive days of this Movement. It is hard to say it, but we cannot fight the problems of tomorrow with the rusty weapons of the past.'[91] The backlash against Wilson's speech was severe. Danny McGarvey hit out at being told 'to put our rule books in the museum. "Onwards to the 'seventies. Forget the hungry 'thirties." There were those of us who said that we might forget the hungry 'thirties but we would never forgive those responsible for them.'[92] Another trade unionist talked about how 'Some of us older people remember 1931 and the pathetic spectacle of our Movement entrapped in a similar spider's web of financial crisis.'[93]

At Labour's annual conference in 1966, Wilson proclaimed that Labour was the 'Party of change, we seek not to conserve, but to transform society' and that 'We cannot afford to perpetuate any dinosaur-type thinking in our own Party.'[94] He suggested that 'technological change' had 'blurred the old divisions between industrial and non-industrial workers.'[95] Echoing Wilson's sentiments, his supporters accused dissenters of wanting to 'hide behind the slogans of the past'.[96] These accusations were not without merit. Speakers opposing the Government's policies made comparisons between the plight of workers in 1966 and the historic struggle of the Tolpuddle Martyrs in 1834.[97] On the subject of Labour's Prices and Incomes Policy, Clive Jenkins, a white-collar trade unionist, declared that 'Our battle flag has on it Tolpuddle, the Chartists, the Combination Laws, Taff Vale, the Osborne judgement and the Trades Dispute Act. Will we add Part IV?'[98] Another trade unionist recalled how he had 'served my time during the twenties and thirties in the ILP, in the Labour Party, like hundreds of others, and I feel today our opinions are not given the consideration they deserve'.[99] Another union delegate argued that the conference should support a motion endorsing free collective bargaining in order to demonstrate that it can 'keep faith with the rank and file, and those great names in history.'[100] Reflecting on the conference, an editorial in *Socialist Commentary* described how members on the left of the party appeared psychologically ill-disposed to engaging with the changed nature of the modern world: 'Mentally and emotionally they live in the past and want to continue living there.'[101]

Deindustrialisation

In 1967, the nostalgically informed backlash against the Government's policies showed no sign of abating. At the National Conference of Labour Women in May 1967, the Chairwoman began her opening address by likening the working-class struggles of the present to those of the past and she talked about how the needs of the movement were 'no less, only different from those which gave the early pioneers of our movement the strength to fight on when there seemed no hope of winning through'.[102] She issued a thinly veiled attack on Labour's current political trajectory: 'Was it for their descendants to be slaves to the managerial age that the Tolpuddle Martyrs were sent into exile?'[103]

Economic and social changes amplified the party's nostalgia. An editorial in the *New Statesman* highlighted how

> Change has been sweeping in the industries which between them employed the great bulk of the working class half a century ago … As craftsmen become technicians or dial watchers, entire occupations vanish, each

with its own status, traditions and psychological satisfactions. Man is a conservative creature and resentment is natural.[104]

Another article noted that

> For the party as a whole there are few words that have more emotive undertones than 'coal'. Much of the ugliness, the hardship and the squalor that gave point to Labour's traditional voice of protest were to be found in the pit townships which became symbols of a grasping and cynical industrialism.[105]

During this period of deindustrialisation, party members routinely made historically rooted statements that emphasised how 'this Labour Movement owes much to the miners. In fact, it is true to say, if we read the history of politics in this country, that if the miners had not stood steadfast for the Labour Party in 1929 and 1931 perhaps we would not have a Labour Government today.'[106] These mnemonic mobilisations placed significant pressure on the party's leadership. In July 1967, when it was suggested in July that Jim Callaghan (the Chancellor of the Exchequer) had over-deflated the economy, Wilson's first instinct was to stop all further pit closures in Britain.[107]

At 1967's Labour Party Conference, the Chairman (John Boyd) attempted to defuse the tensions that existed in the party by making a nostalgic appeal for calm and tolerance. Boyd took it upon himself to 'remind all who may be listening to the words of Keir Hardie spoken in 1903 when he said "Socialism offers a platform broad enough for all to stand upon who accept its principles. It makes war upon a system not upon a class."'[108] This historical emphasis merely served to encourage further discursive deployments of the past. One delegate demanded that Labour 'bring about the birth of a new society that this movement was built to create' and he described how 'in this movement today there is in fact an ever-growing expression of opinion that this Government ought to return to basic socialist principles.'[109] Another CLP delegate from a coal mining area declared that he was seconding a resolution supporting the coal industry because mining areas 'have carried the Labour Party along since the industrial revolution'.[110] In this way, much of the rhetoric that was mobilised by Labour's membership against industrial decline seemed to be informed by the historically orientated idea that was circulating in the wider party that the miners 'have not stayed loyal to the Labour Party through thick and thin for nearly 60 years, to see themselves out on the dole and the mining areas left derelict'.[111]

Shaped by the nature of the intraparty debate that surrounded the emotive issue of deindustrialisation, Wilson's 1967 conference speech was littered with references to the party's industrial past. He claimed that 'No one who was brought up in one of our older industrial areas in the years of the depression – as I was in West Riding, or Wales, Lancashire, the north-east or Scotland or Cumberland or the Black Country – could ever erase those memories from his mind.'[112] He talked about how 'the traditional socialism of this country was created out of the squalor and the inhumanity and the exploitation of that first industrial revolution.'[113] Yet such concessions to the party's industrial heritage could not prevent further resistance to the Labour leadership's policies.

In one of the conference's subsequent debates, selective memories of the past were presented by supporters of the textile industry. These historically defined appeals gave emotional substance to their demand that the textile industry be preserved. Echoing a speech that he had made at the TUC conference in September, Jack Peel (National Union of Dyers, Bleachers and Textile Workers) described how 'we have been giving our best to the economy of this country for many years; and we have also given leaders to the Labour movement, locally, regionally and nationally.'[114] Another delegate stated that the textile workers 'have worked and fought hard for this country. Now they have a right to ask that you help them.'[115] The debate's backward-looking emphasis clearly impacted upon the nature of Frank Donlon's response to the debate. Speaking on behalf of the NEC, Donlon, who was an ex-railway man, was at pains to stress his role in a cotton strike in Manchester in the early 1930s.[116] In an attempt to foster a sense of unity between the nation's textile workers and the Government, he talked about how 'The workers in the cotton industry are the descendants really of those who were massacred at Peterloo, the cotton workers, and they are not now, I do not believe, going to give support to any other than the Government they have placed in power.'[117] By displaying sensitivity towards the past, Donlon attempted to soothe the anger that was being directed towards the Government.

Other supporters of the Government adopted a more ardently anti-nostalgic position on the issue of deindustrialisation. Writing in the *New Statesman* in August 1968, Brian Walden MP described how

> In the world of the past, in which the Labour Party lives and is encouraged to live, the tactics of building a majority out of minorities made some sense. South Wales, Clydeside, Lancashire Trades Councils and coalminers could all be persuaded that the Labour Party existed for them. It was 'their' party.[118]

Walden argued that Labour needed to adapt itself to the realities of modern Britain and broaden its electoral appeal beyond its traditional industrial working-class support base. He declared that, in order to do this, 'The leadership of the Labour Party must banish fear and tame tradition.'[119] Responding to Walden's article, one party member suggested that 'it's not the fundamentals that are wrong or are not relevant – in fact they are more relevant today than they were in the early days of the movement.'[120]

Throughout 1968, opposition to the Government's approach towards Britain's declining industries continued to be expressed through an overtly nostalgic discourse. One delegate at the 1968 Labour Party Conference talked about how 'The men of Peterlee [a coal mining town in Durham] must turn in their graves to see the ruthless wiping out of an industry for which they worked so hard to better the conditions at the beginning of this century.'[121] This particular statement highlighted how Labour's nostalgia could often be divorced from historical reality: the town in County Durham that was being referred to was actually named 'Peterlee' in 1948. More broadly, left-wing Labour politicians like Eric Heffer MP criticised the Government for attempting to disown the party's history. Speaking at the party's annual conference, Heffer proclaimed that 'I believe that we as socialists have got to get back to the ideas of people like James Connolly and others in our movement in the past.'[122] These sentiments were met with applause from the conference's attendees.

Devaluation

The issue of devaluation had long preoccupied the Wilson Governments. In November 1967, the pound was finally devalued. Party members viewed devaluation in a similar manner to the way that they had interpreted the July measures of the previous year. In particular, the Labour Left sought to link the actions of the Government to Ramsay MacDonald's 'betrayal' of the Labour movement in 1931. The week after devaluation, *Tribune* published articles with headlines like 'How Close was Labour to 1931?'[123] Its main editorial declared that 'Not until the archives are open and the Ministers write their memoirs shall we know how close Labour came to another 1931 last week.'[124]

The omnipotence of this historical narrative clearly impacted on the way that senior figures interpreted and responded to events. Richard Crossman (Leader of the House of Commons and a former confidant of Wilson) wrote in his diary on 31 December 1967 that 'This Government has failed more abysmally than any Government since 1931.'[125] George Brown (who, at this stage, held the position of Foreign Secretary) resigned from the Government in March 1968. He likened the unilateral actions of Harold Wilson, Roy Jenkins (who had replaced Callaghan as Chancellor after the devaluation debacle) and Peter Shore to those of Ramsay MacDonald, Philip Snowden and James Henry Thomas in 1931. At the time of his resignation, Brown declared that 'You know, we've all read this history, and we've repeatedly said that if only the Party or the Government had stopped Ramsay, Snowden and Thomas from behaving on their own, the events of 1931 and the subsequent Labour disaster need never have happened.'[126]

The Donovan Commission and *In Place of Strife*

During the late 1960s, nostalgia continued to shape Labour's relationship with the trade unions. Responding to the findings of the Donovan Commission (which highlighted the problem of militant decentralised trade unionism in Britain), the Government called for further union amalgamations and an extension of formal centralised control within the trade union movement.[127] 1968 witnessed the hundredth anniversary of the founding of the TUC. At the TUC's Centenary Pageant in Manchester in June 1968, Wilson declared that 'The TUC has arrived. It is an estate of the realm, as real, as potent, as essentially part of the fabric of our national life, as any of the historic Estates.' He also praised the responsibility that the unions had shown by agreeing 'to surrender to the central organization some part of the historic sovereignty for which they had battled for over a century'.[128] In this way, Wilson referenced the historic struggles of the TUC's past in order to legitimise his calls for reform in the present.

Perhaps inevitably, the past weighed heavily upon the TUC's centennial conference in September 1968. Lord Wright (the TUC's President) began the conference by suggesting that 'nostalgia is not in itself rewarding, and our principal thoughts now must be not of history but of the future.'[129] This advice went largely unheeded by the conference's attendees. Delegates, like Danny McGarvey, were keen to emphasise that

> Yes, we are 100 years old, and not 100 years young, because this movement has experienced and has come through the trials and tribulations of those who went before us. Are we going to cast that aside because somebody says, 'You are not doing it the right way?' We will do things the right way. We want collective bargaining.[130]

Furthermore, trade unionists who opposed the Government's pay policies declared that 'we owe allegiance to the Labour Party, the labour and trade union Movements and the principles laid down 100 years ago. We owe nothing to a Government and leaders who, in the interests of power, have deserted these principles and are determined to impose their will on the free trade union movement.'[131]

The Government's supporters attempted to counter-mobilise nostalgia against these accusations of betrayal. Acting as the fraternal delegate from the Labour Party, Jennie Lee stated that 'you know perfectly well in this Centenary year that the men and women who built our trade union Movement would not have had the courage to stand up to the punishment they had to take if they had been fighting for material things alone.' She pleaded emotionally with the delegates at the conference: 'Do not insult the men of my family, do not insult my grandfather, who went from pit to pit, victimised, when the miners were establishing the 8-hour day for their industry.'[132] Likewise, George Brown told a meeting of trade unionists at the 1968 Labour Party Conference that 'Our policy does mean interfering. That is what Keir Hardie was talking about.'[133] These nostalgic deployments were unsuccessful. In 1968, the annual conferences of both the TUC and the Labour Party voted against the Government's incomes policy.[134]

Barbara Castle's 1969 White Paper *In Place of Strife* was widely interpreted to represent a further attack on Labour's historic relationship with unions. Castle's memoirs highlighted her intention 'to raise the status and rights of trade unions, but I also believed I had the right in return to ask them to accept greater responsibilities in preventing the needless disruption of the country's economic life.'[135] The name *In Place of Strife* was chosen as a direct reference to Bevan's 1952 book *In Place of Fear*.[136] To Wilson's consternation, Castle's proposals for trade union reform were interpreted as being punitive, despite the fact that 'only three of the twenty-seven recommendations involved any use of so called "penal" powers.'[137] The party's inclination to view its Government's policies through the lens of the past contributed to this negative perception. On 3 January 1969, *Tribune* ran a front-page editorial proclaiming 'The Government needs a cooling off period' and it suggested that 'The Government's drift towards self-inflicted destruction is not accidental ... The parallel with 1931 is ominous and hardly needs stressing.'[138] Subsequently, it condemned the Government's White Paper as 'the most far-reaching curbs on the right to strike since the Combination Acts were repealed in 1824'.[139]

Labour's rank-and-file members were incensed by *In Place of Strife*. One party member wrote a letter to *Tribune* that declared that 'Ramsay MacDonald was a novice compared with Harold Wilson and Barbara Castle ... Never were the working classes sold a more despicable set of dishonest persons.'[140] Another letter that was written to the *New Statesman* suggested that the Government's decision to legislate was 'just Tolpuddle all over again'.[141] Party members were quick to remind the Government that Labour 'was founded to represent organised labour in Parliament'.[142] Labour's National Executive Committee passed a resolution against

Barbara Castle's White Paper in March 1969.¹⁴³ Following an emergency meeting of the TUC, Wilson was forced to abandon the White Paper's proposals. *In Place of Strife* had been defeated in a matter of months. *Tribune* compared Wilson's backtracking on *In Place of Strife* to that of Gaitskell on the issue of Clause IV in 1959 and 1960.¹⁴⁴ The two episodes shared a great deal of similarity. In both cases, memories of the past were mobilised effectively against the Labour leadership's policies.

By the end of 1969, there was no indication that Labour members wanted the party to reorient itself away from its nostalgia. At the party's annual gathering in October, Wilson expressed the belief that 'Labour is changing Britain, and changing it for the better. There can be no going back.'¹⁴⁵ Nonetheless, during the conference's debates, delegates routinely displayed an attachment to the past. One speaker talked about how the Jarrow marches were 'indelibly marked on the hearts of all socialists.'¹⁴⁶ The prospective parliamentary candidate for Aylesbury attacked the Conservative Party for having 'murdered towns like Jarrow' and for leaving 'able-bodied men to rot away in valleys like Rhondda' during the 1930s.¹⁴⁷ More nostalgically, a councillor from Rotherham celebrated those 'great regions of this country which have poured out their blood and their treasure for 150 years to make this the most highly industrialised nation in the world'. He also attacked previous Conservative Governments for neglecting Britain's industrial areas.¹⁴⁸ In response to the conference's decidedly backward-looking nature, William Blair from the Electrical, Electronic and Telecommunication Union – Plumbing Trades Union pointedly stated that 'It is no good trying to put the clock back, hiding our heads in the sand and pretending that radical changes in some industrial areas must not take place.'¹⁴⁹ Similarly, speaking at the TUC's 1969 conference, one trade unionist noted that 'We have a long and distinguished history of which we can be proud; but when history cannot be distinguished from the present, then it is not something to be proud of.'¹⁵⁰

Conclusion

If, as O'Hara and Parr have suggested, we are to view Harold Wilson as being 'ahead of his time', then it is also necessary to understand the manner in which the wider party was behind its time.¹⁵¹ The vision of modernity that originated from the Labour leadership in 1963 and 1964 was not shared by the majority of party members. During the years 1964 to 1970, the party's collective nostalgia-identity regularly served to undermine the Labour Government's attempts to modernise the British economy. Party members were largely opposed to any reforms that might affect the party's historic relationship with the unions. They were also, on the whole, suspicious of the new scientific and technological age. Indeed, throughout the period, party members were preoccupied with the preservation of the traditional industries of the past. They were, at best, indifferent and, at worst, hostile to Wilson's desire to plan and develop the scientific and technological industries of the future. A sentimental attachment to the party's traditional industrial heritage and the heroic struggles of a bygone era was central to Labour's political understanding of the present. This sentiment was most pronounced on the left of the party. As Paul Foot noted in 1968, 'Where the Government took action which offended against the old traditions and the old theory of the Labour Left, the Left responded immediately and courageously with clear and untrammelled opposition.'[152]

As the 1960s wore on, the nostalgic backlash against the Government's domestic policies intensified. Having been forced by economic circumstance into pursuing deflationary policies, the Labour leadership was accused of abandoning the traditional industrial working class. Nostalgia and, more broadly, memories of the past were central to these accusations. In response, Wilson and his allies attempted to modify their rhetoric in a manner that was more concessionary to the party's historically orientated identity. However, the Government's approach to Britain's declining industries increasingly came under attack from a rank and file who wanted more proactive policies that sought to preserve and reinvigorate these industries.

There is evidence to suggest that the historically informed backlash against the Government in the mid-1960s impacted upon its political decision making. Faced with a need to reflate the economy in 1967, Wilson's first instinct was to stop any further pit closures. Furthermore, nostalgia clearly shaped the options that were available to the Government with regards to trade union reform. Looking back on the 1964 to 1970 Labour Governments, George Brown noted that 'It is never easy to adjust one's ideas to social change; for a great political party rooted in the past perhaps it is impossible to do so quickly.'[153] Britain was changing at a startling rate but Labour was not. Throughout the social and economic upheavals of the 1960s, the party remained defined by its nostalgic attachment to the past.

Notes

1 D. Butler and A. King, *The British General Election of 1964* (London: Macmillan, 1965), 71.
2 K. O. Morgan, 'The Wilson Years' in N. Tiratsoo (ed.), *From Blitz to Blair: A New History of Britain since 1939* (London: Weidenfield and Nicolson, 1997), 134.
3 B. Pimlott, *Harold Wilson* (London: Harper Collins, 1992), 302.

4. P. Foot, *The Politics of Harold Wilson* (Harmondsworth: Penguin, 1968), 152.
5. J. Tomlinson, *The Labour Governments 1964–70: Vol. 3, Economic Policy* (Manchester: Manchester University Press, 2004), 11.
6. Morgan, 'Wilson Years', 139.
7. Shaw, *Labour Party since 1945*, 105.
8. For a recent collection of essays on Wilson's political record, see A. S. Crines and K. Hickson (eds), *Harold Wilson: The Unprincipled Prime Minister? Reappraising Harold Wilson* (London: Biteback, 2016).
9. G. O'Hara and H. Parr, 'Introduction: The Fall and Rise of a Reputation' in G. O'Hara and H. Parr (eds), *The Wilson Governments 1964–1970 Reconsidered* (London: Routledge, 2006), xii.
10. Cronin, *New Labour's Pasts*, 89.
11. Tomlinson, *Labour Governments*, 173; Pimlott, *Harold Wilson*, 442; A. Cairncross, *Managing the British Economy in the 1960s: A Treasury Perspective* (Basingstoke: Macmillan, 1996), 131. Steven Fielding has adopted a more cultural approach, see S. Fielding, *The Labour Governments 1964–1970: Vol. 1, Labour and Cultural Change* (Manchester: Manchester University Press, 2003).
12. Shaw, *Labour Party since 1945*, 65.
13. C. A. R. Crosland, *The Conservative Enemy: A Programme of Radical Reform for the 1960s* (London: Cape, 1962), 128.
14. M. Barratt-Brown, 'Crosland's Enemy: A Reply', *New Left Review,* March/April 1963, 31.
15. J. Corina, 'Science and Economic Revival', *Socialist Commentary*, March 1963, 13.
16. G. Brown, 'Cotton and its Future' 1963/6, in Labour Party, *Archives of the British Labour Party, Series 2, Pamphlets and Leaflets*, 2.
17. G. Parker, 'Coming to Terms with Reality', *Socialist Commentary*, August 1963, 24.
18. For example, see F. Halliday, quoted in The Trades Union Congress, *TUC Report 1963, Report of the 95th Annual Trades Union Congress held in The Dome, Brighton, September 2nd to 6th 1963* (London: TUC, 1963), 70.
19. J. R. Stanley, quoted in Trades Union Congress, *TUCACR 1963*, 389.
20. E. J. Hill, quoted in Trades Union Congress, *TUCACR 1963*, 396.
21. H. A. Hetherington, 'Meeting with Harold Wilson', 4 September 1963, HETHERINGTON/5, Hetherington Papers, LSE, 4.
22. H. Wilson, quoted in The Labour Party, *Report of the 62nd Annual Conference held in the Spa, Grand Hall, Scarborough, September 30th to October 4th, 1963* (London: The Labour Party, 1963), 134.
23. Wilson, quoted in Labour Party, *LPACR 1963*, 134.
24. *Ibid.*, 140.
25. *Ibid.*, 138.
26. *Ibid.*, 135.
27. A. Woodburn, quoted in Labour Party, *LPACR 1963*, 146.
28. See F. Cousins, quoted in Labour Party, *LPACR 1963*, 146; J. Cooper, quoted in Labour Party, *LPACR 1963*, 190.

29 Doswell, quoted in Labour Party, *LPACR 1963*, 257–258.
30 J. Milhench, quoted in Labour Party, *LPACR 1963*, 258.
31 Editorial, 'Conference Comment: Science and the Party Programme', *Tribune*, 4 October 1963, 3.
32 R. Fletcher, 'Socialism Steps In', *Tribune*, 11 October, 1963, 5.
33 Editorial, 'Impact of Science on Industry', *The Times,* 20 July 1964, 11.
34 F. T. Hawkins, 'What About the Workers?', letter to *Tribune*, 24 January 1964, 2–3.
35 D. McGarvey, quoted in The Trades Union Congress, *TUC Report 1964, Report of the 96th Annual Trades Union Congress held in the Opera House, Blackpool, September 7nd to 11th 1964* (London: TUC, 1964), 548.
36 S. Hopkins, 'Managerial Doubts', letter to *New Statesman*, 18 September 1964, 399.
37 Unnamed writer, 'Coal's Success Story', *Socialist Commentary*, October 1964, 8.
38 See B. Griffiths, 'Jimmy Fell', *Tribune*, 27 March 1964, 12.
39 The Labour Party Science and Industry Sub-Committee Redundancy Group, 'Industrial Training for Adult Workers', April 1964, R. 629, Labour History Archive, Manchester, 1.
40 The Labour Party, 'Manpower Policies in a Changing Society: A Background Note by Reg Prentice for the Meeting of the Trade Union Group', 9 June 1964, RD. 788, Labour History Archive, 1.
41 G. Brown, 'Strategy for Advance', *Socialist Commentary*, January 1964, 6.
42 Editorial, 'The Reluctant Prime Minister', *New Statesman*, 7 February 1964, 193.
43 E. Short, *Whip to Wilson* (London: MacDonald, 1989), 10.
44 The Labour Party, *The New Britain* (London: The Labour Party, 1964), www.labour-party.org.uk/manifestos/1964/1964-labour-manifesto.shtml.
45 Labour Party, *New Britain*.
46 The Labour Party, 'Labour: A Woman's View' (London: The Labour Party, 1964), 1964/29, in Labour Party, *Archives of the British Labour Party, Series 2, Pamphlets and Leaflets*, 4.
47 The Labour Party, 'Welcome to the Labour Party' (London: The Labour Party, 1964), 1964/74, in Labour Party, *Archives of the British Labour Party, Series 2, Pamphlets and Leaflets*, 4.
48 R. Clements, 'Victory for Socialism', *Tribune*, 16 October 1964, 2.
49 H. Wilson. 'Television Broadcast to the Nation on the Economic Situation, 26 October 1964' in H. Wilson, *Purpose in Power: Selected Speeches* (London: Weidenfeld and Nicolson, 1966), 8.
50 H. Wilson, quoted in The Labour Party, *Report of the 63rd Annual Conference held in the Sports Stadium, West Street, Brighton, December 12th and 13th, 1964* (London: The Labour Party, 1964), 112. For Wilson's regret, see H. Wilson, *The Labour Government 1964–1970: A Personal Record* (London: Weidenfeld and Nicolson, 1971), 53.
51 H. Wilson, quoted Labour Party, *LPACR 1964*, 112.
52 *Ibid.*, 117.
53 G. Brown, quoted in Labour Party, *LPACR 1964*, 148.

54　D. Boulton, 'Voices of Socialism: William Morris', *Tribune*, 30 October 1964, 13.
55　A. Arblaster, 'Voices of Socialism: John Ruskin', *Tribune*, 11 December, 1964, 13.
56　G. Rhodes, 'Labour's New Boys', *Socialist Commentary*, January 1965, 18; R. Graydon, 'Baby and Bathwater', *Socialist Commentary*, February 1965, 31.
57　B. Magee 'Labour: The Missing Talents', *New Statesman*, 5 February 1965, 189–190.
58　K. Lomas, 'The MPs Reply', letter to *New Statesman*, 12 February 1965, 233.
59　I. R. Thomas, 'The MPs Reply', letter to *New Statesman*, 12 February 1965, 234.
60　C. H. Bagnall, 'Selecting MPs', letter to *New Statesman*, 19 February 1965, 277.
61　G. G. Jones, 'The Miners are Worried', letter to *Tribune*, 22 January 1965, 2.
62　G. Langham quoted in The Labour Party, 'Report of the Forty-Second National Conference of Labour Women, Barrfields Pavilion, Largs, Ayrshire, March 9th, 10th and 11th, 1965' (London: The Labour Party, 1965), 1965/32, in Labour Party, *Archives of the British Labour Party, Series 2, Pamphlets and Leaflets*, 16.
63　Short, *Whip to Wilson*, 146.
64　Editorial, 'The Great Illusion', *The Times*, 1 May 1965, 11.
65　P. Jenkins, 'Politics of Industry: The Movement of Opinion', *Socialist Commentary*, August 1965, 21.
66　The Department of Economic Affairs, *The National Plan* (London: Her Majesty's Stationery Office, 1965).
67　The Department of Economic Affairs, *Working for Prosperity: The National Plan in Brief* (London: Her Majesty's Stationery Office, 1965), 4.
68　DEA, *Working for Prosperity*, 13; DEA, *Working for Prosperity*, 25.
69　Short, *Whip to Wilson*, 176.
70　Editorial, 'The Plan … That Never Was', *Tribune*, 17 September 1965, 1.
71　G. G. Jones, 'View from the Rhondda', letter to *Tribune*, 24 September 1965, 13; Editorial, 'Questions Which Brown Must Answer', *Tribune*, 24 September 1965, 1.
72　R. Klein, 'Is the Island Going to Sink?' *Observer*, 2 January 1966, 11.
73　For example, see Editorial, 'On to the Commanding Heights', *New Statesman*, 31 January 1964, 149.
74　F. T. Hollocks, quoted in The Trades Union Congress, *TUC Report 1965, Report of the 97th Annual Trades Union Congress held in The Dome, Brighton, September 6th to 10th 1965* (London: TUC, 1965), 487.
75　M. Veitch, quoted in Trades Union Congress, *TUCACR 1965*, 81.
76　A. Patterson, quoted in The Labour Party, *Report of the 64th Annual Conference held in the Empress Ballroom, Winter Gardens, Blackpool, September 27th to October 1st, 1965* (London: The Labour Party, 1965), 240.
77　S. Orme, quoted in Labour Party, *LPACR 1965*, 240.
78　F. T. Blackaby, 'Narrative, 1960–74' in F. T. Blackaby (ed.), *British Economic Policy 1960–74* (Cambridge: Cambridge University Press, 1978), 28.
79　See Cairncross, *Managing the British Economy*, 265.
80　Tomlinson, *Labour Governments*, 173.
81　H. Collins, 'How Close are We to Another 1931?', *Tribune*, 26 August 1966, 5.
82　M. Barratt-Brown, 'Could We Be Back to 1929?', *Tribune*, 16 September 1966, 8.

83 L. W. Dungate, 'The Economic Crisis', letter to *New Statesman*, 29 July 1966, 167.
84 See G. Goodman, *The Awkward Warrior – Frank Cousins: His Life and Times* (London: Davis-Poynter, 1979), 495.
85 P. Crane, 'Old Fashioned Idols: Frank Cousins', *Socialist Commentary*, August 1966, 18.
86 Crane, 'Old Fashioned Idols', 19.
87 G. Goodman, 'Talk with Sir Vincent Tewson', 26 January 1975, MSS.169/48, Goodman Papers, Modern Records Centre, 1.
88 G. Goodman, 'Talk with Richard Marsh', 19 November 1973, MSS.169/48, Goodman Papers, Modern Records Centre, 2.
89 J. O'Hagan, quoted in The Trades Union Congress, *TUC Report 1966, Report of the 98th Annual Trades Union Congress held in the Opera House, Blackpool, September 5th to 9th 1966* (London: TUC, 1966), 79.
90 For example, see A. Roberts, quoted in Trades Union Congress, *TUCACR 1966*, 81.
91 H. Wilson, quoted in Trades Union Congress, *TUCACR 1966*, 400.
92 D. McGarvey, quoted in Trades Union Congress, *TUCACR 1966*, 467.
93 T. J. Smith, quoted in Trades Union Congress, *TUCACR 1966*, 471.
94 H. Wilson, quoted in The Labour Party, *Report of the 65th Annual Conference held in the Top Rank Entertainments Centre, Brighton, October 3rd to October 7th, 1966* (London: The Labour Party, 1966), 163.
95 Wilson, quoted in Labour Party, *LPACR 1966*, 162–163.
96 W. Blair, quoted in Labour Party, *LPACR 1966*, 170.
97 D. McGarvey, quoted in Labour Party, *LPACR 1966*, 233.
98 C. Jenkins, quoted in Labour Party, *LPACR 1966*, 216.
99 E. Patterson, quoted in Labour Party, *LPACR 1966*, 218.
100 A Gibson, quoted in Labour Party, *LPACR 1966*, 224.
101 Editorial, 'Our Gradual Revolution', *Socialist Commentary*, November 1966, 3.
102 M. Miller, quoted in The Labour Party, 'Report of the Forty-Fourth National Conference of Labour Women, Cliffs Pavilion, Southend on Sea, May 16th, 17th and 18th, 1967' (London: The Labour Party, 1967), 1967/37, in Labour Party, *Archives of the British Labour Party, Series 2, Pamphlets and Leaflets*, 14.
103 Miller, quoted in Labour Party, 'Report of the Forty-Fourth National Conference of Labour Women', 15.
104 Editorial, 'Luddites or Just Human?', *New Statesman*, 30 June 1967, 893.
105 M. Coady, 'Fall Out From the Pits', *New Statesman*, 30 June 1967, 894.
106 B. King, quoted in Labour Party, *LPACR 1966*, 152.
107 B. Castle, diary entry for 22 July 1967 in B. Castle, *The Castle Diaries 1964–70* (London: Weidenfeld and Nicolson, 1984), 280.
108 J. Boyd, quoted in The Labour Party, *Report of the Sixty-Sixth Annual Conference of the Labour Party, Scarborough, 1967, October 2nd to 6th* (London: The Labour Party, 1967), 118.
109 E. Loyden, quoted in Labour Party, *LPACR 1967*, 190.
110 M. Quinn, quoted in Labour Party, *LPACR 1967*, 203.
111 H. Collins, 'The Next Crisis', *Tribune*, 17 November 1967, 1.

112 H. Wilson, quoted in Labour Party, *LPACR 1967*, 215.
113 *Ibid.*, 216.
114 J. Peel, quoted in The Trades Union Congress, *TUC Report 1967, Report of the 99th Annual Trades Union Congress held in The Dome, Brighton, September 4th to 8th 1967* (London: TUC, 1967), 556; J. Peel, quoted in Labour Party, *LPACR 1967*, 265–266.
115 F. Hilson, quoted in Labour Party, *LPACR 1967*, 265.
116 F. Donlon, quoted in Labour Party, *LPACR 1967*, 267.
117 *Ibid.*, 268–269.
118 B. Walden, 'What Labour Needs is Guts' *New Statesman*, 9 August 1968, 158.
119 Walden, 'What Labour Needs', 158.
120 H. Marks, 'Walden's Solution' letter to *New Statesman*, 16 August 1968, 201.
121 N. Crawford, quoted in Labour Party, *Report of the Sixty-Seventh Annual Conference of the Labour Party, Blackpool, 1968, September 30th to October 4th* (London: The Labour Party, 1968), 276.
122 E. Heffer, quoted in *LPACR 1968*, 197.
123 G. Sinclair, 'How Close was Labour to 1931?', *Tribune*, 24 November 1967, 4.
124 Editorial, 'What Last Weekend Meant for British Socialism', *Tribune*, 24 November 1967, 1.
125 R. H. S. Crossman, diary entry for 31 December 1967 in R. H. S. Crossman (A. Howard ed.), *The Crossman Diaries: Selections from the Diaries of a Cabinet Minister, 1964–1970* (London: Cape, 1979), 386.
126 Brown, *In My Way*, 179.
127 For more on the Donovan Report, see W. H. Fraser, *A History of British Trade Unionism: 1700–1998* (London: Macmillan, 1998), 217–219; J. McIroy, *Trade Unions in Britain Today* (Manchester: Manchester University Press, 1995), 237–238; C. Wrigley, *British Trade Unions, 1945–1995* (Manchester: Manchester University Press, 1997), 65–77.
128 Wilson, *Labour Government*, 533.
129 L. Wright, quoted in The Trades Union Congress, *TUC Report 1968, Report of the 100th Annual Trades Union Congress held in the Opera House, Blackpool, September 2nd to 6th 1968* (London: TUC, 1968), 94.
130 D. McGarvey, quoted in Trades Union Congress, *TUCACR 1968*, 564.
131 W. Lindley, quoted in Trades Union Congress, *TUCACR 1968*, 566.
132 J. Lee, quoted in Trades Union Congress, *TUCACR 1968*, 444.
133 G. Clark, 'Mr Brown Tells Unions to Grow Up', *The Times*, 1 October 1968, 10.
134 Trades Union Congress, *TUCACR 1968*, 572; Labour Party, *LPACR 1968*, 153.
135 Castle, *Fighting all the Way*, 416.
136 *Ibid.*, 417.
137 Wilson, *Labour Government*, 591.
138 Editorial, 'The Government Need a "Cooling Off Period"', *Tribune*, 3 January 1969, 1.
139 Editorial, 'How Many Warnings Does the Government Need?', *Tribune*, 4 April 1969, 1.
140 R. Thomas, 'MacDonald and Wilson', letter to *Tribune*, 24 January 1969, 8.

141 J. Stewart Cook, 'Governments and Unions', letter to *New Statesman*, 2 May 1969, 620.
142 J. Rawson, 'Labour's Crisis', letter to *New Statesman*, 4 April 1969, 479.
143 B. Castle, diary entry for 26 March 1969 in Castle, *Castle Diaries*, 625–626.
144 R. Clements, 'How Important Was Last Week's Victory – Another Clause Four?', *Tribune*, 27 June 1969, 1.
145 H. Wilson, quoted in The Labour Party, *Report of the Sixty-Eighth Annual Conference of the Labour Party, Brighton, 1969, September 29th to October 3rd* (London: The Labour Party, 1969), 199.
146 A. Leary, quoted in Labour Party, *LPACR 1969*, 238.
147 J. Mitchell, quoted in Labour Party, *LPACR 1969*, 242.
148 S. Crowther, quoted in Labour Party, *LPACR 1969*, 239.
149 W. Blair, quoted in Labour Party, *LPACR 1969*, 243.
150 R. Rosser, quoted in The Trades Union Congress, *TUC Report 1969, Report of the 101st Annual Trades Union Congress held in the Guildhall, Portsmouth, September 1st to 5th 1969* (London: TUC, 1969), 489.
151 O'Hara and Parr, 'Introduction', xii.
152 Foot, *Politics of Harold Wilson*, 315.
153 Brown, *In My Way*, 90.

3

Labour's Alternative Economic Strategy, 1970–83

A significant section of the Labour Party blamed the party's 1970 General Election defeat on the policies and performance of Harold Wilson's 1964 to 1970 Labour Governments. In 1970, as James Cronin has described, 'There was a widespread and vague sense within the party that Labour's defeat had been largely self-inflicted, that the loss was perhaps a fitting rebuke for failures in government, and that it might require a rethinking of party policy and strategy.'[1] According to Martin Pugh, for many party members, 'The 1970 defeat was the signal to release the accumulated resentment over the government's record since 1964 and the prime minister in particular.'[2] Within the Labour Party, disaffection with the policies and the political record of the 1964 to 1970 Wilson Governments fuelled the rise of the party's left wing.[3] It was in this political climate that Labour's Alternative Economic Strategy (AES) was formulated.

The AES's conceptual origins lay in the subcommittees of Labour's NEC during the party's period in opposition between 1970 and 1974.[4] Its policies were embodied in *Labour's Programme 1973*, *Labour's Programme 1976*, and Labour's 1983 General Election Manifesto, *The New Hope for Britain*. The AES envisaged a widespread extension of public ownership. *Labour's Programme 1973* argued that a future Labour Government should gain control of twenty-five of Britain's leading companies (as well as those in which the Government had already heavily invested).[5] Stuart Holland was the economist who became most closely associated with the development of the AES. Holland believed that a high level of state control was necessary in order to combat the rise of multinational power and to rejuvenate the stuttering British economy.[6] He suggested that 'Recent acceleration in the trend to monopoly and multinational capital has eroded Keynesian economic policies, and undermined the sovereignty of the capitalist nation state.'[7] Holland argued that public ownership offered a means by which Britain could reverse recent global trends and develop a socialist economy. The Government was to gain a majority shareholding stake in new dynamic growth industries. This process of nationalisation was to be facilitated by a National Enterprise Board.[8]

Holland's initial vision of the AES was heavily influenced by state holding and planning institutions in European countries like France and Italy.[9] His exploration of the possibilities of alternative European models of public ownership was less insular than the understanding of the strategy that would become dominant within the party. Over time, withdrawal from the European Economic Community (EEC) became a central component of the AES. The AES's supporters fought ardently for a 'no' vote at the 1975 referendum on Britain's membership. The 1980 Labour Party Conference demanded Britain's withdrawal from the EEC.[10] Increasingly, Labour opposed the perceived free-market capitalism of the EEC. By the mid-1970s, protective import controls were deemed to be a necessary prerequisite to the successful implementation of the AES.[11] The AES also advocated increased industrial democracy and workers' control in British industry. These proposals were interlinked with the AES's promotion of public ownership and they were underpinned by the idea that 'it would be easier to pioneer and develop the institutions and the operation of industrial democracy in a centrally controlled industry run in the spirit of public service than in a disparate one operated under the urge of the maximisation of profit.'[12]

The AES has been portrayed by both historians and political scientists as a modern, progressive, and forward-looking strategy. A consensus has formed around the idea that modernity influenced the AES's polices and shaped Labour's programmatic commitments. Mark Wickham-Jones has argued: 'The Alternative Economic Strategy marked a radical departure in the kind of social democracy that Labour advocated. The adoption of the AES indicated a break with Labour's Revisionist past.'[13] Stephen Haseler has declared: 'By the late 1970s it [Labour] had become wholly unrecognisable. It had broken with its past. It was as if a new political party had been born.'[14] Furthermore, historians who have written about the AES have emphasised the role of political factions or a small number of policymakers.[15] They have ignored the emotional resonance of the AES within the wider party in favour of conducting highly focused studies on the strategy's policies and the political actors involved in the construction of these policies. Thus, the policies that were contained within the AES have been viewed largely through the lens of the theoretical and deliberative discussions that are perceived to have taken place in the party's policy committees during the early 1970s. This chapter examines the way that nostalgia shaped Labour's AES. It does so by looking at the three major components of the AES that I have outlined: public ownership, EEC withdrawal, and industrial democracy.

The AES was devised at a point in British history at which the past has been understood to have exerted a particularly strong influence on the nation's culture. Raphael Samuel noted that a 'historicist turn in national life' had been 'amplified in the 1970s by a whole series of separation anxieties' that had developed from the changing nature of British society.[16] However, as this book has already shown, Labour's strong historical impetus predated the British heritage and tradition boom of the 1970s.[17] Moreover, Labour's nostalgia-identity was defined by symbols, figures, and events that were highly specific to the party's own past. In this chapter, I suggest that it was this nostalgia-imbued identity that ensured that preservation and restoration, not modernisation, lay at the heart of Labour's AES.[18]

Public ownership

Despite his commitment to economic innovation and his promotion of new and dynamic growth industries, Holland's approach to Britain's ailing traditional industries was characterised by ambiguity. He blurred the distinction between old and new industries and declared that 'The modern manufacturing sector of today is the traditional manufacturing of tomorrow. Moreover, today's traditional industry may be modernized through new techniques of production, greater capital-intensity, and so on.'[19] Holland suggested that coal and steel, two publicly owned industries at the heart of Labour's historic identity, could play an important role in improving the economic climate and reducing the 'long-term deficit on the visible balance of trade' in Britain.[20] Additionally, he also argued that, by developing key manufacturing industries, the future economic growth of Britain's traditional industries could be secured.[21]

Significantly, it was these elements of Holland's economic analysis that the Labour Party seized upon. An economic interpretation of Britain that stressed the continued viability of Britain's traditional industries was embraced by the party's membership. The AES was understood not as a blueprint by which to modernise the British economy, but as a means by which to preserve and restore a particular vision of the past. Such an interpretation was facilitated by the nature of the political discourse that surrounded the AES from an early stage in its development. Preservation, not modernisation, lay at the heart of the way that the strategy was discursively framed: Labour's Industrial Policy Sub-Committee declared that 'our industrial policies are not intended to be judged by the criteria of industrial efficiency.'[22]

The past was mobilised to legitimise the party's economic approach: 'There are many strands of Socialist analysis and belief which throughout the history of our movement have made the theme of the public ownership of our material industrial resources central to the achievement of a Socialist society.'[23] There was a strong sense that the past could provide guidance for the present. *Labour's Programme: Campaign Document 1974* stated that 'the Labour Party is proud of the contribution that we made to the nation's salvation at critical times in our history, and it is in the same mood that we approach the interlocking crises of the 1970s.'[24] *Labour's Programme 1973* discussed the need to preserve employment in the traditional industries of coal, steel, and shipbuilding.[25] In much the same way, the February 1974 Manifesto appeared preoccupied with declining industrial occupations. It demanded that 'with the utmost urgency, the coal industry must be given a new status, perspective, and security.'[26] Increasingly, the AES's advocates argued that the strategy was 'designed to halt the process of de-industrialisation'.[27]

The emotional context of such statements should not be dismissed. Nostalgia shaped the political identities of the AES's leading advocates. Tony Benn talked about how his father 'went to the 1889 dock strike on his father's shoulders'.[28] He noted the 'tremendous emotive overtones'[29] that a visit to the former shipyard of the Jarrow marchers held for him and he referred to a need to 'return to the spirit of 1926'.[30] Nostalgia flourished in and around Benn's public appearances. Describing one speech to a Young Socialists' rally in London in 1971, one journalist noted: 'Earlier generations would no doubt have listened with nostalgia to the chants of "Victory to the working class!" "Nationalise!" and nodded recognition at the posters "TUC! Prepare for the general strike" and "Smash Capitalism." There was even a contingent of twenty from Jarrow.'[31]

Benn quickly became the AES's figurehead. He was the politician who most effectively articulated Labour's historical identity. His tendency to construct present policies in terms of their relationship to the past was apparent in his two main books during this period: *Arguments for Socialism* (1979) and *Arguments for Democracy* (1981). Ostensibly modern, these works attempted to offer political guidance for the future. However, Benn expressed his political positions through a historically orientated discourse. In *Arguments for Socialism*, he described how 'today it is frequently said that the Labour Party is moving further to the Left than can be justified by its origins. This is not so'.[32] Benn talked about the political programme of the Chartists and how 'we can find the same aspirations in the moving words of Clause IV of the Labour Party Constitution'.[33]

Above all, Benn located the AES within the context of a history of British working-class struggle and those workers who 'have fought for what they believe in, organised others to join them and have done so against immense odds'.[34] By referring to the Peasants' Revolt, the Levellers, the Chartists, Robert Owen, and the Webbs, Benn mobilised nostalgia for the heroic struggles of and symbolic figures from the British labour movement's past in order to promote the idea that democratic socialism was 'very much a home-grown British product which has been slowly fashioned over the centuries. Its roots are deep in our history.'[35] Similarly, *Arguments for Democracy* located the AES-supporting Labour Party within the historical context of the trade-union struggles against the Combination Acts, the Chartists, the formation of the Labour Representation Committee, and the adoption of the 1918 constitution.[36]

Benn deployed positively idealised memories of an era of perceived party unity in his attacks on those who opposed the AES's proposals to extend public ownership. In 1976, James Fenton of the *New Statesman* wrote that Benn had declared that

> If you consider the Labour tradition to be like a sedimentary rock … and you drill down from the present period, through the fossilised bodies of the Marquands, the Hattersleys, the Jenkinses and Gaitskells, you come to a level at which the party was united. The undisputed tenets of that time are the left-wing beliefs of today.[37]

When members of Labour's right wing split to form the Social Democratic Party (SDP) in March 1981, it was noted that Benn 'compares the SDP with Ramsay MacDonald and refers to the fact that Attlee once compared MacDonald with Hitler and Mussolini' and that he recalled 'the struggles in London over six centuries. "Wat Tyler [leader of the English Peasants' Revolt of 1381] would certainly not have been endorsed by the organisation sub-committee of the Labour Party."'[38]

Benn's constant referrals to the past and his frequent attendance at commemorative events corresponded with his ever-increasing popularity in the party.[39] Written in 1979, one letter to *Tribune* declared that 'if I believed in the transmigration of souls, I would say that Tony Benn is none other than Percy Bysshe Shelley here to wreak vengeance on the heads of the heirs of the perpetrators of Peterloo.'[40] Three years later, another writer to the same paper stated: 'It wasn't the MacDonalds, the Snowdens, the Woodrow-Wyatts, the Robens, the Marshs or the latest batch of Jenkins Minstrels who have kept the light of socialism going. It was always people like George Lansbury, Aneurin Bevan and Tony Benn who have served the party before self who have kept socialism alive in this country.'[41] In 1981, the *Guardian* commented that, at a speech commemorating the six hundredth anniversary of the Peasants' Revolt, 'Benn slipped easily into the role of Wat Tyler.'[42]

Judith Hart, an influential party figure close to Benn and an advocate of public ownership, noted that 'a folk memory of the early struggles, a recognition of the essential relationship between economic and political freedom has consistently united the Party and the trade unions.' Critically, she argued that 'there is here a deep collective memory of struggle and a scarcely understood shared past experience which is exclusively British. Pre-Marxist as I say. Pre-Fabian.'[43] Hart believed that the AES's commitment to public ownership was the product of this collective memory and that it was 'the message of the people whether articulated by the Chartists, by the early trade unionists, by Tawney and his contemporaries or by Labour Party conference. We must continue, and intensify, the fight to bring economic power ... into the area of public responsibility and accountability.'[44]

Within the party, the AES's attachment to public ownership was often characterised as nostalgic by its opponents. Publications like *Socialist Commentary* dismissed the notion that 'all we need to do is to return to the old dogmas, old slogans.'[45] Labour's nostalgic orientation was also widely noted by contemporary observers. Writing in the *Guardian*, Simon Hoggart declared that Labour's 'members do almost everything for reasons of sentiment or nostalgia or both.'[46] Similarly, the journalist David McKie, reporting on a constituency party meeting in Rhondda in 1973, described the 'heavily nostalgic conversation, looking back repeatedly to the grim but politically gratifying battles of the thirties.' McKie noted the deeply embedded belief that 'the fire and passion and Socialist conviction of the great days of the movement have been lost and must somehow be recaptured.'[47]

Positively idealised memories of symbolic figures from Labour's industrial past were mobilised against senior party figures who opposed widespread public ownership. Attacking comments made by Roy Jenkins, one Labour Party member wrote to *Tribune*: 'This is what we in the Labour movement ought to be striving for: the New Jerusalem that William Blake wrote about, that Keir Hardie dreamed about, that Michael Foot and Tony Benn now speak about.'[48] Writing in 1975, almost a year after Labour had regained power, another activist mocked the failure of the party's leaders to implement the AES: 'Keir Hardie never went to Parliament to make money or become a Lord: he went to put through the policy for which he was elected.'[49] As the 1970s progressed, despite the Labour leadership's rejection of the AES's central tenets (highlighted by the decision to seek an International Monetary Fund loan in 1976), supporters of the strategy remained undeterred.[50]

Defeated by Margaret Thatcher's Conservative Party, Labour returned to opposition in 1979. Michael Foot was elected leader of the Labour Party in November 1980. Foot had frequently expressed his anger at the Conservative Government for allowing 'the great industries to collapse' and he had argued that 'it is the Labour movement of this country, reawakened and reinvigorated, which can serve and save the people of this country.'[51] The nostalgia that drove Foot's response to contemporary politics was evident on the campaign trail in 1983. Covering a visit by Foot to Liverpool, the journalist David Pallister described how

> it was a nostalgic return to the city where Mr Foot joined the Labour Party 49 years ago. 'Poverty is coming to our country in a way most people never thought they would see again' he said. Liverpool was suffering under Conservative policies just as it had done in the 1930s.[52]

At another point during the campaign, Pallister was struck by the way that Foot, speaking at the Aneurin Bevan memorial stones near Tredegar in South Wales, 'stood there, the curator of the Labour Party's conscience and tradition, regretting the days long gone when political orators held huge meetings spellbound for two hours. For anyone under 35 it was a history lesson, eloquently put and tinged with nostalgia.'[53]

Foot wrote the foreword to Labour's 1983 General Election Manifesto, *The New Hope for Britain*. He declared that there was a desperate need in Britain 'to rebuild our shattered industries.'[54] Such notions were located in a static understanding of economic and societal progression that was firmly rooted in the past: 'The Labour movement – the Labour Party and the trade unions acting together – came into being, as one of our poets Idris Davies said, to end "the long Victorian night." It was a fight to introduce civilised living standards into the world of ruthless, devil-take-the-hindmost individualism.'[55] *The New Hope for Britain* was fundamentally shaped by Labour's historical orientation. Its immediate origins lay in *Labour's Draft Manifesto 1980* and *Labour's Programme 1982*, both of which seemed as concerned with propping up the declining industries of the past as they were with creating the growth industries of the future.[56] In 1981, a campaign strategy note suggested that Labour should hold itself at least partially responsible for the public's perception that it was 'concerned only to defend the traditional or declining sectors of the economy'.[57] Despite this perception, *Labour's Programme 1982* declared that 'at the heart of this new Programme lies our socialist economic strategy. Our aim is to rebuild our industrial base.'[58] It stated the party's intent to 'end the decline of steel' and envisaged 'a highly competitive and efficient coal industry playing a central role in Britain's energy future'.[59] Furthermore, *Labour's Programme 1982* argued that Labour's central goal of rebuilding

Britain's 'industrial base' would only be possible because, in the words of Clause IV of the party's 1918 constitution, 'As a socialist party we are committed as our long term-goal to the "common ownership of the means of production, distribution and exchange."'[60]

The sentiments that were contained within *Labour's Programme 1982* were echoed in Labour's 1983 Manifesto. *The New Hope for Britain* reinforced the idea that Labour's priority in government would be to 'save jobs and stop the further destruction of industry.'[61] It talked, in a less tentative manner than *Labour's Programme 1982*, about giving 'priority to the coal industry'.[62] This focus on the need to arrest and reverse industrial decline occurred at the expense of the presentation of any real vision of modernity and of the construction of policies concerned with developing Britain's new and expanding growth sectors. One document, written by Geoff Bish (the Labour Party's Research Secretary), noted that Labour was approaching the General Election with 'many policy gaps' and that 'with some of these – such as science and technology or consumer protection – the lack of content in our policies may prove to be embarrassing.'[63] In another document, Bish declared that, in the area of science and technology, 'we have no real policy at all.'[64] The party's attachment to Britain's traditional industries emerged victorious over the development of any policies regarding governmental intervention in new scientific or technological industries. The past triumphed over modernity.

Labour suffered a significant defeat at the 1983 General Election. The party obtained its smallest share of the vote since 1918 and its lowest-ever average number of votes per candidate.[65] Within the party, opponents of the AES's commitment to public ownership were in no doubt as to why defeat had occurred. Speaking at the TUC's annual conference in 1983, Frank Chapple argued that, in the future, the party's 'appeal will have to be in touch with the times in which we live. Just as 19th century economics have proved no answer to the problems of the 20th century, so neither are 19th century politics.' Moreover, Chapple suggested that 'We will have to stop wishing that the World was like it once was, and face up to what it is … We will have to appeal to the new working class and not cling to old fashioned definitions of 50 years ago.'[66] In a similar manner, Austin Mitchell MP argued that Labour must reassess its historic commitment to public ownership and he stated that 'the new electorate has to be reached by new materials, not treated as if it were a working class movement of the twenties.' Mitchell declared that 'we found ourselves appealing to an electorate of 1983 in the language of 1883' and he noted that 'political Parties can die just like other prehistoric monsters which failed to evolve with the times.'[67]

The European Economic Community

The vast majority of AES supporters were adamantly opposed to membership of the EEC. Their opposition manifested itself in their campaign for a 'No' vote at the June 1975 referendum. Anti-EEC rhetoric was often informed by an attachment to past political achievements and struggles. Benn argued that membership of the EEC would destroy 'literally at a stroke, fundamental democratic rights which the people of this country fought for hundreds of years to establish.'[68] Elsewhere, when talking about the need for a referendum, Benn suggested that Britain would 'lose ... our traditions of democracy' if it was taken into the EEC without consent from the British electorate.[69] Increasingly, the EEC was portrayed by Stuart Holland as a capitalist clique that threatened Britain's traditional industries. He argued that none of its policies, such as the regional development fund, were able to meet the needs of Britain's traditional industries.[70] This concern was echoed amongst rank-and-file AES supporters. The notion that 'with [the] older industries such as leather and textiles, entry into the Common Market ... would mean increased unemployment ... history ordained that the Labour Movement would have an historic role and therefore have an historic task' fed the anti-EEC but pro-traditional industry sentiment of the era.[71] Activists expressed the concern that 'the very logic ... of the E.E.C. can bring our steel and coal industries to eventual death.'[72]

EEC membership seemed to encourage a deep-seated and emotional fear among AES supporters. Sentiments like 'the last person to tell this country that we could not go it alone was Adolf Hitler ... I did not go six years without a banana as a schoolboy for nothing' were indicative of the manner in which the issue was often articulated through a historically orientated discourse.[73] Furthermore, nostalgia for the heroic struggles of the British labour movement's past was regularly deployed against the idea of EEC membership. At the TUC's Annual Congress in 1970, one delegate from the National Union of Agricultural and Allied Workers declared: 'My Union and its members, [are] the descendants of the Tolpuddle Martyrs from whom this great Movement draws its roots' and called upon the conference to support a motion rejecting EEC membership.[74] In turn, supporters of EEC membership suggested that the AES's approach to Europe was backward-looking. At the following year's annual TUC conference, one white-collar trade unionist argued that 'Living in the past is the surest way to kill the future.'[75] In 1975, the Young European Left group noted that 'many of the fears expressed on the Left reflect an out-of-date analysis of the way to build socialism.'[76]

Tribune ardently supported EEC withdrawal. Its arguments for withdrawal were consistently framed by the past. In 1971, when Labour was facing a pro-European revolt over the issue of EEC membership, Francis Flavius wrote: 'If Roy Jenkins, Labour's deputy leader, and some members of the Shadow Cabinet go into the Prime Minister's lobby this Thursday ... there will be no precedent for it. The only comparable incident was the decision of Ramsay MacDonald in 1931.'[77] *Tribune* focused on the impact of EEC membership on the traditional industries of the past rather than on the growth sectors of the future. Contributors regularly expressed their concern that EEC membership would lead to further decline in Britain's traditional industrial base and that there would be an influx of a 'new range of highly profitable, low wage, service industries—"Candy-floss industry."' It was argued that 'the biggest danger of Britain's entry in the Common Market is this process of losing much of our manufacturing industry in exchange for "candy floss."'[78] In 1975, with the referendum date of 5 June closing in, industrial scare stories became more frequent and *Tribune* ran front-page headlines like 'Steel Jobs: Market Rules Forbid Rescue.'[79]

By the mid-1970s, the idea that EEC membership prevented the implementation of selective import controls had crept into the political rhetoric of AES supporters. Michael Hatfield noted in *The Times* in 1976 that 'with the growth of economic difficulties the left believes that the alternative must be broad-based import controls'.[80] In contrast to the University of Cambridge's Department of Applied Economics, which argued that import controls were needed to improve the balance of payments and to keep unemployment down, import controls were interpreted primarily as a means by which Britain could protect its traditional industrial heritage.[81] Clive Jenkins, from the Association of Scientific, Technical and Managerial Staffs' (ASTMS) white-collar union, argued at Labour's annual conference in 1975 that 'if the Italians can have import deposit schemes ... and the French can slap a levy on Italian wine, I think we can protect the heartland of our British industry.'[82]

As the decade progressed and Britain's traditional industries continued to decline, the desire for protective controls hardened. The sense of fear surrounding the potential loss of these industries was palpable: at the party's conference in 1980, one trade unionist declared that 'the speed of Britain's economic and industrial decline has accelerated to a frightening pace ... The campaign for an alternative economic strategy is of immense importance. Such a strategy must include import controls.'[83] Import controls were understood as the best means of arresting and reversing industrial decline. The international consequences of import controls and the effect that they would have on industries in developing nations were largely ignored. This position was shaped by an emotional attachment to the party's industrial past. One writer in the party noted the 'traditional cries on which the Labour Party relies to arouse the loyalties of the faithful. Whereas the slums of Calcutta do not arouse altruistic emotions, the road to Wigan Pier does.'[84]

Writing in the *Observer* in 1976, Alan Day described 'the disturbingly puritanical nostalgia among some members of the Labour Party for the Attlee years with its rationing and bureaucracy.' Day argued that 'In fact our import controls at that time were not part of an attempt to create a tight little autarchic island but part of a world-wide reaction to the post-war dollar shortage.'[85] In this way, opponents of import controls declared that it would 'be a serious defeat for the Left if it became identified with the cause of all that is backward and inward-looking.'[86] They suggested that the need for autarky was indicative of the inability of the AES to deliver a modern and competitive economy.

It is remarkable how little the intraparty debate concerning EEC membership developed between 1976 and 1981. AES supporters continued to argue that membership of the EEC had compromised Britain's ability to protect its traditional industries.[87] By condemning the EEC's policy of 'survival of the fittest', they essentially accepted that such industries should be propped up regardless of their economic efficiency.[88] During the early 1980s, Labour's position on EEC withdrawal hardened. Whereas the *Draft Manifesto 1980* argued that Labour would only leave the EEC if attempts to change its views and policies failed, *Labour's Programme 1982* declared that, if Labour was elected, withdrawal would occur immediately and there would be no need for another referendum: 'The verdict of the electorate at a general election, we believe, is the decisive mandate on which the next Labour government can renegotiate our withdrawal.'[89]

Opening the annual conference of the TUC in 1982, Alan Sapper, President of the TUC, exhibited the kind of nostalgia that observers and contemporaries had noted was informing Labour's desire for EEC withdrawal. He attacked the fact that 'large sections of our alternative economic strategy could be considered illegal were we to introduce it while we are still members of the EEC' and, significantly, he then went on to elaborate: 'it is so easy for us to forget the wider aims of our Movement, something that I would express as the gleam at the top of the mountain. That gleam is the kind of society and the kind of world that has been the aspiration of generation after generation of those who served our Movement.'[90]

Labour's Programme 1982 argued that EEC membership would nullify the AES. It declared that, while Article 12 of the European Treaty would prevent the implementation of import controls in order to protect British industry and manufacturing, Articles 90 and 92 would stop Labour from adopting a wide-reaching programme of public ownership and planning that would be reliant on 'selective aids to industry'.[91] Above all, EEC membership was perceived to be accelerating the decline of the nation's traditional industries. *The New Hope for Britain* proclaimed that 'the next Labour government, committed to radical, socialist policies for reviving the British economy, is bound to find continued membership a most serious obstacle to the fulfilment of these policies.'[92] However, this commitment to 'radical socialist policies' represented something of a misnomer. The economic policies that were contained within the AES had, increasingly, been articulated through a nostalgic discourse.

Industrial democracy and workers' control

Industrial democracy was central to the AES. During the 1970s, advocates of industrial democracy argued that 'the very scale of the [economic] crisis makes possible the canvassing of measures of a radical nature, which can no longer be dismissed as utopian or "extremist."'[93] They talked about the advantages of a new means of 'socially progressive control' that would allow workers 'to run things in ways best suited to their own aims and ideals … in modern Britain'.[94] For Holland, industrial democracy and workers' control formed critical components of a broader strategy that aimed to 'transform the injustice, inequality and inefficiency of modern capitalism.'[95] Accordingly, he suggested that workers should 'be invited to submit proposals for the diversification and expansion of their companies'.[96] It was argued that, by giving workers greater involvement in the workplace, industrial productivity and economic performance could be enhanced and new ways to expand the economy would be developed. Workers' control was portrayed as an innovative means to release the unfulfilled potential of British industry.[97] Yet, as I will show, far from being radical and modern, the AES's proposals concerning industrial democracy were understood primarily through the lens of the past.

In the early 1970s, many of the ideas concerning industrial democracy that circulated in the party had their origins in the highly influential Institute for Workers' Control (IWC). One of the IWC's leading figures, Ken Coates, often deployed a contradictory discourse that expressed the notion that workers' control was something new and modern – 'We add something new' – but that also simultaneously mobilised mnemonic constructions of the past in order to support his ideas.[98] At an early workers' control conference in 1967, Coates argued that 'we carry with us the spirit of the shop stewards of the first world war, of the syndicalists and industrial unionists of 1910 onwards, of the guildsmen and the first communists who pioneered ideas of workers' control.' He then stated that 'we carry on from farther back, from the Grand National Consolidation Trades Union of 1834, from Robert Owen, from founders of socialism and trade unions.'[99] From an early stage, Coates's ideas were located within the emotional parameters of Labour's nostalgia-identity.

The past provided guidance for the workers' control movement in Britain. Many of the ideas that were understood to offer contemporary solutions had their origins in memories of the industrial working class of the past. In one article in *Tribune*, Coates talked about how

> among the public sector unions there exist dozens of traditional proposals for industrial democracy ... The miners have the old Miners' Federation of Great Britain programme which was put before the Sankey Commission [an investigation in 1919 into the hours, wages, and ownership of the coal industry] ... All these schemes are 50 years old now, but they are still more 'modern' than the National Coal Board.[100]

Similarly, a report from an IWC miners' seminar in *Workers' Control Bulletin* declared:

> Today we are coming near to the truth seen by the miner William Straker in 1919 who in his evidence to the Sankey Commission said: 'the unrest is deeper than can be reached by pounds, shillings and pence ... The root of the matter is the straining of the spirit of man to be free.[101]

In the same issue, Coates referred to the story of the Rhondda Socialists, who, after World War I, wrote the text 'Industrial Democracy for the Mines.' He proclaimed that this text was

> a trail-blazing document which has inspired imitations on many sides: Hull busmen, dockworkers, steel men, and many others in our times have come to take up its challenge. It is to be hoped ... that the work of the Rhondda Socialists will be seen to receive its consummation in these, later efforts.[102]

Written in the past, literature by traditional industrial workers provided guidance for the present.

Significantly, in the mid-1970s, despite rising levels of both white-collar and female employment,[103] the pages of *Workers' Control Bulletin* were filled with articles and pictures celebrating male traditional industrial working-class occupations. In one issue in 1974 alone, almost half of the paper's twelve pages were taken up with coal mining–related stories and features.[104] Tellingly, at the IWC Miners' Conference in April 1974, Coates stated that 'miners are the key people in the argument for workers' control.'[105] In this way, Britain's declining traditional industrial workforce was central to the discourse originating from the IWC. The past was deployed by advocates of workers' control at the Labour Party Conference. Delegates made statements like 'Since the time of Robert Owen we have had, and still have, many examples of workers controlling their working lives in whole or in part successfully.'[106] In the same way, documents circulating in the NEC's policy departments referred to 'the historical fight to democratise our political system.'[107] Benn talked about how the labour movement must 'take up its historic task again.'[108] In 1976, the prospective Labour candidate for Fareham wrote in *Labour Weekly* that 'men have looked at their place of work, just as Owen, Morris and Hardie did, and they have found its ownership, its management, its greed and pursuit of wealth, totally unacceptable.'[109] Within the party, nostalgia for a bygone era of male traditional industrial working-class prominence, struggle, and unity and the associated symbolic figures of this era were central to the case for increased worker participation in industry.

Industrial democracy was advocated via a political discourse that was almost exclusively concerned with the male-dominated industries of the past. The expansion of white-collar employment and the increase in female employment were rarely discussed. Labour appeared out of touch with modern economic developments. At a time when the women's movement was flourishing in Britain, the AES and its policy commitments were articulated through the language of traditional male industrial employment. In an early speech on industrial democracy in 1968, Benn talked of how 'When a man enters the factory gate in the morning he sheds much of his dignity with his overcoat.'[110] He went on to make frequent references to 'the democracy of the workshop'.[111] Significantly, in this speech and in many of his speeches during the early 1970s, Benn referred to the person exploited by the authoritarian nature of the workplace, almost uniquely, as being a male industrial worker. In another speech on workers' control addressed to the Amalgamated Union of Engineering Workers in 1971, Benn argued that 'The new grey flannel brigade with their degrees in business studies, familiar with the language of accounting and computers, and their shiny offices away from the dirt and noise of the factory floor are still often too remote.'[112] Benn tied in the idea of workers' control not with shiny offices but with dirty and noisy factory floors. His rhetoric seemed strangely detached from Britain's increasingly white-collar economy.

When new white-collar unions were mentioned by the AES's advocates, it was with hesitancy and reluctance. This was not the case with their traditional industrial counterparts. Ken Coates noted that the 'radicalism of the major growth unions in the white-collar sector' reflected the new mood of militancy. However, he then went on to state with a degree of suspicion that this militancy 'by no means correlates with the mass of membership opinion in the organisations concerned'.[113] Such suspicions were shared by the industrial trade unions, which felt that their dominance was threatened by the growth of the new white-collar unions. Anti-nostalgic comments at the annual TUC conference from white-collar trade unionists like Clive Jenkins (ASTMS), who noted that 'What we have [in the trade union movement] is a muddle which is based on ancient patterns of nineteenth century trade and organisation, a pattern of industrial archaeology', did little to alleviate these fears.[114] Yet the omnipotence of Labour's nostalgia-identity also forced unions like ASTMS to locate themselves within more acceptable historical parameters. On another occasion, Clive Jenkins attempted to express the aims of his union in terms that were acceptable to these parameters, and he declared that putting aside sectional interest was 'worthy of the aims, hopes and aspirations of those pioneers who gathered in the Memorial Hall, Farringdon Street, on February 27, 1900'.[115]

Writing in *Workers' Control Bulletin*, Audrey Wise questioned the dominance of male industrial workers within the political discourse of her contemporaries. Wise asked, 'Have you ever noticed that jobs threatened by closures are always "men's jobs" even when many are actually women's jobs? And that strikers are always "the lads" and "solid to a man" even when a good number of them are women? And that trade unionists always have "wives and families" even though about a quarter of them are women?'[116] Articles like this were rare in the 1970s. AES supporters wrote letters that questioned: 'How many women possess the breadth and depth of mind to understand political philosophy, economics and the social sciences generally? How many appreciate what socialism is and what it could do for the world?'[117] Manifestly sexist, this letter's publication in *Tribune* suggested that there were those who thought it expressed a legitimate point of view.

By the early 1980s, little had changed and the AES and its ideas of industrial democracy and workers' control remained conceptualised around the male traditional industrial worker. This did not go unnoticed by feminists in the party. Writing in *Tribune* in 1981, Patricia Hewitt and Harriet Harman criticised the fact that the 'debate about the alternative economic strategy has been almost wholly confined to male trade unionists and economists.'[118] Similarly, Diana Gilhespy noted the way that the AES seemed to speak only to and about male workers, and she argued that 'making sure that women are involved in the alternative economic strategy – both as initiators and beneficiaries – is important not only for women but also the whole Labour movement.'[119] Thus, right up until the 1983 General Election, the AES was attacked for its failure to engage with the sizable female workforce that existed in Britain. There were left-wing thinkers who displayed an understanding of the significance of these changes. In 1978, Eric Hobsbawm declared: 'Since 1951 the number of married women technically described as "occupied" has gone up from about one-fifth to about half. This is a major change in the composition of the working class.'[120] Nevertheless, the impact of women upon Labour's AES remained negligible.

In 1977, Labour released the Bullock Report. Among other proposals, it suggested that an equal number of workers and shareholders should make up the boards of those companies employing more than two thousand people.[121] Advocates of workers' control on the left of the party were critical of both its content and extent.[122] However, the main significance of the Bullock Report was its insignificance in shaping the dominant political discourse of the Labour Party. Primarily, this failure occurred because, within the party, the ideas that underpinned industrial democracy and workers' control were the product of an abstract nostalgia for a male traditional industrial working class that was unaligned to any concrete policy proposals. Industrial democracy's resonance with Labour's past legitimised its political application in the present. Neil Kinnock's response to the Bullock Report was typical: 'The ideal of industrial democracy is as old as socialism.'[123]

Indeed, the idea of industrial democracy remained defined by its location within Labour's nostalgia-identity. This led to confusion about the idea itself. Joe Gormley, leader of the National Union of Mineworkers, asked, 'I am from a nationalised industry and I ask myself a question when people talk about workers' control. What the hell do we mean?'[124] In the wider party, ambiguous statements like 'Industrial democracy has to be developed in accordance with the requirements and the history of the labour movements in each particular industry' did little to allay this confusion.[125] As late as 1981, Labour's policy committees on industrial democracy seemed unfocused and their policies appeared poorly thought out and ill-defined. One of these committees noted that 'discussions on industrial democracy are often bedevilled by different, though related issues being brought into the argument the wrong way or being mixed up together.'[126] Moreover, if the relationship between the AES's policies concerning industrial democracy and widespread public ownership were ill-defined, it was because they were increasingly being articulated through an abstract nostalgic discourse. Delegates at the party conference made such statements as:

> Comrades, I come from Clydeside and I will finish with a quote from John Maclean, the red Clydeside leader, because it seems to me that his words,

said in 1919, are appropriate for this Conference to hear today. He said then: 'Capitalism is in the last ditch. Let us cover over this dripping monster and prepare the way for worldwide, workers-owned and controlled economic solidarity.'[127]

Rather than offering concrete policy proposals, Benn continued to emphasise the historical importance of industrial democracy. In *Arguments for Socialism*, Benn wrote that 'The ideas of workers' control have roots going deep into the history of our movement'.[128] Benn quoted a miner who gave evidence to the Sankey Commission in 1919 – 'We must have industrial democracy, in order that men may be free'– and he argued that 'This is a very remarkable statement, from a working miner, of the aspirations which led so many of his fellow workers to press for public ownership, raising hopes which have not been realised by the structure of nationalisation which we have adopted.'[129] In a similar fashion, in *Arguments for Democracy*, Benn both expressed and reinforced the sense of nostalgic legitimacy that surrounded the idea of industrial democracy when he declared, 'From time immemorial, through the Chartist campaigns and up to the present day, the Labour movement at grass roots level has always fought to extend democratic control.'[130]

Labour's 1983 Manifesto did little to clarify the idea of industrial democracy or to move it away from a conceptualisation that was heavily rooted in the past. The policy documents and drafts that shaped the 1983 Manifesto argued that industrial democracy was needed in order to 'rebuild industry'.[131] Like the ideas of public ownership and EEC withdrawal, industrial democracy was understood as a means by which to preserve Britain's traditional industries. *The New Hope for Britain* declared that one of Labour's main aims was 'to rebuild British industry, working within a new framework for planning and industrial democracy'.[132] The AES's programmatic commitments to industrial democracy were shaped by an emotional commitment to a bygone era.

Conclusion

Historians have undervalued the extent to which the past impacted on the Labour Party's understanding of its Alternative Economic Strategy. Previous studies on the AES have stressed its radical nature. They have suggested that the AES was defined by its modernity. In this chapter, I have disputed this dominant understanding and have argued that the AES's programmatic commitments were shaped by a nostalgic attachment to the past.

Significantly, during the 1970s and early 1980s, as many commentators noted, Labour seemed to be fundamentally in thrall to its historically orientated identity. All of the AES's leading advocates were, to varying degrees, influenced by the party's distinctive collective nostalgia. This nostalgia took three interrelated forms: nostalgia for an era in which Britain's male traditional industries lay at the forefront of the British economy; nostalgia for the heroic male traditional industrial working-class struggles and unity of this era; and nostalgia for the historical symbols and figures that were perceived to represent this era of male traditional industrial working-class prominence, unity, and struggle. Tony Benn proved himself to be particularly adept at channelling this nostalgia in a way that increased support for the AES. Furthermore, Benn's increasing popularity in the party directly related to his close association with (and his ability to articulate) this nostalgia.

Stuart Holland's initial vision of the AES displayed a degree of ambiguity toward the past and, in particular, toward Britain's traditional industries. However, an interpretation of the AES that was more recognisably characterised by nostalgia became dominant within the party. In turn, this interpretation shaped the AES's political development. Over time, the predominance of nostalgia served to eradicate any sense of modernity that was contained in Holland's earlier version of the AES. Labour decisively rejected the aspects of Holland's vision that prioritised economic modernisation over industrial preservation and restoration: this left the scope for a modernising and progressive strategy for economic rejuvenation greatly diminished. The AES's policies were understood to represent mechanisms for the restoration of the traditional industries of the past rather than blueprints for the development of the growth sectors of the future.

Economic strategies are often as much emotional constructs as they are carefully thought-out programmatic commitments. Public ownership was central to the party's AES between 1970 and 1983. The idea of nationalisation, as envisaged in Clause IV of Labour's constitution, resonated within the party's nostalgia-identity. Party members interpreted the policies on public ownership that were contained within the AES as a means by which to restore the British male traditional industrial working class of the past. Primarily, the EEC was seen as a barrier to this restoration. EEC membership was anathema to the majority of party members because they believed that it would compromise the policies contained within the AES and, thus, accelerate the decline of the British male traditional industrial working class. The outcome was that widespread public ownership was accepted and the EEC was rejected. At their most extreme, such as in the case of industrial democracy and workers' control, the AES's policies became characterised not by their political content, but by their nostalgic resonance. Nostalgia became the policy.

Onlookers described how Labour appeared to be out of touch with the realities of modern Britain. With its wholehearted commitment to the AES, the 1983 General Election Manifesto, *The New Hope for Britain*, represented something akin to a nostalgic apotheosis. Fighting an election on the basis of policies that were heavily rooted in the past and explicitly designed to preserve and restore the traditional industries associated with Britain's industrial heritage, Labour performed poorly at the polls. To the advantage of Margaret Thatcher's Conservative Party, the economic strategy that was offered by Labour to the electorate in 1983 was both a reflection and a cause of the limited appeal of the party at this point in its historical development. Between 1970 and 1983, nostalgia shaped the political trajectory of the AES. It also, ultimately, directed Labour to a catastrophic electoral defeat.

Notes

1. Cronin, *New Labour's Pasts*, 118.
2. M. Pugh, *Speak for Britain: A New History of the Labour Party* (London: The Bodley Head, 2010), 345.
3. See Panitch and Leys, *End of Parliamentary Socialism*, 16.
4. See P. Bell, *The Labour Party in Opposition, 1970–1974* (London: Routledge, 2004).
5. Cronin, *New Labour's Pasts*, 136.
6. S. Holland, *Strategy for Socialism: The Challenge of Labour's Programme* (Nottingham: Spokesman Books, 1975), 27.
7. S. Holland, *The Socialist Challenge* (London: Quartet Books, 1975), 9.
8. See Shaw, *Labour Party since 1945*, 113.
9. For example, see S. Holland, 'Inflation and Price Control: Note on the French Programme Contracts', February 1973, RD. 605, Labour History Archive, Manchester.
10. The Labour Party, *Report of the Annual Conference and Special Conference of the Labour Party 1980* (London: The Labour Party, 1980), 126.
11. Wickham-Jones, *Economic Strategy and the Labour Party: Politics and Policy-Making*, 74.
12. M. Hatfield, *The House the Left Built: Inside Labour Policy-Making, 1970–1975* (London: Gollancz, 1978), 28.
13. Wickham-Jones, *Economic Strategy and the Labour Party*, 7.
14. S. Haseler, *The Tragedy of Labour* (Oxford: Blackwell, 1980), 8.
15. In particular, see P. Seyd, *The Rise and Fall of the Labour Left* (Basingstoke: Macmillan, 1987); Wickham-Jones, *Economic Strategy and the Labour Party*.
16. Samuel, *Theatres of Memory Volume 1*, 150.

17 See also C. Griffiths, 'Remembering Tolpuddle: Rural History and Commemoration in the Inter-War Labour Movement', *History Workshop Journal*, 44 (1997), 144–169; Lawrence, 'Labour – The Myths It Has Lived By', 341–366.
18 This chapter reproduces material from R. Jobson, 'A New Hope for an Old Britain? Nostalgia and the British Labour Party's Alternative Economic Strategy, 1970–83', *The Journal of Policy History*, 27:4 (2015), 670–694.
19 S. Holland, *Capital Versus the Regions* (London: Macmillan, 1976), 178.
20 Holland, *Socialist Challenge*, 147.
21 S. Holland, 'The New Economic Imperatives: The State Holding Company, Planning and Policy Coordination, Planning Strategy, Tactics and Techniques – A Summary of RD. 271, RD. 315 and RD. 442', November 1972, RD. 473, Labour History Archive, 2.
22 The Labour Party Industrial Policy Sub-Committee, 'The Contribution to the Green Paper', 19 April 1972, RD. 336, Labour History Archive, 1.
23 The Labour Party, *Labour's Programme 1973* (London: The Labour Party, 1973), 30.
24 The Labour Party, *Labour's Programme: Campaign Document 1974* (London: The Labour Party, 1974), 1.
25 Labour Party, *Labour's Programme 1973*, 32, 35.
26 The Labour Party, *Let Us Work Together – Labour's Way Out of the Crisis* (London: The Labour Party, 1974). www.labour-party.org.uk/manifestos/1974/Feb/1974-feb-labour-manifesto.shtml.
27 T. Benn, F. Morrell and F. Cripps, 'A Ten-Year Industrial Strategy for Britain', April 1975, RE. 126, Labour History Archive, 1.
28 T. Benn, diary entry for 31 July 1972 in T. Benn (R. Winstone ed.), *Office Without Power: Diaries 1968–1972* (London: Arrow, 1988), 442.
29 T. Benn, diary entry for 11 May 1970 in Benn, *Office Without Power*, 277.
30 T. Benn, diary entry for 18 January 1972 in Benn, *Office Without Power*, 397.
31 J. Windsor, 'Drizzle Fails to Dampen Youth', *The Guardian*, 8 November 1971, 20.
32 T. Benn (C. Mullin ed.), *Arguments for Socialism* (London: Cape, 1979), 23.
33 Benn, *Arguments for Socialism*, 33.
34 *Ibid.*, 44.
35 *Ibid.*, 146.
36 T. Benn (Chris Mullin ed.), *Arguments for Democracy* (London: Cape, 1981), 49.
37 J. Fenton, 'Is This Mr Benn's Party?' *New Statesman*, 1 October 1976, 434.
38 R. Gott, 'By the Left', *The Guardian*, 14 December 1981, 17.
39 For example, see Benn's speech on Saturday 15 May 1976 at Burford Church, Oxford, commemorating the execution of three Levellers in 1649, recorded in T. Benn, 'The Levellers', *Tribune*, 14 May 1976, 5, 8–9.
40 S. H. Pierce, '"Benn for Leader" campaign', letter to *Tribune*, 17 August 1979, 11.
41 A. H. Williams, 'Gaitskell Never Won an Election', letter to *Tribune*, 30 July/6 August 1982, 10.
42 C. Brown, 'Wat Every Revolutionary Should Know Now', *The Guardian*, 5 May 1981, 4.
43 J. Hart, 'The Folk Memory of Early Struggles', *Tribune*, 29 July 1977, 5.

44 J. Hart, 'Democracy in Conflict with Capitalism', *Tribune*, 12 August 1977, 4.
45 Editorial, 'The Significance of Leadership', *Socialist Commentary*, January 1973, 1.
46 S. Hoggart, 'Callaghan the Dauphin Holds Himself Aloof', *The Guardian*, 25 March 1976, 13.
47 D. McKie, 'Labour's Scent of Victory', *The Guardian*, 25 September 1973, 16.
48 P. Coane, 'In Reply to Roy Jenkins', letter to *Tribune*, 2 August 1974, 10.
49 R. Roberts, 'Labour Turncoats', letter to *Tribune*, 17 January 1975, 10.
50 See Cronin, *New Labour's Pasts*, 185.
51 M. Foot, quoted in Labour Party, *LPACR 1980*, 12, 13.
52 D. Pallister, 'Foot Finds some Market Cheer', *The Guardian*, 18 May 1983, 2.
53 D. Pallister, 'Labour Leader Beached by the Tide of History', *The Guardian*, 9 June 1983, 2.
54 The Labour Party, *The New Hope for Britain: Labour's Manifesto 1983* (London: The Labour Party, 1983), 4.
55 Labour Party, *New Hope for Britain*, 5.
56 The Labour Party, *Labour's Draft Manifesto: Issued on the Authority of the National Executive Committee* (London: The Labour Party, 1980); The Labour Party, *Labour's Programme 1982* (London: The Labour Party, 1982).
57 The Labour Party Campaign's Committee, 'A Note on Campaign Strategy by the Research Secretary', February 1981, RD. 723, Labour History Archive, 4.
58 Labour Party, *Labour's Programme 1982*, 15.
59 *Ibid.*, 55, 62.
60 *Ibid.*, 48.
61 Labour Party, *New Hope for Britain*, 14.
62 *Ibid.*, 15.
63 The Labour Party National Executive Committee, 'The General Election Campaign: A Note on Priorities from the Research Secretary', October 1982, RD. 2522, Labour History Archive, 5.
64 The Labour Party Home Policy Committee, 'Programme of Work, 1982–83: A Note from the Research Secretary', November 1982: RD. 2539, Labour History Archive, 1.
65 D. Butler and D. Kavanagh, *The British General Election of 1983* (London: Macmillan, 1984), 289.
66 F. Chapple, quoted in The Trades Union Congress, *Report of the 115th Annual Trades Union Congress held in the Opera House, Blackpool, September 5th to 9th 1983* (London: TUC, 1983), 360.
67 A. Mitchell, 'Labour Must Choose between Ideological Purity and Impotence', *Tribune*, 24 June 1983, 2.
68 M. Hatfield, 'Labour Party Chiefs Plan to Challenge Benn for Making "Divisive" Speeches', *The Times*, 25 September 1972, 2.
69 T. Benn, 'Exchange of Letters with Dr Mansholt (President of the European Commission)', 28 March 1972, in T. Benn, *Speeches* (Nottingham: Spokesman Books, 1974), 117.
70 Stuart Holland, *The Regional Problem* (London: Macmillan, 1976), 91.

71 D. Hughes, quoted in Labour Party, *LPACR 1971*, 119.
72 R. Briginshaw, quoted in Labour Party, *LPACR 1971*, 319.
73 A. Judge, quoted in Labour Party, *LPACR 1971*, 336.
74 R. Bottini, quoted in Trades Union Congress, *TUC Report 1970: Report of the Proceedings of the 102nd Annual Trades Union Congress held in the Dome, Brighton, September 7th to 11th 1970* (London: TUC, 1970), 683.
75 R. A. Grantham, quoted in Trades Union Congress, *TUC Report 1971: Report of the Proceedings of the 103rd Annual Trades Union Congress held in the Opera House, Blackpool, September 6th to 10th 1971* (London: TUC, 1971), 476.
76 The Young European Left, 'The Left, the Referendum and the Future of Europe', *Socialist Commentary*, May 1975, 4.
77 F. Flavius, 'A Vote for European Socialism: Roy Jenkins', *Tribune*, 29 October 1971, 3.
78 H. Marks, 'Birmingham Faces a "Candy Floss" Future', *Tribune*, 10 November 1972, 8.
79 M. Walsh, 'Steel Jobs: Market Rules Forbid Rescue', *Tribune*, 9 May 1975, 1.
80 M. Hatfield, 'Pressure for Control of Imports Is Growing', *The Times*, 13 October, 1976, 2.
81 See Department of Applied Economics, *Economic Policy Review: February 1975, No. 1* (Cambridge, 1975), 3; and *Economic Policy Review: March 1976, No. 2* (Cambridge, 1976), 14.
82 C. Jenkins, quoted in The Labour Party, *Report of the Seventy-Fourth Annual Conference of the Labour Party, Blackpool, 1975, September 29th to October 3rd* (London: The Labour Party, 1975), 192.
83 B. Switzer, quoted in Labour Party, *LPACR 1980*, 28–29.
84 M. Goydor, *Socialism Tomorrow: Fresh Thinking for the Labour Party*, Young Fabian Pamphlet 49 (London: The Fabian Society, 1979), 10.
85 A. Day, 'Don't Try to Be Too Protectionist', *The Observer*, 3 October 1976, 11.
86 Editorial, 'The Case Against Import Controls', *New Statesman*, 17 February 1978, 205.
87 For example, see Benn, *Arguments for Socialism*, 99.
88 Benn, *Arguments for Socialism*, 102.
89 Labour Party, *Labour's Draft Manifesto 1980*, 31; Labour Party, *Labour's Programme 1982*, 235.
90 Alan Sapper, quoted in The Trades Union Congress, *Report of the 114th Annual Trades Union Congress held in the Conference Centre, Brighton, September 6th to 10th 1982* (London: TUC, 1982), 426, 427.
91 Labour Party, *Labour's Programme 1982*, 231.
92 Labour Party, *New Hope for Britain*, 205.
93 S. Bodington, J. Eaton, M. Barratt-Brown, and K. Coates, *An Alternative Strategy for the Labour Movement* (Nottingham: Spokesman for the Institute of Workers' Control, 1975), 7.
94 *Ibid.*, 9, 12.
95 Holland, *Socialist Challenge*, 12.

96 Holland, *Strategy for Socialism*, 72.
97 *Ibid.*, 75.
98 T. Topham (ed.), *Report of the 5th National Conference on Workers' Control and Industrial Democracy held at Transport House, Coventry on June 10th and 11th, 1967* (Hull: The Centre for Socialist Education, 1967), 78–79.
99 Topham (ed.), *Report of the 5th National Conference on Workers' Control*, 78.
100 K. Coates, 'Labour and Industrial Democracy', *Tribune*, 8 September 1972, 7.
101 S. Bodington, 'Democratising the Mining Industry: The Miners New "Next Step"', *Workers' Control Bulletin*, 4 May 1974, 2.
102 K. Coates, 'How They Wanted to Democratise the Mines', *Workers' Control Bulletin*, 4 May 1974, 8.
103 Between 1901 and 1991 services increased from 34 per cent of UK employment to 70 per cent. C. Lindsay, 'A Century of Market Change: An Overview of Labour Market Conditions in the Previous Century', *Labour Market Trends* 111 (March, 2003), 137. By 1981, women constituted 38.9 per cent of the workforce. D. Gallie, 'The Labour Force' in A. H. Halsey and J. Webb (eds) *Twentieth-Century British Social Trends* (Basingstoke: Macmillan, 2000), 292.
104 *Workers' Control Bulletin*, 1 June 1974.
105 K. Coates is quoted speaking at the IWC Miners' Conference in Nottingham by *The Miner* in April 1974, 'Miners Demand Workers' Control', *Workers' Control Bulletin*, 1 June 1974, 8.
106 M. Saunders, quoted in The Labour Party, *Report of the Seventy-First Annual Conference of the Labour Party, Blackpool, 1972, October 2nd to 6th* (London: The Labour Party, 1972), 125.
107 The Labour Party Home Policy Committee, 'Economic Strategy Growth and Unemployment: A Statement by the National Executive Committee of the Labour Party', 25 January 1972, RD.165, Labour History Archive, 21.
108 T. Benn, 'Mr Heath's Confrontation: The Political Consequences', *Workers' Control Bulletin*, 2 February 1974, 7.
109 B. Townsend, 'The New Workers' Co-Ops Show Us the Way Forward', *Labour Weekly*, 13 February 1976, 10.
110 T. Benn, 'Industrial Democracy', speech given at the Industrial Society lunch, 21 November 1968, in Benn, *Speeches*, 11.
111 *Ibid.*, 14.
112 T. Benn, 'Thinking About Workers' Control', speech given at the Annual Delegate Meeting of the Amalgamated Union of Engineering Workers, Foundry Section at the Winter Gardens, Morecambe, 27 May 1971 in Benn, *Speeches*, 18.
113 K. Coates and T. Topham, *The New Unionism: The Case for Workers' Control* (Harmondsworth: Penguin Books, 1974), 43.
114 C. Jenkins, quoted in Trades Union Congress, *TUCAR 1971*, 393.
115 C. Jenkins, 'White and Blue-Collar Workers Have More in Common than the Enemies of Trade Unionism Think', *Tribune*, 29 April 1977, 6.
116 A. Wise, 'Women Want a Different Economy', *Workers' Control Bulletin*, 16 February 1973, 3.
117 D. Hudson, 'Unbalanced Women Voters?', *Tribune*, 20 April 1979, 14.

118 P. Hewitt and H. Harman, 'Women and the Alternative Economic Strategy', *Tribune*, 26 June 1981, 2.
119 D. Gilhespy, 'Women and the Alternative Strategy', *Tribune*, 19 March 1982, 5.
120 E. Hobsbawm, 'The Forward March of Labour Halted?', *Marxism Today* 22:9 (September, 1978), 282.
121 See Wickham-Jones, *Economic Strategy and the Labour Party*, 142–143.
122 See K. Coates and T. Topham, *The Shop Steward's Guide to the Bullock Report* (Nottingham: Spokesman Books, 1977).
123 N. Kinnock, 'Bullock and the Left', *New Statesman*, 11 February 1977, 175.
124 J. Gormley, quoted in The Labour Party, *Report of the Seventy-Sixth Annual Conference of the Labour Party, Brighton, 1977, October 3rd to October 7th* (London: The Labour Party, 1977), 195.
125 J. Mordecai, 'Fight for the Socialist Alternative: Minority LPYS 1977 Conference Document' (1977–78), in The Labour Party (S. Bird ed.), *The Archives of the British Labour Party, Pamphlets and Leaflets: Part 6: 1970–1979* (Reading: Harvester, 1999), 10–11.
126 The TUC – Labour Party Liaison Committee Sub-Committee on Industrial Democracy and Planning, 'Industrial Democracy: An Introductory Note by the Joint Secretaries', March 1981, RD. 761, Labour History Archive, 2.
127 B. Wylie, quoted in Labour Party, *LPACR 1977*, 170.
128 Benn, *Arguments for Socialism*, 42.
129 *Ibid.*, 60.
130 Benn, *Arguments for Democracy*, 215.
131 The Labour Party, 'Draft Synopsis of "Plan for Recovery,"' February 1983, RD. 2646, Labour History Archive.
132 Labour Party, *New Hope for Britain*, 6.

4

Reinventing the Labour Party, 1983–92

Introduction

New Labour's 'year-zero' approach to politics and its advocacy of the idea that it represented a fundamental rupture with the party's past meant that it was never entirely comfortable locating the genesis of its 'modernising' programme in the years during which Neil Kinnock was party leader. As we shall see in the next chapter, Tony Blair made it clear that he believed he (and, effectively, John Smith before him) had inherited a party that was still in thrall of its nostalgia. Central to this analysis was the notion that, despite some important contributions to party modernisation, Kinnock had been a somewhat reluctant 'moderniser' and that, under his leadership, the rate of 'change' had been too slow and the extent of reform had been too limited in scope.[1] According to New Labour, Kinnock's party had failed to break significantly with its attachment to the past. Looking back on the outcomes of Labour's post-1987 policy review, Peter Mandelson scathingly retitled 1989's *Meet the Challenge, Make the Change* 'Skirt the Challenge, Hint at Change'.[2]

Academics have been divided over the nature, impact and legacy of Kinnock's leadership of the party. Critics have attacked the perceived synthetic nature of Labour's new professionalised 'modern' image during these years. Moreover, they have suggested that, under Kinnock, an increasingly hollowed out and careerist party was left 'without roots in the working class or in the communities it claimed to represent'.[3] These analyses have emphasised Kinnock's marginalisation of the Left and the emergence of 'a new kind of party' that served as a precursor to the New Labour years.[4] In such studies, the argument has been that Kinnock enacted a significant but negative break with the party's past. Other studies have been more cautious and have suggested that

Kinnock's reforming and modernising zeal was restrained by events and circumstances.⁵ However, it is notable that the year 1985 and, in particular, the 1985 Labour Party Conference, regularly appear in the academic literature as points at which Kinnock 'was finally able to stamp his personal authority upon the Labour Party and set the agenda for its development'.⁶ In a similar manner, the policy review that was initiated after the 1987 General Election defeat has also been described as an important turning point in Labour's political development.⁷

Nevertheless, in all cases, the role played by party nostalgia in shaping the form, extent and parameters of party modernisation during the Kinnock years has been undervalued and underexplored. Furthermore, modernisation – the pursuit of new policies and objectives based on an interpretation of contemporary and future developments – has often been analysed in a way that has suggested that it was pursued in an emotional vacuum, albeit one that was filled with disputes over either pragmatic or ideologically based concerns. The aim of this chapter is to provide a more critical and nuanced discussion of the 1983 to 1992 Labour Party's relationship with its past than has hitherto been provided.

1983 Labour Leadership Election

With his personal roots in the coalmining communities of South Wales and his political origins on the Left of the party, it was perhaps unlikely that Neil Kinnock would attempt to overturn the type of attachment to the past that had informed Labour's trajectory during the period in which it had advocated its Alternative Economic Strategy. However, after Labour's 1983 General Election defeat, a number of significant voices, both inside and outside of the party, argued that Labour needed to reinvent itself in line with modern social and economic developments. In an influential essay entitled 'Labour's Lost Millions', the Marxist historian Eric Hobsbawm built on his earlier analysis in 'The Forward March of Labour Halted' by outlining why, in electoral and political terms, Labour had to move on from its traditional industrial working-class past. Hobsawm's analysis was emphatic: 'The working class has changed. The country has changed. The situation has changed.'⁸ Similar points were made by senior Labour politicians. In a speech to the Tower Hamlets Fabian Society, Peter Shore declared that Labour 'must apply democratic socialism to the problems of today and tomorrow – not of yesterday'.⁹

These sentiments were not necessarily shared by Labour Party members. Letters of support that were sent to Kinnock after the 1983 General Election defeat and during his leadership campaign indicate that he was understood to be a candidate who would keep the party connected with its historical roots. One of these communications argued that Labour had lost because it was not backward-looking enough:

> Can I make a suggestion in helping the Labour Party to win the next election in 4 yrs time. Could you possibly educate the first time voter & second, come to that, in the history of the Labour Party. How it was founded so that Labour is not a dirty word ... Do this near the next general election especially.[10]

Another Labour supporter, who was writing to wish Kinnock luck, focused on the industrial struggles of the early twentieth century and her experiences as a 'school girl in 1912, the year of the miners' big strike ... The miners today owe my father's generation a lot, and my mother's too. Please don't let them [the Conservative Party] take away our National Health. Our young ones don't realise what a loss that will be.'[11]

Indeed, there is little evidence to suggest that the 1983 defeat enacted a grassroots reorientation away from nostalgia. In Bristol, the defeated and departing Tony Benn was given the 'text of a miners' hymn from the old days of the Bristol mines' as a leaving present. The *Red Flag* was played as he left Bristol's Transport House.[12] Kinnock's political rise can be attributed, at least in part, to his own personal nostalgic resonance and his ability to use his oratorical skills to locate himself firmly within the party's nostalgia-identity. Mo Mowlam, who would later become a MP in 1987, described Kinnock's 1983 leadership campaign speech at the People's Theatre in Newcastle as 'one of the best speeches I have heard, because of the degree of emotional commitment in it. It made me think it must be how another inspiration of mine, Ellen Wilkinson, had sounded in her speeches when she led the Jarrow marchers down to London in 1936.'[13]

Similarly, at the party's annual conference in 1983, Michael Foot, the outgoing Labour leader, described how he believed that his successor had 'the true spirit of Aneurin Bevan in him'. Foot then went on to reminisce about how he had been 'to hear Nye speak in 1937 when the hunger marchers came to London. It was in Trafalgar Square and, I think, it was 10 November 1937 – 1936 or 1937 – at any rate, it was the day before Armistice Day.'[14] This comparison with Bevan, a politician with whom Kinnock shared geographical, social and political origins, was one that the new leader was keen to cultivate and reinforce. In his first conference speech as leader, the audience applauded as Kinnock declared: 'If we want guidance in how to win, we look no further than the man you would expect me to quote on this day of all days, Aneurin Bevan, my fellow countryman, my fellow townsman, my inspiration.' Interestingly, however, the Bevan quote that Kinnock chose that day spoke of the dangers of speaking 'the old false categories'.[15]

Despite his oratorical tendency to allude to the past, Kinnock clearly understood that the party needed to modernise its image. In a private conversation with the journalist Hugo Young in February 1984, he seemed wary of the need to focus on 'presentation' and appeared 'well attuned to the extreme importance of it in modern politics'.[16] At this stage, Kinnock had not yet either recognised or defined nostalgia explicitly as a barrier to party modernisation, but he certainly perceived it to be a powerful emotion that could shape political development. At the 1983 annual conference, he proclaimed, both boldly and mistakenly, that 'the labour movement is made up of today's people, who borrow nothing from nostalgia, whether for the 1950s and 1960s or for the 1920s or the 1820s.'[17] Elsewhere, he argued that nostalgia was the preserve of the Conservative Party and that 'the task of the Labour Party is a much more arduous one than that of the Tory Party. It is always more difficult to argue convincingly for a development in the future not yet within the experience of people than to mobilise nostalgia.'[18]

1984–85 Miners' Strike

The first significant test of Kinnock's leadership arrived in the form of the 1984–85 Miners' Strike, a strike in an industry renowned for its nostalgic symbolism. In 1983, an unsympathetic article in *The Economist* had described nostalgia as 'the curse of the mineral that first made industrial Britain great.'[19] More specifically, as I have shown in preceding chapters, the miners and, in particular, memories of their past heroic struggles were central to Labour's nostalgia-identity. Within the party, the strike that began on 12 March 1984 and ended almost one year later was, perhaps unsurprisingly, interpreted largely through the lens of this existing shared understanding of the past.

Throughout the strike, the actions of the miners and their union, the National Union of Mineworkers, were routinely portrayed by party figures as 'historic' and part of a long tradition of heroic struggle. Speaking as Chair of Labour's 1984 annual conference, Eric Heffer paid tribute to the striking miners and he declared that

> Today, we are being forced to fight for our rights, as the peasants did in 1381, as the Levellers and Diggers did during the English Revolution, as the early trade unionists did in the late 17th and early 18th centuries, as the Chartists did in the 1830s and as the early Socialists and Radicals did in the late 18th century when they began to propagate the alternatives to the sweated labour of the capitalist system.[20]

At the same conference, Jim Mortimer (Labour's General Secretary) discussed the relationship between extra-parliamentary industrial struggles and the parliamentary party. Mortimer argued that there was 'no conflict between the two – both are necessary. That was the meaning of the life of Keir Hardie – he was a workers' leader who voiced the workers' demands, but he was also the leader of the labour movement in parliament.'[21]

Positively charged idealised memories of the 1926 Miners' Strike (the centrepiece of that year's General Strike) characterised the party's understanding of the 1984–85 dispute. In a literal sense, nostalgia for 1926 provided financial capital for the strike – support groups sold pictures of A. J. Cook (the General Secretary of the Miners' Federation of Great Britain) and other images from 1926 – but it also provided political capital for the strike's advocates.[22] In 1984, speakers at the party's annual conference drew on nostalgia in order to shape the outcome of the debates. Arthur Scargill referenced the 1926 strike whilst moving a successful composite paying 'tribute to the historic struggle of the miners in 1984'.[23] In the same debate, a councillor from Ogmore elicited applause and cheers from her audience by referring to her memories of the heroic struggles of the miners and their families in 1926 and drawing parallels with the present situation.[24] A similar speech by the same speaker, delivered at the Welsh regional conference in May 1984, had received coverage in *Labour Weekly*.[25] At times, the mobilisation of nostalgia on behalf of the miners took a rather surreal turn: at Labour's annual conference, in the debate on the policing of the strike, one party member declared that he was 'sorry that we got rid of the pit ponies. Pit ponies and a few whippets would have chased these buggers back to the Metropolitan area long before now.'[26]

One of the most interesting aspects of the party's understanding of the 1984–85 strike was the way in which individuals and groups were assigned mnemonic forerunners from 1926. The 1926 miners' leader, A. J. Cook, became Arthur Scargill; the 1926 breakaway Spencer Union became the Union of Democratic Mineworkers;[27] the miners in 1926 were perceived as having been let down by the TUC and Labour Party in the same way that they were being 'betrayed' in the present.[28] Furthermore, this nostalgic reimagining of the 1926 strike also shaped the behaviour of the 1984–85 dispute's participants. Individuals and groups acted out their mnemonically assigned roles. Writing for the *New Statesman* in August 1984, Geoffrey Goodman (Industrial Editor for the *Daily Mirror*) noted that the 1926 Miners' Strike 'remained engrained on the contours of Labour Movement history as firmly as the Chartists or even the Peasants' Revolt' and his analysis went on to highlight the way that 'Today Arthur Scargill is compared (and compares himself) with

A. J. Cook whose legend he salutes with a special adulation. It's a kind of reincarnated symbolism.'[29] News items in Labour Party publications reinforced this sense that the 1984–85 strike represented a re-enactment of the events of 1926. One story in *Labour Weekly* described how 'History has repeated itself in Enfield where during the general strike of 1926 local families took in the children of striking south Wales miners.'[30] Other articles highlighted the way that memories of the female support groups and networks of 1926, held by women who were described as looking 'back nostalgically at the 1926 strike', were shaping the actions of their modern counterparts in 1984.[31] The past and present became blurred. Nostalgia had a contemporary agency.

Kinnock has routinely been described as a 'miner's son who must have felt the agonies of the strike in his gut'.[32] Yet he was also conscious of the electoral need for the party to broaden its appeal beyond its traditional industrial heartlands and was concerned about the issues of democracy that surrounded the strike (the NUM did not hold a national strike ballot). The archival evidence suggests that, rather than supporting the miners with either emotional or nostalgic rhetoric, Kinnock attempted to pursue a rational approach throughout the dispute. One internal document, written by John Reid (Kinnock's researcher and adviser) in December 1984, outlined a number of potential strategic options that included various emotive approaches, but noted that Kinnock should be able to commit to presenting 'the rational case' for coal with relative ease because he had 'been doing it consistently for nine months in any case'.[33] Kinnock's handwritten inserts into the first draft of his speech to the 1984 Durham Miners' Gala were indicative of his belief that it was necessary to emphasise rationality and reason rather than sentiment: 'There is not a coal miner alive who doesn't know when a pit is gone, finished, unworkable.'[34] Likewise, in a letter to the communist trade unionist Ken Gill, Kinnock was keen to stress that 'In speech after speech, I have outlined the rational, logical case for sustaining coal.'[35]

However, the 1984–85 Miners' Strike raised three issues that Kinnock was seemingly unable to address without recourse to the rhetorical deployment of the past. The first of these issues concerned extra-parliamentary action. In his speech at the TUC's annual conference in September 1984, Kinnock argued that political change must be brought about by peaceable and democratic means. He declared that 'general elections – and only general elections – are for changing governments in this country … This Congress has never, in its 116 years of history, preached or practised any other creed.'[36] When addressing Labour's annual conference, he outlined how a similar 'question' about the best way to enact political change had been 'faced by our movement in the

1930s; and they came back with the answer that the democratic road was the only route for British socialism.'[37] The second issue centred on the use of violence by striking miners. In a speech in Aberavon in November 1984, the TUC's General Secretary Norman Willis described how he had 'marched proudly behind many miners' banners and I know that there will never be one that praises the brick, the bolt or the petrol bomb ... such acts if they are done by miners are alien to our common trade union tradition.'[38] Kinnock was quick to support Willis's analysis. Speaking in the aftermath of the death of a South Wales taxi driver, he declared that violence 'disgraces our country and the traditions and temperament of our movement'.[39] The third issue was the potential retrospective reimbursement of the striking miners by a future Labour Government. On this issue, Kinnock argued both publicly and privately that none of the precedents that had been offered by supporters of reimbursement stood up to historical scrutiny.[40] In the end, the party was unpersuaded and the 1985 Labour Party conference carried a motion supporting the miners' retrospective reimbursement.[41]

Kinnock's approach to the 1984–85 Miners Strike provoked a nostalgic backlash within the party. His condemnation of picket-line violence was contested by an article in *Tribune* that cited 'the old Chartist slogan ... "Peaceably if we may. Forcibly if we must"' and emphasised the role played by working-class aggression in previous historical disputes. The same article also described the behaviour of the Yeomanry Cavalry during the 1819 Peterloo Massacre and the shooting of striking miners in Featherstone in Yorkshire in 1893 as part of 'the tradition now being carried out by Margaret Thatcher, Leon Brittan, television and the press.'[42] Politicians on the Left of the party also contested Kinnock's interpretation of the past. Writing in *Tribune*, Hugh Macpherson noted that, when questioned about picket-line violence, Benn was 'liable to depart on a Cook's Tour of the Diggers, the Levellers, the Chartists, the Polish trade union movement and the ownership of the British press'.[43] Similarly, at Labour's 1985 annual conference, in a seemingly targeted attack on Labour's leader, Joan Maynard made the 'connection between the miners and my old farmworkers' union. I am thinking of the Tolpuddle Martyrs. Remember, comrades, they broke the law as well.'[44] Her audience applauded this historical comparison.

Thus, rather than defusing tensions, the few references to the past that Kinnock made during the dispute heightened the sense of betrayal felt amongst party members. One letter, published in Labour's *New Socialist* magazine, attacked Kinnock's condemnation of picket-line violence. The writer argued that 'the lessons of history are either completely unknown or ignored by Neil Kinnock ... Now in the latest attempt to smash the

NUM he joins in the loudest baying. What hypocrisy when he referred to his mining family connections and lead [sic] the "Here We Go" miners' song at the Tolpuddle [150th anniversary] celebrations!'[45] A version of the same letter was published in *Tribune*.[46] Kinnock was also subjected to unwelcome historical comparisons. As the academic David Howell noted, one of the banners at the South Wales Miners' Rally in Aberavon in November 1984 asked 'Where is Ramsay McKinnock?'[47]

The Militant Tendency

As stated in this chapter's introduction, the 1985 Labour Party Conference Leader's Speech has been interpreted as a turning point in the party's political development. In his 2012 memoirs, Jack Straw deemed it '*the* speech of the last four decades'.[48] In this speech, Kinnock famously attacked the actions of Liverpool's Militant-led council and, in particular, 'the grotesque chaos of a Labour council hiring taxis to scuttle round a city handing out redundancy notices to its own workers.'[49] From 1985 onwards, the Labour leadership, having identified the organisation as a serious threat to Labour's democracy since the mid-1970s,[50] redoubled its efforts to expel leading figures of the Trotskyite so-called Militant Tendency from the party. These actions have become central to popular narratives surrounding Kinnock's attempts to modernise the Labour Party. They have been understood as part of a broader move to isolate and expunge the far-Left from the party. This narrative has suggested that the Militant Tendency was expelled in order to modernise Labour into a viable electoral force. However, regardless of the political and electoral necessity of these actions, the process of isolating and 'othering' Militant actually served to reinforce Labour's attachment to past. Critically, history and nostalgia lay at the heart of the construction of the Militant 'other'.

It is highly significant that, after delivering the famous lines about Liverpool City Council in his 1985 Leader's Speech, Kinnock drew applause from his audience by citing Bevan's criticism of ideological 'purists'.[51] Instrumental references to the past provided political capital for speakers and writers when they were presenting the case against Militant. In the context of Kinnock's 1985 conference speech, these references worked when they were perceived as genuine and failed when they were not. Reflecting on the speech after the conference, Frances Morrell (leader of the Inner London Education Authority) stated that 'the very positive aspect of Neil Kinnock's speech was his ability to describe the "old time religion" … it had a lot of warmth, a lot of generosity, a lot of, if you like, emotionally based values that he clearly feels very deeply, and therefore they are convincing when you hear them.'[52] Others were less convinced. Eric Heffer walked out of the speech in protest. In comments reported in the media, Robert Parry (Labour MP for Liverpool) declared that 'Kinnock today showed that he's the biggest traitor since Ramsay MacDonald.'[53]

On other occasions, Kinnock pursued a similar approach. Ostensibly modern in its political message and outlook, Kinnock's 'Future of Socialism' speech to the Fabian Society in November 1985 described how 'The harsh electoral reality is that Labour cannot rely merely on a combination of the disposed, the "traditional" and increasing figmentary working class and minority groups for the winning of power.'[54] Throughout the speech, Kinnock implied that the Militant Tendency was holding the party back: 'The Labour Party must no longer allow others to usurp what are surely its legitimate claims and aims. Above all, it must reassert democratic socialism as an effective body of values for modern needs rather than the ghost from the past.'[55]

However, the nature of Kinnock's argument and the way in which it was framed against a group that had decided to 'opt for a parasitical life inside the mass labour movement', shaped the speech in unintended and contradictory ways.[56] Kinnock mobilised the past in order to locate Militant (and the far-left in general) outside of the party's tradition and heritage. These deployments of the past were carefully considered: outline drafts of the speech stated that 'the objectives and methods of the ultra-left are irrelevant and repugnant to the traditions of Democratic socialism.'[57] Kinnock referred to, amongst other people, the early Fabians, Bevan, Richard Tawney, G. D. H. Cole, Robert Owen and William Morris. The paradoxical outcome of these historical references was that a speech that was concerned with modernisation and the future ended up being framed and characterised by an attachment to the past. Writing in the *Guardian*, Hugo Young noted that the speech was problematic because it spoke to the party rather than to the electorate and 'did not flinch from seeing the future in terms of the past'.[58]

Kinnock was drawing on a historically informed construction of Militant that was well-established. Since 1981, the anti-Militant Labour Solidarity Campaign had argued that 'Labour is not a revolutionary party and never has been … Labour's roots are in the free trade union movement.'[59] At Labour's annual conference in 1982, Militant was described by the party's General Secretary as alien to the Left's traditions.[60] Other speakers were more emphatic in their analysis:

> We have seen an uncontrollable Frankenstein of programmed robots nibbling away at the foundations of this great labour movement. We have

seen thousands of our supporters bewildered and perplexed, crying out for a return to the traditional democratic socialism of Bevan, Griffiths, Attlee and Robert Owen, socialism through the medium of the ballot box.'[61]

At the same conference, Michael Foot asked the party to protect the constitution 'given to us by our forebears' and denied that the attacks on Militant had historical antecedents in the expulsions of Stafford Cripps and Bevan in 1939.[62] Such sentiments were echoed by Tom Sawyer at the height of the Liverpool controversy in 1986 when he argued that 'People have said that it happened to Michael Foot, it happened to Nye Bevan, it happened to Stafford Cripps. I think that does a great disservice to the memories of these men.'[63]

This mnemonic construction of the Militant 'other' was so closely tied to Labour's nostalgia-identity that even Benn, who was opposed to expelling the organisation, inadvertently echoed it in a speech to a Militant rally at Wembley in October 1984. In this speech, Benn declared that 'over many centuries, from the Peasants' Revolt, through the English Revolution and the Tolpuddle Martyrs right up to today, similar battles have been fought and won. We should never forget the home-grown nature of much of our own socialist tradition.'[64] Indeed, throughout the 1980s and early 1990s, the idea that the Militant Tendency was antithetical to the British socialist tradition that had spawned the Labour Party consistently reoccurred in the public rhetoric of Labour politicians and activists. Discussing the suspension of the MP Terry Fields (a suspected member of Militant) at Labour's annual conference in 1991, a delegate from Liverpool declared that Labour needed to be protected from the organisation: 'This issue is not about witch hunts; it is about traditions, the traditions of the Labour Party.'[65] Ultimately, modernity did not defeat Militant, but Labour's historically orientated identity did.

Jobs and industry

When attempting to locate critical turning points in the development of Kinnock's Labour Party, historians and political scientists have tended to overlook the party's Jobs and Industry Campaign.[66] The political significance of the outputs that were generated by this campaign should not be understated. Kinnock's 1986 book *Making Our Way* marked a fundamental break from the type of restorative nostalgia that had characterised party policy during the period in which it had advocated its Alternative Economic Strategy. This book exhibited little in the way of an idealised and sentimental attachment to Britain's traditional industrial past. Kinnock argued that 'New technological developments render old skills and old factories redundant with frightening speed. Yet to try to prevent that change would endanger the economic future of the whole country.'[67] Britain's traditional industries were almost completely absent from the analysis that was presented. Instead, Labour's central industrial objective was stated as the building of 'a competitive, innovative, modern industrial sector in Britain'.[68] This objective would go on to inform Labour's policy documents *New Industrial Strength for Britain*, *New Skills for Britain* and the 1987 General Election Manifesto.[69]

From the outset, the Jobs and Industry campaign operated around the central premise that 'We must appear relevant and modern. Our cloth cap image must be shed. "The future" must be a continual theme.'[70] Critically, *Making Our Way* represented an explicit and direct attack on the party's nostalgia. Kinnock declared that the decline of Britain's traditional industrial working-class communities should not 'mean that a socialist movement should wallow in nostalgia for the old days of terraced housing, minimal healthcare and few educational opportunities. Only those who never knew it could really long for it. Socialism is dedicated to progress.'[71] Importantly, this statement represented the point at which Kinnock tied in his long-held notion that nostalgia could be politically problematic with the resistance to modernisation that existed in the party. It was also a response to the growing trend of political opponents mobilising nostalgia against reform. During 1986, nostalgia was regularly deployed by those who resented the party's trajectory under Kinnock. Eric Heffer's book *Labour's Future: Socialist or SDP Mark 2?* framed the new strategy being pursued by Kinnock as a betrayal of Labour's history. Heffer's argument was replete with quotes from figures from the party's past. Keir Hardie appeared more times in the footnotes than any other author. Throughout the book, Heffer declared that Labour must return to the principles that had defined the party's founding moments.[72]

However, the relationship between Labour's Jobs and Industry campaign and the party's nostalgia was by no means straightforwardly oppositional. Tensions between the past and the present became obvious during the Jarrow 86 campaign. Jarrow 86 was 'designed both to commemorate and celebrate the fiftieth anniversary of the historic Jarrow march in October 1936 *and* to actively campaign on the issue of unemployment in 1986.'[73] Attempting to follow the route of the original 1936 marches, the 1986 campaign's central aim of 're-creating this historic event' meant that it had a restoratively nostalgic dimension.[74] From the outset, the lines between past and present were intentionally blurred. Along the route, a play focusing on contemporary issues was designed to be performed to music from 1936 'with the historical and contemporary alternating' and meetings were to be held in front of reproduced banners from the original marches.[75]

Internal party correspondence between the party's General Secretary's office and Kinnock's advisory team suggests that a sense of unease existed about the potentially backward-looking nature of the Jarrow 86 campaign. The need for 'continuous party involvement in the publicity surrounding the tour in order to ensure that it is forward looking' was emphasised.[76] If the idea was to make the march forward-looking, it was not realised. The manner in which Jarrow 86 was conflated with the Jobs and Industry campaign primarily served to legitimise the party's nostalgia for its traditional industrial past. At Labour's annual conference in 1986, a delegate from Jarrow seconded a composite on economic and industrial policy. He stressed the similarities with 1936 and urged his audience to support the 1986 marches. His speech was met with 'Applause and cheers'.[77] Roy Hattersley asked the conference 'to support the Jarrow March not only in memory of what we fought for in the past, but in recognition of what we have to go on fighting for until the day of the next General Election and beyond.'[78] In this way, much of the party's rhetoric felt at odds with the anti-nostalgic policy orientation that was outlined in the Jobs and Industry campaign's main outputs.

1987 General Election

To a certain extent, *Making Our Way*'s anti-nostalgic language was informed by the broader efforts to modernise the party's image that were taking place at the same time. Image modernisation became a key component of the Labour leadership's electoral strategy. In 1985, this drive for modernisation was accelerated by the appointment of Mandelson as Director of Communications and the ever-increasing influence of Philip Gould's consultative Shadow Communications Agency. Both Mandelson and Gould would later be at the forefront of the New Labour project.

Reflecting on his role during this period, Mandelson has described how his job was 'to make everything about Labour look and sound modern too'.[79] His actions were often met with a backlash that contained notably nostalgic elements. After Eric Heffer had viewed the launch of the 'Freedom and Fairness' campaign, his anger was uncontrollable: '"It's disgraceful," he muttered ... "It's more than disgraceful. It's disgusting! The NEC never approved this. Where's the Red Flag? What is 'Putting People First'?"... This was *not* the Labour Party he had joined, he fumed.'[80] Mandelson's work also involved replacing and reinventing established nostalgic symbols. Famously, at Labour's 1986 annual conference, in a move that provoked a great deal of hostility amongst the party's rank-and-file, the red flag was replaced by a red rose.[81] In retrospect, perhaps optimistically, Kinnock viewed this change as important in reshaping attitudes within the party in a manner more conducive towards reform.[82] At the time, he was less sure about other changes. Just before the 1986 conference, Mandelson was called into Kinnock's office: 'His wife was there too, looking upset and worried. Neil was holding up one of our salmon-pink [conference] wallets. "Do you really think the mineworkers' delegation are going to prance around conference holding *this*?" … "You can't do it. There'll be a riot."'[83]

Despite the aforementioned symbolic changes, the reorientation of the party's image away from the past was by no means complete by 1987. Certainly, Labour's election campaign contained recognisably nostalgic tropes. Speaking to the Welsh Labour Party conference in Llandudno in May 1987, Kinnock mobilised memories of traditional industrial working-class struggle when he asked the question 'Why am I the first Kinnock in a thousand generations to be able to get to university?' Kinnock went on to ask 'Did they lack talent; those people who could make wonderful, beautiful things with their hands; those people who could dream dreams, see visions?' He emphasised both the psychological and physical strength of 'those people who had such a sense of perception as to know in times so brutal, so oppressive, that they could win their way out of that by coming together … those people who could work eight hours underground and then come up and play football.'[84]

Tensions between the past and the present were highlighted when extracts from this speech were included in the modern-looking Party Election Broadcast that was dubbed 'Kinnock – The Movie'.[85] Alastair Campbell has described the way that, when the speech was initially delivered, Kinnock's oratory 'moved sections of his audience to tears'.[86] There is little evidence to suggest that Labour's PEB enacted a comparable response outside of the party. Furthermore, when Denis MacShane MP viewed the much-hyped broadcast retrospectively, he was both underwhelmed and struck by the fact that 'All the images were of the past, most of the language was of pain, poverty and privation. There was nothing on success, on modernisation, on the future.'[87] Undoubtedly, the Llandudno speech undermined Kinnock's attempts to portray the Conservatives as 'living in a time warp. They would need a Dickens to do them justice.'[88]

In the aftermath of the party's 1987 election defeat, a number of Labour politicians argued that Kinnock needed to move quickly to jettison policies and strategies that remained the product of a sentimental attachment to the past. Austin Mitchell declared that 'our old approaches are as out of fashion as Keir Hardie.'[89] Peter Shore, in an unpublished interview with the *Daily Telegraph*, stated that Labour's 'real problem' was that 'it reflected those parts of the country – the old industrial north and the inner cities – where everything was old and out of fashion.'[90] Other figures in the party deployed memories of the past to legitimise the need for reform in the present: speaking at the party's annual conference in 1987, John Willman from the Fabian Society described how 'When the Labour Party was formed, socialists knew the future ... We are [now] constantly surprised at developments in the economy and in society. Our only remedy often seems to be back to the future ... For a party of change we have become very conservative.'[91]

Policy review

After the 1987 election defeat, the Labour leadership moved quickly to initiate a wide ranging review of the party's policies. At an elite level, the review was clearly understood to represent a necessary step towards party modernisation. From the beginning, internal party correspondence and memoranda described how the review would be 'rooted in the realities Britain will face in the 1990s: Britain as it will be, not Britain as we would like it to be.'[92] One document written by Geoff Bish (the party's policy director) in July 1987 emphasised the party's need for forward-looking policies that 'do not look as though they have been simply dusted down or reworked from Labour's programmes of 1976 and 1982'.[93] With the party's Policy Review Groups (PRGs) working closely with Gould's Shadow Communications Agency, the review's early outputs were couched in the language of modernity. At times, this language seemed almost overbearing: published in the document *Social Justice and Economic Efficiency*, the Productive and Competitive Economy Policy Review Group's first report contained the word 'New' in nine of its eleven sub-headings.[94] In contrast to the AES's policies, the emphasis was on developing new industries and harnessing new technologies to make the British economy more competitive.[95] Moving the report for the NEC at the party's 1988 annual conference, Tom Sawyer argued that Labour's new orientation needed to seem 'relevant ... to a new generation of people who do not even remember Harold Wilson or Jim Callaghan, never mind Keir Hardie and Clement Attlee.'[96] Moreover, in the report's foreword, Larry Whitty (the party's general secretary) made it clear that the statements from the PRGs that followed were explicitly designed to 'look forward to the Britain of the 1990s'.[97] In a similar manner, the statement *Democratic Socialist Aims and Values*, endorsed by the NEC in March 1988, stressed that the party needed to adapt its ideological approach in order for it to respond to the societal and economic changes that would take place in the future.[98]

This language of modernity did not connect with the wider party. Throughout the policy review, Tony Benn expressed a static model of political development. He acknowledged that a number of social and technological changes had taken place, but he also argued that these changes did not 'really alter the underlying faith which brought the Labour movement into existence'.[99] When challenging Kinnock for the party's leadership in 1988, Benn wrote articles and statements criticising the Labour Leader's hostility to the past.[100] When the policy review's findings were brought before the NEC in May 1989, Benn condemned 'The Productive and Competitive Economy' report for not engaging with the party's history and he declared that it represented a betrayal of Labour's beliefs akin to the actions of Ramsay MacDonald in 1931. Kinnock replied that 'there was no need for a historical analysis; it would daunt us.'[101] Benn was not the only politician who criticised the review in this manner. At the inaugural Socialist Conference that was held in Chesterfield in October 1987, Eric Heffer rejected his label as a 'dinosaur', but he also made an appeal to younger members to remember the party's history and to 'work as our forefathers did, and our mothers, to bring about a transformation of society.'[102] At the same conference, Ken Livingstone argued that little had changed about the 'class nature of society' and he too compared Kinnock to Ramsay MacDonald.[103] Labour party members echoed these sentiments with letters to publications like *Tribune* that stressed the applicability of the situation in the 1930s to the present and accused the party of ignoring the lessons of the past.[104]

At the 1988 Labour Party Conference, both *Democratic Socialist Aims and Values* and *Social Justice and Economic Efficiency* were attacked for representing an abandonment of Labour's historical roots. To applause from his audience, Arthur Scargill condemned 'the Filofax brigade with the philosophy of the yuppies' and he declared that 'The document "Aims and Values" is a clear departure from the basic principled position of our party and our forefathers who created it … I believe our Labour pioneers got it right. They wanted to change society.'[105] Supporting Scargill, a delegate from Bristol talked about how 'In 1922, a Labour MP was sent for the first time from my constituency to alleviate oppression, to challenge poverty, and it is on that basis – the basis of common ownership – that we stand here united.'[106]

Within the party, there were certainly people who believed that the opposition to Labour's direction under Kinnock was being fuelled by nostalgia. In June 1987, one letter writer to *Tribune* noted that Labour's hostility to change seemed to stem from the tendency of party members to 'over-romanticise the undoubted poverty and deprivation associated with the struggles that took place 60 years ago'.[107] Commenting on why he would be voting for Kinnock in the 1988 leadership contest, David Blunkett stated that democratic socialism 'cannot be achieved by living on nostalgia, or by ignoring the reality of the opinion polls'.[108] In a widely reported speech, delivered at the *Tribune* rally at the party's annual conference in 1988, Ron Todd (leader of the Transport and General Workers' Union) exhibited a level of suspicion of the 'modernisers and reformers, with sharp suits and cordless telephones, clipboards and scientific samples'. However, significantly, he also confronted those who found 'a melancholy pleasure in nostalgia'. He went on to describe how 'The Labour Party's nostalgic faction isn't small ... The nostalgics look back to a misty past, which never really existed, when the party stood for true socialist values, when no one cared about opinion polls, advertising, and all the rest of the flim-flam.'[109]

Without a doubt, this nostalgia shaped the manner in which power elites supported the policy review. Nostalgia represented something that had to be negotiated; it could not be circumvented. Launching the review at Labour's annual conference in 1987, Kinnock quoted Bevan (again) and proclaimed that 'We, in our time, face the challenge of the realities spoken of by Bevan.'[110] His speech's tendency to call on the past to legitimise the present was noted by David McKie in the *Guardian*.[111] During the review, other commentators suggested that, due to his personal attachment to the party's symbols, traditions and rituals, Kinnock would be unable to enact a decisive break with Labour's nostalgia.[112] His foreword in *Meet the Challenge, Make the Change* was certainly more conciliatory towards the party's identity than the policy solutions that the document prescribed. Although his statement was largely orientated towards the future, Kinnock outlined how the policy reviewers had 'looked back to gain inspiration from the great accomplishments of the past and to be instructed by the most successful'.[113]

Nevertheless, this historical emphasis, rather than representing a spontaneous outpouring of emotion, should be viewed as an instrumental attempt to legitimise the overall forward-looking nature of the review. Other senior 'modernisers' pursued a broadly similar approach. Contradicting his speech from the previous year, Tom Sawyer moved the policy review at the 1989 annual conference with the explanation that 'we have renewed our policies so that we are, in Bevan's phrase, "the partners and not the creatures of social reality."'[114] In this way, contentious policies that were likely to be interpreted as incongruent with Labour's nostalgia-identity, paradoxically, needed to be cloaked in the veil of the past.

Towards the 1992 General Election

Labour proceeded towards the 1992 General Election with a set of policies that represented a decisive break from the party's nostalgically informed AES. Labour's policy documents proclaimed that 'unlike the Tories ... we are Looking to the Future.'[115] A new outward-facing approach, which looked to industrial success stories abroad, emphasised the need to modernise British manufacturing and to make sure that the workforce had the training and skills that were required for new technologically advanced jobs.[116] This approach was also designed explicitly to meet the demands of the changing nature of British society and, in particular, the ever-increasing number of female, part-time and self-employed workers in Britain.[117] Yet, at the same time, Labour's focus groups repeatedly provided evidence that suggested that the party was still associated with the past. Images of Kinnock in nostalgically charged situations, including singing with Welsh miners' choirs, served to repel swing voters who believed that the Labour leader needed 'to do more for *all* the people not just folksy people in pubs and Welsh miners'.[118] With such criticisms in mind, Kinnock's team drew up strategy documents that aimed to 'Liberate NK from the shackles of the past.'[119]

Without a doubt, these efforts were hampered by both Kinnock's personal attachment to Labour's internal culture and his need to display sensitivity towards the party's nostalgia-identity in order to secure political capital. When the Labour leader got up to sing 'Comrades in Arms' with a Welsh choir at 'Welsh night' at the 1990 Labour Party Conference, one journalist described how 'the lady next to me actually fell over with excitement. Drenched in nostalgia, the Welsh delegates revelled in old socialist hymns, and forgot that such things as image advisers existed.'[120] At the 1991 annual conference, in a speech that stressed that Labour would win the forthcoming election by 'looking at a future instead of reaching for the past', Kinnock began by quoting the poet Idris Davies.[121] In a rather contradictory manner, such acts served to reinforce the type of backward-looking orientation that, elsewhere, Kinnock routinely suggested was holding the party back.[122]

In the years running up to the 1992 General Election, opposition to Kinnock's reforms was often martialled behind an emotional commitment to staying 'true' to Labour's past. This occurred across a range of issues; for example, at the party's annual conference in 1990, one delegate who was speaking against the use of One Member, One Vote in trigger ballot reselections asked 'is this what our forefathers fought for – designer socialism?'[123] In the same debate, another delegate suggested that the proposed changes would take Labour back to the

1890s and he argued that it was important that 'we remind ourselves of where we come from' in order not to betray the ideals of the party's founders.[124] Furthermore, during a discussion about the party's position on trade union rights, delegates appeared to ignore Tony Blair's request for the party to 'leave the past to those who live in it' by repeatedly making appeals to Labour's traditions.[125]

The past was also evoked by those seeking political change. At times, these evocations involved a direct contestation of the party's male-orientated nostalgia. In 1991, Loraine Monk, who sat on the NEC's Women's Committee, criticised the lack of female representation within the party via a series of questions that asked 'Where is Keir Hardie's sister? Bevan's sister? Neil Kinnock's sister? We need to encourage those fundamental ideas as well.'[126] At other times, simplistic binary historical references were made that contrasted Labour's new economic strategy with a Conservative Party that 'hankers after the society of the 1890s'.[127]

In all cases, historically framed analyses served to legitimise, sustain and reinforce the broader backward-looking emphasis that existed within the party and to provide the emotional climate in which nostalgia could flourish. Such an environment had its advantages for party elites: nostalgia represented a resource that could be used to mobilise rank-and-file activists. In 1990, the Labour Party's official newspaper published a letter calling for members to campaign and vote at the next General Election for the generation who 'grew up in the economic depression of the 20s and 30s' and 'who in 1945 gave us a landslide Labour victory'.[128] In an article appearing on election day in 1992, Michael Foot argued that victory could be 'worthy of the men and women who against infinitely fiercer odds, prepared the way for the establishment of the party in the year 1900, [and] worthy to be set aside the 1945 victory'.[129]

Clearly, tensions existed between the pursuit of modern policies and strategies that targeted the electorate and an electoral strategy that required the mobilisation of an overtly nostalgic membership. At the party's rock concert-style Sheffield Rally on 1 April 1992 – an event made famous by Kinnock's multiple cries of 'We're alright' – these tensions were manifestly obvious to onlookers. Speaking at the rally, Barbara Castle's comparisons between 1945 and 1992 'nearly brought the house down'.[130] An article in the *Sunday Times* reported that Castle's intervention represented a 'risky exercise in nostalgia, not to be carried too far'.[131] Taking to the stage afterwards, Kinnock's speech began by outlining the way that the party was 'looking to the future', but this emphasis was not sustained. In order to attack the Conservative Party, Kinnock quoted Percy Bysshe Shelley. Before long, he was recalling his upbringing in South Wales.[132] One journalist wrote that, taken as a whole, the event was a 'mix of sound, light, nostalgia, glitz and real political punch'.[133] Significantly, the Sheffield Rally highlighted the fact that a party that offered policies that were explicitly designed to meet the challenges of the future still retained an identity that was firmly rooted in the past. The electorate was unsure. Ultimately, this uncertainty about whether or not Labour had fully broken with its past was one of a number of factors, including John Smith's last minute so-called 'Tax bombshell', that contributed to the party unexpectedly losing the 1992 General Election.

Conclusion

New Labour argued that the Kinnock era was a period of limited modernisation. This critique contained a degree of accuracy. However, when the years 1983 to 1992 are analysed within a framework that examines the party's relationship with nostalgia, it becomes apparent that important changes took place. Kinnock and his allies were able to negotiate Labour's nostalgia-identity in a manner that allowed them to reorient the party's programmatic commitments away from the past.

Aided by a long period in opposition, party policy was successfully isolated from nostalgia. The key turning point was the 1985–86 Jobs and Industry Campaign. The 1986 book *Making Our Way* jettisoned the type of nostalgia for traditional working-class industries that had previously shaped the party's AES between 1970 and 1983. This trajectory was maintained throughout the policy review era. To a large extent, political developments and electoral necessity had increased the need for this reorientation. Whilst defeat at the 1983 General Election proved that policies informed by nostalgia could no longer deliver electoral success, the failure of the 1984–85 Miners' Strike demonstrated that groups that lay at the heart of the party's nostalgia-identity were now unable to help to facilitate political change in the way that they had done in the past (most notably, during Ted Heath's 1970 to 1974 Government).

When assessed within the context of party nostalgia, other episodes do not represent the kind of 'modernising' turning points that academics have hitherto described them to be. In particular, Kinnock's attacks on the Militant Tendency relied on the historical 'othering' of the entryist group and, thus, actually served to reinforce the party's attachment to the past. More generally, the Labour leadership's relationship with nostalgia was complex and, at times, contradictory. One of the central paradoxes of Labour politics has been the way in which power elites have had to frame change and reform within the parameters and language of the past – thereby sustaining the very same nostalgia that they seek to overturn. This contradiction ran throughout the Kinnock era. In 1992, Labour's identity, an identity with which Kinnock clearly felt a degree of personal affinity, remained shaped by a positively charged idealised attachment to the past. Therefore, when placed in their historical context, the changes that were made to the political role played by Labour's nostalgia during these years should be described as limited but significant.

Notes

1. Blair, *A Journey*, 49.
2. P. Mandelson, *The Third Man* (London: Harper Press, 2011), 118.
3. R. Heffernan and M. Marqusee, *Defeat from the Jaws of Victory: Inside Kinnock's Labour Party* (London: Verso, 1992), 1.
4. Panitch and Leys, *End of Parliamentary Socialism*, 218.
5. See T. Jones, 'Neil Kinnock's Socialist Journey: From Clause Four to the Policy Review', *Contemporary Record*, 8:3 (1994), 573; M. Westlake (with I. St. John), *Kinnock: The Biography* (London: Little, Brown and Company, 2001), 427.
6. Westlake, *Kinnock*, 343.
7. M. J. Smith, 'Neil Kinnock and the Modernisation of the Labour Party', *Contemporary Record*, 8:3 (1994), 559; Shaw, *Labour Party since 1945*, 181–182.
8. E. Hobsbawm, 'Labour's Lost Millions', *Marxism Today*, October 1983, 10.
9. P. Shore, 'Speech to Tower Hamlets Fabian Society at Oxford House, Bethnal Green on Monday 26 September 1983', SHORE/16/19, Peter Shore Papers, LSE.
10. Letter of support from Brighton Labour Party member dated 20 June 1983, KNNK/2/1/10, Neil Kinnock Papers, The Churchill Archives Centre, University of Cambridge.
11. Letter of support from Glasgow Labour supporter dated 19 June 1983, KNNK/2/1/10, Kinnock Papers, Churchill Archives.
12. T. Benn, diary entry for 30 July 1983 in T. Benn (R. Winstone ed.), *The End of an Era: Diaries 1980–90* (London: Hutchinson, 1992), 311.
13. M. Mowlam, *Momentum: The Struggle for Peace, Politics and the People* (London, Hodder and Stoughton, 2002), 33.
14. M. Foot, quoted in The Labour Party, *Report of the Annual Conference of the Labour Party 1983* (London: The Labour Party, 1983), 116.
15. N. Kinnock, quoted in Labour Party, *LPACR 1983*, 30.
16. H. Young, 'N. Kinnock, Lunch, *The Times*, 29 February 1984' in H. Young (I. Trewin ed.), *The Hugo Young Papers: Thirty Years of British Politics – Off the Record* (London: Penguin, 2008), 202.
17. N. Kinnock, quoted in Labour Party, *LPACR 1983*, 249.
18. Extract from E. Hobsbawm's interview of N. Kinnock from *Marxism Today*, 'Agenda: Why Labour Can Sound Tunes of Glory', *The Guardian*, 1 October 1984.
19. 'Some Miners Strike against Geology', *The Economist*, 5 March 1983, 25.

20 E. Heffer, quoted in The Labour Party, *Report of the Annual Conference of the Labour Party 1984* (London: The Labour Party, 1984), 4.
21 J. Mortimer, *LPACR 1984*, 263.
22 'Boost for Miners', *Labour Weekly*, 31 August 1984, 13.
23 A. Scargill, quoted in *LPACR 1984*, 32.
24 M. Williams, quoted in *LPACR 1984*, 42.
25 'Oppose the Closures', *Labour Weekly*, 25 May 1984, 4.
26 M. Quinn, quoted in *LPACR 1984*, 48.
27 See S. Newens, 'The Breakaway Miners' Union', letter to *Tribune*, 6 April, 1984, 10.
28 See Editorial, 'The TUC Must Stand Up for the Miners', *Tribune*, 31 August 1984, 1.
29 G. Goodman, 'Feedback: Parallels with 1926', *New Statesman*, 10 August 1984, 19.
30 D. Cordwell, '1926 Revisited', *Labour Weekly*, 31 August 1984, 4.
31 J. Copley, 'Fighting for Their Lives' and 'One Step Further in the Struggle', *Labour Weekly*, 6 July 1984, 10–11.
32 J. Lloyd, *Understanding the Miners' Strike*, Fabian Tract 504 (London: Fabian Society, 1985), 38.
33 J. Reid, 'Labour Party – NUM Meeting: Thursday 6 December [1984]', KNNK/15/2/9, Kinnock Papers, Churchill Archives, 2.
34 'Durham Miners' Gala, 14/7/84: Draft 1, KNNK/15/2/48, Kinnock Papers, Churchill Archives, 3.
35 N. Kinnock, letter to K. Gill entitled 'Address to the Trades Union Congress', KNNK/15/2/9, Kinnock Papers, Churchill Archives, 1.
36 N. Kinnock, quoted in The Trades Union Congress, *TUC Report 1984, Report of the 116th Annual Trades Union Congress held in Brighton Centre, Brighton, September 3rd to 7th 1984* (London: TUC, 1984), 459.
37 N. Kinnock, quoted in *LPACR 1984*, 103.
38 TUC Press Release, 'A Copy of the Speech Made by Norman Willis to Striking Miners in Aberavon, 13 November 1984', ORME/5/3, Stanley Orme Papers, LSE, 4.
39 N. Kinnock, 'Speech to Labour Rally in Stoke', *Labour Weekly*, 7 December 1984, 8.
40 See N. Kinnock, quoted in The Labour Party, *Report of the Annual Conference of the Labour Party 1985* (London: The Labour Party, 1985), 154 and N. Kinnock, 'Letter to Ron Todd' dated 26 September 1985, KNNK/15/2/48, Kinnock Papers, Churchill Archives, 2.
41 *LPACR 1985*, 156.
42 D. Goodman, 'Picket-Line Violence: The Lessons of History', *Tribune*, 12 October 1984, 11.
43 H. Macpherson, 'Asking the Wrong Questions', *Tribune*, 7 September 1984, 4.
44 J. Maynard, quoted in *LPACR 1985*, 165.
45 M. Gray, 'Kinnock's Need for a History Lesson', letter to *New Socialist*, December 1984, 47.

46 M. Gray, 'Neil Kinnock and the Miners', letter to *Tribune*, 2 November 1984, 10.
47 D. Howell, 'Labour and the Miners', *New Socialist*, March 1985, 20.
48 J. Straw, *Last Man Standing* (London: Macmillan, 2012), 158.
49 N. Kinnock, *LPACR 1985*, 128.
50 See M. Crick, *The March of Militant* (London: Faber, 1986), 103
51 N. Kinnock, *LPACR 1985*, 128.
52 S. Weir, 'Follow our Leader: Stuart Weir Talks to Four People', *New Socialist*, November 1985, 34.
53 'Heffer Walks Out Over Liverpool Attack', *The Times*, 2 October 1985.
54 N. Kinnock, *The Future of Socialism*, speech delivered on 12 November 1985, Fabian Society 509 (London: Fabian Society, 1986), 2.
55 Kinnock, *Future of Socialism*, 3.
56 *Ibid.*, 10.
57 'Democratic Socialism – Now', KNNK/16/1/23, Kinnock Papers, Churchill Archives, 3.
58 H. Young, 'The Quest for Kinnock the Statesman', *The Guardian*, 14 November 1985.
59 The Labour Solidarity Campaign, 'You, the Labour Party and the Militant Tendency' (London: The Labour Solidarity Campaign, 1982), SHORE/13/142, Shore Papers, LSE, 2.
60 J. Mortimer, quoted in *LPACR 1982*, 41.
61 R. Ormonde, quoted in *LPACR 1982*, 47–48.
62 M. Foot, quoted in *LPACR 1982*, 52.
63 S. Weir, 'To Move against Militant?', *New Socialist*, April 1986, 13.
64 T. Benn, 'Never Forget that Much of Our Socialist Tradition is Home Grown', *Tribune*, 26 October 1984, 5.
65 B. Navarro, quoted in The Labour Party, *Conference Report: Ninetieth Annual Conference of the Labour Party* (London: The Labour Party, 1991), 8.
66 The exception is Wickham-Jones, 'Economic Strategy and the Labour Party', 215–216, 219.
67 N. Kinnock, *Making Our Way: Investing in Britain's Future* (Oxford: Basil Blackwell, 1986), 191.
68 Kinnock, *Making Our Way*, 49.
69 The Labour Party, *New Industrial Strength for Britain* (London The Labour Party, 1987); The Labour Party, *New Skills for Britain* (London: The Labour Party, 1987); The Labour Party, *Manifesto: Britain Will Win with Labour* (London: The Labour Party, 1987).
70 The Labour Party, 'Labour's Jobs and Industry Campaign, 1985: Section: "Where We Start From"', CSC 1/11/84, KNNK/2/1/65, Kinnock Papers, Churchill Archives, 7.
71 Kinnock, *Making Our Way*, 192.
72 For example, see E. Heffer, *Labour's Future: Socialist or SDP Mark 2?* (London: Verso, 1986), 62.
73 'A Unique Combination: An Initial Report from Jarrow 86' (Cambridge: The Electric Press Factory, 1986), KNNK/2/1/65, Kinnock Papers, Churchill Archives, 1.

74 'A Unique Combination', 4.
75 *Ibid.*, 5–6.
76 T. Manwaring, letter to P. Hewitt dated 12 March 1986, KNNK/2/1/65, Kinnock Papers, Churchill Archives.
77 S. Hepburn, quoted in The Labour Party, *Report of the Annual Conference of the Labour Party 1986* (London: The Labour Party, 1986), 25.
78 R. Hattersley, quote in *LPACR 1986*, 27.
79 Mandelson, *Third Man*, 92.
80 *Ibid.*, 88.
81 For example, see N. Waterfield, 'Alive and Kicking', letter to *New Socialist*, May 1987, 63.
82 N. Kinnock, 'Reforming the Labour Party 1983–92', *Contemporary Record*, 8:3 (1994), 542.
83 Mandelson, *Third Man*, 92.
84 N. Kinnock, 'Llandudno, May 15 – Speech to Welsh Labour Conference', quoted in The Labour Party, *The Future We Offer: Neil Kinnock's speeches in the 1987 general election* (London: The Labour Party, 1987), 6.
85 The Labour Party, 1987 Party Election Broadcast, www.youtube.com/watch?v=SFgjCP6qpfU.
86 Labour Party, *Future We Offer*, 3.
87 D. MacShane, 'Labour Cannot Win Unless It Makes a Historic Compromise with Capital.' *Tribune*, 21/28 August 1987, 4.
88 N. Kinnock, 'Speech in Birmingham, May 19 on the Afternoon of the Manifesto Launch', quoted in Labour Party, *Future We Offer*, 10.
89 A. Mitchell, 'Rebuilding the Coalition', in The Fabian Society, *Labour's Next Moves Forward*, Fabian Tract 521 (London: Fabian Society, 1987), 26.
90 G. Turner, Unpublished interview with Peter Shore dated 10 July 1987, SHORE/16/19, Shore Papers, LSE Archive, 1.
91 J. Willman, quoted in *The Labour Party, Report of the Eighty-Sixth Annual Conference of the Labour Party 1987* (London: The Labour Party, 1987), 12.
92 'Policy Review; Key Themes', KNNK/2/2/8, Kinnock Papers, Churchill Archives, 1.
93 Home Policy Committee, 'Policy Development for the 1990's', PD1052/July 1987, KNNK/2/2/1, Kinnock Papers, Churchill Archives, 2.
94 The Labour Party, *Social Justice and Economic Efficiency: First Report of Labour's Policy Review for the 1990s* (London: The Labour Party, 1988), 5–7.
95 Labour Party, *Social Justice*, 3–4.
96 T. Sawyer, quoted in The Labour Party, *Report of the Eighty-Seventh Annual Conference of the Labour Party 1988* (London: The Labour Party, 1988), 16.
97 Labour Party, *Social Justice and Economic Efficiency*, 1.
98 The Labour Party, *Democratic and Socialist Aims and Values* (London: The Labour Party, 1988).
99 National Executive Committee, 'The Aims and Objectives of the Labour Party: A Note by Tony Benn', KNNK/2/2/1, Churchill Archives, 1.
100 See T. Benn, 'Back to the Future', *New Socialist*, Summer 1988, 12.
101 T. Benn, diary entry for 8 May 1989 in Benn, *End of an Era*, 562.

102 E. Heffer, 'Organise for Socialism', *Socialist Organiser*, 29 October 1987, 12.
103 A. Thornett, 'Capitalism in Crisis: *Don't* be Part of It', *Labour Briefing*, 10 November 1987, 1.
104 See E. Pittman, 'Thirties Lessons', *Tribune*, 19 February 1988, 11.
105 A. Scargill, quoted in Labour Party, *LPACR 1988*, 21.
106 P. Tatlow, quoted in Labour Party, *LPACR 1988*, 21–22.
107 A. Brooke, 'Labour Must Attract All Progressive Voters', letter to *Tribune*, 19 June 1987, 10.
108 D. Blunkett, 'A Division of Friends that Unites Enemies', *The Guardian*, 23 April 1988.
109 R. Todd, 'Change the Party – But Never Forget Labour's Real Values', *Tribune*, 14 October 1988, 4.
110 N. Kinnock, quoted in *LPACR 1987*, 46.
111 D. McKie, 'Brighton Sketch', *The Guardian*, 30 September 1987.
112 See D. Marquand, 'Labour Must Break with Labourism to Provide a Socialist Alternative for Britain', *The Guardian*, 29 March 1988.
113 The Labour Party, *Meet the Challenge, Make the Change: A New Agenda for Britain* (London: The Labour Party, 1989), 8.
114 T. Sawyer, quoted in The Labour Party, *Report of the Eighty-Eighth Annual Conference of the Labour Party 1989* (London: The Labour Party, 1989), 14.
115 N. Kinnock, foreword to The Labour Party, *Looking to the Future: A Dynamic Economy, A Decent Society, Strong in Europe* (London: The Labour Party, 1990), 4.
116 See The Labour Party, *Building a World Class Economy: Modern Manufacturing Strength* (London: The Labour Party, 1991); The Labour Party, *Manifesto: It's Time to Get Britain Working Again* (London: The Labour Party, 1992).
117 The Labour Party, *Opportunity Britain: Labour's Better Way for the 1990s* (London: The Labour Party, 1991), 37.
118 R. Glenn, 'Focus Group Report: No More Mr Nice Guy or, Time to Start Playing the Game', 19 and 22 February 1990, KNNK/3/4/1/4, Kinnock Papers, Churchill Archives, 16.
119 Strategy document: 'Operation Liberation', KNNK/3/4/1/4, Kinnock Papers, Churchill Archives, 3.
120 K. Saunders, 'How to Keep the Nouveau Red Flag Flying', *The Sunday Times*, 7 October 1990.
121 See N. Kinnock, quoted in The Labour Party, *LPACR 1991*, 129–130.
122 For example, see H. Young, 'N. Kinnock, 18 January 1990', Young, *Hugo Young Papers*, 289.
123 S. Lewis, quoted in The Labour Party, *Conference Report: Eighty-Ninth Annual Conference of the Labour Party* (London: The Labour party, 1990), 15.
124 T. Serjeant, quoted in *LPACR 1990*, 17.
125 T. Blair, quoted in *LPACR 1990*, 75; A. Mawson, quoted in *LPACR 1990*, 78; F. Winders, quoted in *LPACR 1990*, 79.
126 L. Monk, quoted in *LPACR 1991*, 102.
127 M. Beckett, quoted in *LPACR 1990*, 52.

128 J. Mansfield, 'Votes for Heroes', letter to *Labour Party News*, September/October 1990, 5.
129 M. Foot, 'Reasons to Be Cheerful', *Tribune*, 9 April 1992, 12.
130 P. Anderson, 'Labour Finds its Winning Formula', *Tribune*, 9 April 1992, 6.
131 P. Millar, 'Mega-Neil Gets High on Decibels', *The Sunday Times*, 5 April 1992.
132 N. Kinnock, 'Sheffield Rally Transcript', KNNK/3/4/1/49, Kinnock Papers, Churchill Archives.
133 N. Timmins, 'Rousing Spectacular Delivers a Political Punch', *The Independent*, 2 April 1992, 8.

5

The New Labour era, 1992–2010

New Labour emphasised the nostalgic and backward-looking dimensions of Old Labour and, up until this point, the analysis presented has centred on an assessment of the validity of these claims. This chapter will move on to assess New Labour's relationship with the same type of nostalgia that it believed had previously limited the party's political progression. As highlighted in this book's introduction, the idea that New Labour actively distanced itself from the past has been put forward by both historians and political scientists. James Cronin has argued that the 'rejection of the past was … central to New Labour's emerging identity.'[1] Similarly, studies that have suggested that Blairism represented an ideological accommodation of Thatcherism have tended to imply that New Labour was historically rootless.[2]

Nevertheless, the notion that New Labour was an ahistorical entity that was uniformly hostile to the past has been contested. Nick Randall has argued that New Labour mobilised selective memories in an attempt to separate the party from its past.[3] Furthermore, Richard Toye has stated that 'The charge that the key figures in New Labour are ignorant of their own party's history is quite wrong.' Instead, Toye has suggested that Tony Blair's 'view of history' stemmed from the idea of a 'lost' historical progressive alliance between social democrats and liberals that was presented by David Marquand in *The Progressive Dilemma* in 1991.[4] More recently, Emily Robinson has also challenged the perception that New Labour had no use for history. Robinson has provided evidence that has shown that Blair's historical interest in New Liberalism predated Marquand's book.[5] She has outlined the way in which, during their successful attempt to reform Clause IV in 1995, members of the New Labour project gained a strategic advantage by framing their political opponents as nostalgic whilst, simultaneously, portraying themselves as heirs to a longer-term historical 'progressive consensus'.[6]

However, Blair's rhetorical deployment of a New Liberal past was only one aspect of New Labour's complex relationship with nostalgia. This chapter will chart New Labour's interaction with the unique nostalgia-identity that has been outlined in preceding chapters. The extent to which New Labour was either able or willing to overturn this sentimental and idealised attachment to the past will be assessed. Although previous academic accounts have emphasised the deployment of memory by party elites, this chapter will also analyse the degree to which New Labour's trajectory and political development were shaped by a broader nostalgia that operated in the party during this period.

John Smith as party leader

John Smith became leader of the Labour Party in July 1992. Amongst other reasons, reports suggested that Labour had lost the 1992 General Election because it was perceived as 'old fashioned' by the British people.[7] Certainly, the party that Smith inherited was characterised by a preoccupation with the past. Letters appeared in Labour-aligned magazines that stressed the need for workers to have ownership of and control over their industries in line with the model 'pioneered by Robert Owen in the 1820s'.[8] Speakers at the party's annual conference in 1992 (Smith's first conference as leader) referred to historical figures and events like Keir Hardie and the 1936 Jarrow Marches.[9] One delegate argued that the conference should hold a collection so that copies of *The Ragged Trousered Philanthropists* could be bought for the party's policy makers.[10] Drinking mugs were available that celebrated the one hundredth anniversary of Hardie's election as an MP.[11] Speakers blamed the 1992 General Election defeat on the electorate for not understanding the party's historic principles.[12]

Reporting on Labour during this period, Hugo Young noted that the nature of the party's internal culture meant that its members were 'uncommonly attached to the past'.[13] Another journalist described how 'Behind Labour's post-Kinnock image of sharp suits and Filofaxes, the reality is desperate nostalgia for Clause Four socialism.'[14] Labour was, according to the Director of the new Demos think tank, 'more prone to nostalgia, than almost any other major party in Western Europe'.[15] This nostalgically informed identity also continued to influence the actions and oratory of Labour politicians. When faced with the Conservative Government's Coal and Rail Transfer Bill in June 1992, Benn rushed to the House of Commons to give a speech that drew on 'a leaflet issued by the Mining Federation of Great Britain about casualties in the pits between 1927 and 1934'.[16] On a debate on the coal industry at Labour Party Conference in 1993, Dennis Skinner described how the party owed 'a debt to the miners, not just for recent years but throughout the decades and centuries. They have been at the forefront of every struggle and they will be in the future.' His speech was particularly well-received.[17]

Like Kinnock, Smith exuded a personal nostalgic resonance that gave him a broad appeal across the party. Benn believed Smith to be a new Attlee.[18] Smith deployed memories of the party's founding moments in order to energise his speeches.[19] He was cautious about directly confronting the party's nostalgia. During the period in which Smith was leader, Jack Straw worked on and published a pamphlet that, in order to counteract accusations of Labour being 'trapped in the past', advocated the reform of Clause IV of the party's 1918 constitution.[20] Straw argued that the clause's writers would be shocked to find that their words were still adhered to with such 'reverence' in 1993.[21] Smith was very hostile to this pamphlet. Commenting on its first draft, he declared that Clause IV '"should be allowed to whither on the vine." It was a "sentimental souvenir, best ignored"' and urged Straw not to proceed with his work.[22] Retrospectively, Straw has suggested that Smith's 'political roots in the Scottish Labour Party' and 'industrial west Scotland' meant that the Labour leader was unable to view Clause IV as the political liability it had become.[23]

On other issues, Smith appeared to be a more ardent moderniser. Writing in the *Sunday Times* in June 1993, Martin Jacques argued that the case for revising the Labour-union link and introducing One Member One Vote (OMOV) was obvious to everyone apart from a Labour Party whose internal debates seemed 'to be no more than an exercise in nostalgia for some bygone era'.[24] Nostalgia was perceived as an impediment to OMOV's implementation. Yet, paradoxically, nostalgia also provided an important source of political capital for the politicians who were advocating these reforms. At the party's annual conference in 1993, in order to increase support for OMOV, Smith and his allies mobilised memories of the historic role played by the trade unions in Labour's founding moments. OMOV was portrayed as a point of historical continuation: a strengthening, rather than a weakening, of this historic link.[25] In a debate that was routinely framed by the past, this historical narrative was contested. One speaker condemned people within the movement who 'either do not know or conveniently forget just why the Labour Party was set up in the first place. It was set up by trade unions and socialist societies' and she asked her audience if the party was now prepared to 'betray that tradition'?[26] Other delegates described OMOV as anathema to Labour's founding constitution.[27] More generally, speakers demanded that the party should 'not forget our fine history'.[28]

In the debate's key speech, John Prescott came to the aid of the party's leadership. Prescott disputed the moderniser-traditionalist dichotomy that had surrounded the issue of OMOV and he argued that it was perfectly possible to hold 'traditional values' and still support the proposals.[29] The reforms were carried by a narrow margin. Reporting critically on the event, *The Economist* described how, OMOV aside, the party had come to represent an intellectual 'Jurassic Park' with the conference's fringe meetings seeming particularly 'desperate in their aridity and futile class-ridden nostalgia'.[30]

Tony Blair becomes leader

Following John Smith's unexpected death on 12 May 1994, the *Guardian* wrote that 'In this new situation there will be few rewards for caution and none at all for nostalgia. The choice should be between active alternatives rather than safety first.'[31] An internal debate ensued amongst the party's 'modernisers' about whether either Tony Blair or Gordon Brown should stand in the forthcoming leadership election.[32] Interestingly, at this stage, both Blair and Brown made speeches that contained overtly backward-looking content. On 25 May 1994 the *Independent* reported that Brown had delivered a speech to Welsh party members with a 'revivalist tone'. At around the same time, Blair had given a speech on 'youth crime' that had suggested that he would 'have to articulate a much more concrete and bold programme for government if his Utopia is to be accepted as more than a wistful nostalgia.'[33]

The fact that, at this point, both Blair and Brown were giving speeches of this nature should not come as a surprise. Due to the nostalgic tendencies of the party's rank-and-file members, a degree of electoral necessity underpinned this type of rhetoric. The April/May edition of *Labour Party News* (the party's official magazine) published a letter from an eighty-year-old member that described the heroic struggles of the 1930s and expressed concern that the party was now 'lacking in "soul"'. The writer went on to 'welcome, perhaps in LPN, a few nostalgic articles on their experiences in the 1930s, which might help some of the present-day activists to hear a bit more about the paths we trod.'[34] The editors duly obliged: they produced a request for similar letters and published one in a subsequent edition of the magazine.[35]

Ultimately, Blair became the modernisers' candidate. His successful leadership campaign was based on a promise to 're-build by applying our traditional democratic socialist principles to the modern world'.[36] At this stage, the language that he used was ambiguous enough towards the party's past to offer a broad appeal across the party. Watching

Blair's acceptance speech on 21 July 1994, Tony Benn believed that the new leader had drawn on his wife's biography of Keir Hardie (a book that Blair had reviewed warmly in October 1992) and he was impressed.[37] Elsewhere, Blair was quick to build a historical narrative that portrayed his modernising agenda as a return to the Left's 'true identity and historic mission'.[38]

In an attempt to signal to the electorate that the party had changed, Blair's first Leader's Speech at Labour's annual conference was much more uncompromisingly anti-nostalgic in tone. He proclaimed that 'It is time to break out of the past and break through with a clear, radical and modern vision for Britain.'[39] His line 'community is not some piece of nostalgia' was picked up by the media.[40] Taken as a whole, his speech differed markedly from the rhetoric of the conference's other speakers. In contrast to Blair, Arthur Scargill declared that he had come to the conference to 'preach an old time socialist religion. If it was good enough for Keir Hardie, it is good enough for me!'[41]

Clause IV

As outlined in this book's introduction, Blair's successful attempt to revise Clause IV of the party's 1918 constitution was widely interpreted as representing an attack on the party's nostalgia. Alastair Campbell recorded that, in the days before the 1994 annual conference, Blair explained to his team that reforming the clause would act as a 'signal to the outside world that we're serious about change'.[42] His advisers were uncertain about how to frame the issue, but they clearly viewed this reform as an opportunity to distance New Labour from the party's traditional industrial working-class past: 'Peter Hyman suddenly chipped in: did you know there are more Indian waiters in Britain than there are coal miners?'[43]

During his 1994 Labour Party Conference speech, Blair did not mention Clause IV explicitly. Campbell briefed the media about Blair's true intentions after the event.[44] Towards the end of the 1994 conference, the extent of the challenge that lay ahead was highlighted by the party's reaffirmation of its commitment to public ownership. Delegates voiced their support for a pro-Clause IV composite in overtly nostalgic ways. The speaker moving the composite demanded that his audience 'raise the scarlet standard high and keep the red flag flying here.'[45] Another delegate talked about how the principles underpinning the clause 'founded our great victories in the past and should be the basis of our new strategies.'[46]

Faced with a potentially widespread backlash against the proposed reform of Clause IV, party elites did not attempt to overturn the party's attachment to the past. Instead, they operated within the existing parameters of Labour's nostalgia-identity to rework a historical narrative that was more conducive to change. Thus, at the 1994 conference, Larry Whitty asked the party not to 'belittle the intellectual achievements of our forebears', but he also described how the party's 1918 constitution had been written in a deliberately vague and pragmatic manner at a time of political upheaval and chaos.[47] In January 1995, a special 'Clause IV' issue of *Labour Party News* was published for party members. It contained the party's consultative questionnaire and a number of arguments both for and against reform. In this magazine, Alan Johnson (General Secretary of the Union of Communication Workers) argued that 'Were Sidney Webb … alive today he would be the first to recognise the need for change.'[48]

In the same way that Kinnock had deployed notions of timeless but historical 'values' in order to isolate Militant and to provide a platform for programmatic change, when talking to their party, Blair and his allies used similar 'values' to portray the reform of Clause IV as a point of historical continuity and not rupture. Blair reassured members that 'in proposing to replace Clause IV, John Prescott and I do not plan to discard any values held dear by the Labour movement.'[49] The party's new deputy leader John Prescott, who was proving to be a valuable asset because of his personal nostalgic resonance, concurred that the jettisoning of Clause IV was 'not a rejection of our traditional values'.[50]

It has been argued that, within Labour, there was a degree of acceptance of the need to reform Clause IV and that opposition to change was informed by a belief that the clause remained relevant and applicable to the modern world.[51] Without a doubt, there were submissions to the party's internal consultative process that suggested that Clause IV's 'language is archaic' and that the clause was 'out of date'.[52] However, further analysis of these submissions also indicates that a widespread hostility to change existed. Moreover, opposition to reform was frequently shaped by a form of restorative nostalgia. Responding to the party's questionnaire, one CLP branch noted that the clause was 'a historic part of our roots. It is symbolic.'[53] Another branch described how 'a lot of Labour Party members have a deep attachment to Clause 4 Part IV.'[54] Rejecting the proposed reform, a branch from north-east England declared that 'Clause IV is responsible for the standard of living that developed after 1918 when it was written. We should be making prospective members aware of this.'[55]

Individual party members submitted responses to the consultation that argued that the world had not changed since 1918 and that 'the class system, economic and social inequality all remain broadly as they were then.'⁵⁶ There was also a sense that the attempts that had been made by party elites to rework the past to their advantage might have backfired. The attached notes on one submission read 'Sidney Webb: How does Alan Johnson know, I should think he is turning in his grave.'⁵⁷ Another submission implored the Labour leadership to 'stop using John Prescott in his emotional blackmail speeches. Our party was built on democracy and them that don't like it should leave.'⁵⁸

The Labour Left argued that the proposed reform of Clause IV meant that 'The Labour Party was in danger of losing its identity.'⁵⁹ In a statement that was published in both *Labour Party News* and *Socialist Campaign Group News*, Benn described how the clause had 'deep roots in our history'. He went on to declare that it was the 'dream of socialism' that had brought people into the party during the 1920s and 1930s and he asked 'Today we are told that the bad old days are gone – but have they?'⁶⁰ In response to these deployments of the past, a shadow industry spokesman suggested that Tony Benn 'seems to suffer a nostalgia not only for the Webbs and 1917, but also for his heyday in the early eighties'.⁶¹ Yet Benn was not alone in framing the issue in terms of its relationship to the past. Writing in *Socialist Campaign Group News*, Diane Abbott proclaimed that 'The Blairite project is not modern in any respect – it is as old as Ramsey McDonald [sic].'⁶²

In a similar manner, in order to restate the continued relevance of 'Common Ownership' and Clause IV, Ken Coates produced a book that extensively referenced individuals and groups from the British labour movement's history. As Coates himself noted, 'this is very old hat, and Mr Blair and his bright young acolytes will take great pleasure in pointing out that much of it has been said before. We must find ways of continuing to say it.'⁶³ Within the party, there were also those who believed that, whilst the clause was not a useful guide for policy, 'Flags and banners, poems and songs, heroic images and memories of past triumphs have a role in sustaining the party faithful ... If that is what Clause 4 is about ... then I am in favour of it.'⁶⁴ Elsewhere, Benn warned David Miliband (Blair's Chief of Policy) that, although the Labour leader's attempts to revise the clause would probably succeed, it would be '"at a fairly considerable price. It's like taking crucifixes out of a church. It just separates you from your traditional background."'⁶⁵

Benn correctly predicted that Blair's attempt to reform Clause IV would be successful but, as the remainder of this chapter will illustrate, he underestimated the resilience of the party's nostalgia-identity. Clause IV was altered at a Special Conference on 29 April 1995. At this conference, speakers advocating change emphasised that reforming the clause did not 'mean we have to forget our past.'⁶⁶ Blair was careful to state that he had 'pride in our past' and that 'The ghosts of our history no longer rattle our chains but they are there, with their spirit, to guide us and our country.'[67] Nevertheless, Lew Adams from the Associated Society of Locomotive Engineers and Firemen expressed the wider concerns of party members, albeit with a slightly strange emphasis, when he asked 'What's to be next? Is it to be the red flag? That's what really worries me.'[68]

Towards the 1997 General Election

Members of the New Labour project explicitly sought to overturn the party's nostalgic orientation. In popular understandings of the period, the rewriting of Clause IV has come to symbolise New Labour's anti-nostalgic impetus. Although Blair and his allies were forced to veil this reform in a language that was actually fairly conciliatory to the past, victory provided New Labour with a platform from which to go on to present itself to the British electorate as the party of modernity and change. Framed around the concept of Britain as a 'young country', Blair's speech at the 1995 Labour Party Conference directly repudiated nostalgia in a programmatic sense. In this speech, he argued that 'Keir Hardie did not manage to achieve a minimum wage and nor did Attlee, Wilson, Callaghan or anyone else, but this next Labour government will introduce a statutory minimum wage for Britain.'[69]

In the mid-1990s, Blair was not the only Labour politician who attacked the party's nostalgia. In a 1996 speech to the Nexus think tank, Robin Cook, who became foreign secretary in 1997, condemned Labour's 'unhealthy nostalgia for a vanished society' and he declared that 'It is important that we resist the attractions of a retreat to a sepia-tinged Hovis socialism.'[70] Other Labour politicians, who would later accept important cabinet positions under Blair, made attacks on Old Labour's perceived nostalgia in certain policy areas.[71]

When he was not talking to his party, Blair was routinely hostile to the past. In his foreword to Labour's 1997 manifesto, Blair emphasised the way in which many of the 'conflicts' that had been at the centre of British politics in the past had 'no relevance to the modern world – public versus private, bosses versus workers, middle class versus working class.'[72] Delivering a speech to the Confederation of British Industry's annual conference, he declared that 'Once free from [Labour's] historical baggage, we can address the future with confidence. This we now do.'[73] When speaking to the Japan Federation of Economic Organisations, Blair informed his audience that 'I have no time for living in the past. Many of the political struggles of the twentieth century will seem odd to the children of the twenty-first century.'[74]

In private, Blair often suggested that his lack of roots in Labour's history and traditions made him less susceptible to the nostalgia that operated in the wider party.[75] However, he was not completely averse to using memories of the past in an instrumental manner. Occasionally, such deployments manifested themselves in his attempts to micromanage his parliamentary team. Prescott reports that Blair responded to his refusal to back him during the furore that followed Harriet Harman's decision to send her child to a selective school with the demand that '"You should be like Ernest Bevin, supporting Attlee."'[76]

More significantly, Blair used nostalgia for Labour's 1945 General Election victory to legitimise his own strategic positioning of the party and unflinching commitment to electoral success. Writing in *Labour Party News* on the fiftieth anniversary of the victory, Blair argued that 'The lesson of 1945 should be clear: democratic socialism can be both practical and popular.' His commentary piece was positioned next to a number of personal nostalgic reflections from party members who had experienced the 1945 election.[77] Blair also used the 1945 Attlee Government's fiftieth anniversary to outline the type of Marquandian historical narrative that, as shown in this chapter's introduction, other academics have described. In a speech to the Fabian Society in July 1995, Blair argued that 'Democratic Socialism in Britain was indeed the political heir to the radical Liberal tradition.'[78] He declared that, at the beginning of the twentieth century, the fledgling Labour Party and the wider labour movement had placed political 'demands on the Liberal Party. These were the forces that were eventually to swamp the Liberals, but for a time they found political manifestation in the rise of New Liberalism.'[79]

Given the hostility to the past that Blair expressed on other occasions and the total absence of this historical narrative from his commentary piece on the 1945 election in the party's internal magazine, it is possible to overstate the way in which this argument was the product of genuine historical convictions. It is no coincidence that Blair expressed these sentiments when he was seeking to make overtures to the Liberal Democrats and their supporters. During the brief moment in 1997 when it looked like members of the Liberal Democrats might be brought into the Labour Government, Blair told Labour Party Conference 'I know some of you are a bit nervous about what I am doing with the Liberal Democrats – although not half as nervous as they are. Since this is a day for history, I will tell you why. My heroes are not only Ernie Bevin, Nye Bevan and Attlee, they are also Keynes, Beveridge and Lloyd George.'[80]

Blair also exhibited a broadly communitarian nostalgia that contained noticeably nationalistic elements. *The Economist* noted the increasing influence of communitarianism on Blair and his team of advisers. Moreover, it stated that 'Communitarians prefer not to look closely at the past that we have lost: their appeal is partly to nostalgia, which can tolerate only so much analysis.'[81] At times, this nostalgia appeared to manifest itself in Blair's speeches. At Labour's 1996 conference, he recalled how

> When I was growing up the family was strong, the sense of social responsibility was strong, crime was low. There was a national ethos and spirit that had won us the war and stayed with us in peace. What was strong then is fragile now. National purpose faltering, our feeling of collective responsibility starved of expression, the family unsupported.[82]

Reporting on this conference, the *Independent* noted that this 'strongly nostalgic passage' felt at odds with Blair's 1995 'young country' speech.[83] On other occasions, Blair dipped into Labour's established collective memories to pull out historical examples that centred on the manner in which 'Early socialists like Robert Owen understood very clearly that a society which did not encourage people voluntarily to carry out their responsibilities to others would always be in danger of slipping either into the anarchy of mutual indifference ... or the tyranny of collective coercion.'[84] According to Blair, New Labour had 'returned' Labour to 'its roots' by 'rediscovering the ideas of community, mutuality and solidarity that were the foundation of the party'.[85]

Blair and his allies were forced to deny that they held a sentimental attachment to the communities of the past. These protestations were indicative of a concern that the ideas that were being presented bordered on the nostalgic. Blair's 1994 declaration that 'community is not some piece of nostalgia' was echoed by his supporters. In his 1997 book *Why Vote Labour?*, Tony Wright stated that the 'post-war world has changed almost out of recognition. It would be no more than a sentimental exercise in nostalgia to recall it, except for the fact that it provides a reminder of where the Labour Party came from and what it has always stood for.'[86] Once again, it is necessary to question the extent to which New Labour's brief dalliance with a broadly communitarian nostalgia had genuinely expressive origins. This particular type of engagement with the past performed a useful instrumental function. It helped to generate public support for Labour's social agenda and to demonstrate that the party understood the British electorate's concerns about the current state of British society.

New Labour in power

It is tempting to view New Labour's emphatic success at the 1997 General Election as the apex of the party's modernisation. In the aftermath of victory, Blair stated that Labour's massive majority was 'not a mandate for dogma or for doctrine, or for a return to the past, but it was a mandate to get those things done in our country that desperately need doing for the future.'[87] However, there is little evidence to suggest that Labour's wider identity had been reoriented towards the future. At the start of the 1997 election campaign Benn had visited a village that was established by the Chartist Feargus O'Connor in 1847. Witnessing the local party's historic ritual to select their election candidate in the village's churchyard, Benn had noted that 'Every day Blair tells us Labour has changed, but when you see the local Labour parties they haven't changed at all.'[88] Similarly, reporting on the May Day rally in Blaenau Gwent in the immediate aftermath of Labour's election victory, an article in the *Independent* noted the continued reverence for the past that existed amongst Labour's rank-and-file and it described how 'Nostalgia comes easily in places where memories are long and values are handed down from generation to generation.'[89]

After 1997, this sentimental attachment to the past was merely pushed further underground by the New Labour project. An internal culture that was overtly nostalgic continued to exist beneath the public veneer of modernisation and change that was presented by party elites. Left-wing groups and publications provided an outlet for this nostalgia. Letters to *Socialist Campaign Group News* contrasted the days in which MPs like Clement Attlee, Aneurin Bevan, Michael Foot and James Maxton 'travelled the country, addressing public meetings, facing approval and questioning – and hostility – from all sections of the electorate' with the new 'army of "spin doctors" and mysterious backroom "advisers"'.[90] Blair's attempts to attract Liberal Democrats into the party were also derided in historical terms: 'A merger is not going to happen and any leader who tries to affect one is likely to end up like Ramsay MacDonald.'[91] After standing down from parliament in 2001, Tony Benn embarked on a lecture tour that combined 'nostalgia, humour, common sense, ideology and idealism'. It whimsically recalled an era when 'Britain produced goods rather than services.' The tour did 'sell out business across the country.'[92]

Writing in the *Guardian* in September 1998, Jonathan Freedland described 'the nostalgia for those symbols of Old Labour, reminders of the time when Labour – for all its rough, untelegenic edges – felt like it belonged to them [the party's members], rather than the sleekly competent board of management in charge today.'[93] Nostalgically informed tensions simmered beneath the surface. After Labour's second successive victory in 2001, an umbrella group was established under the name of the 'Campaign for Real Labour' by organisations and individuals, including Roy Hattersley, who were critical of New Labour's trajectory. Hattersley had previously argued that Blair 'cannot convincingly claim that it [New

Labour] is a party which "Keir Hardie, Attlee and Wilson would sign up for"'.[94] At the Campaign for Real Labour's inaugural meeting, one speaker declared '"we want the old Labour Party back."'[95]

It is possible to track the significant role that nostalgia continued to play through an analysis of the speeches that were made by New Labour elites. Instrumental nostalgic references indicated the important grip that the past retained on the party. On occasions when he found himself short of political capital, Blair deployed positively idealised memories that were congruent with the party's industrial working-class nostalgia-identity. Speaking in Methyr Tydfill, Blair 'invoked the spirit of Keir Hardie to insist there was no distinction between the party's heartland and middle Britain.'[96] In 2001, Blair proclaimed to his party that 'our aims as a government would be recognisable to every Labour leader from Keir Hardie onwards.'[97]

Under New Labour, the party's annual conference became carefully stage-managed and the level of dissent expressed by party members diminished.[98] Nevertheless, the event remained a forum for nostalgia. In order to legitimise Labour's trajectory, the past was frequently evoked by both party power elites and supportive rank-and-file speakers. At 1997's Labour Party Conference, Gordon Brown justified his programme to modernise the British economy with references to Labour's history: 'It was because a century ago Keir Hardie looked at the world as it was, and saw what a new world could be that he broke with the old order, set politics on a new modern path and he founded the Labour Party.'[99] At this conference, in order to generate support for the party's policies and programmatic commitments (which included the structural rearrangements to Labour's policy-making process that were proposed by 'Partnership in Power'), Brown, Hazel Blears and John Prescott all cited Nye Bevan.[100]

There is also anecdotal evidence that suggests that a more spontaneous and expressive nostalgia continued to influence the behaviour of Labour MPs, albeit in a fairly limited manner. Chris Mullin viewed 1998's Minimum Wage Bill as 'old-fashioned class war'. Writing in his diary, he noted that 'There was a spring in my step as I walked through the "Aye" lobby. I even found myself humming "The Red Flag" until Steve Hepburn called out, "A bit early for that yet, Chris. We don't know the rate."'[101] When he became Secretary of State for Wales in October 2002, Peter Hain was 'photographed holding aloft a statuette of Nye Bevan which had sat on the mantel shelf of my office as Europe Minister'.[102] Certain groups continued to hold an emotional grip on Labour politicians. Inspired into action by the film *Brassed Off*, John Prescott announced at the 1997 Durham Miners' Gala that he would pursue new policies for Britain's coalmining communities.[103] According to *The Economist*, the energy policies that subsequently emerged from the Government harked back to the party's 'Old Labour roots' and contained a degree of 'nostalgia for coal'.[104]

Centennial anniversaries

New Labour's attempts to reorient the party away from the past were hindered by two significant centenary events. Whilst the one hundredth anniversary of the foundation of the Labour Representation Committee took place in February 2000, the one hundredth anniversary of the official establishment of the 'Labour Party' in Parliament was commemorated in February 2006. In the preface to *The Labour Party: A Centenary History*, Michael Foot noted the Labour leadership's hostility to the party's past. He suggested that Tony Blair and his allies would argue that only limited lessons could be learnt from discussions of Labour's historical development.[105] In fact, the emotionally charged nature of Labour's centennial celebrations forced members of the New Labour project to engage with the party's history in a fairly direct manner.

Brenda Etchells opened the 1999 Labour Party Conference with a speech that declared 'Whilst we must never forget our roots ... our party, the Labour Party, has always been about a better future, not nostalgia for the past.'[106] Thereafter, Margaret McDonagh (the party's General Secretary) used memories of the past to legitimise the party's trajectory in the present: 'I am certain that the founding fathers of our party would be proud of how we have translated their values into action.'[107] This type of historical legitimisation ran throughout the conference. Brown gave a speech that acknowledged 'the inspiration that comes ... from the achievements of our pioneers that we celebrate in this centenary year' and he positioned New Labour as a natural outgrowth of the 'vision' of these 'pioneers'.[108] In a similar manner, Blair talked about how Keir Hardie and other figures from the party's past would be 'proud' of New Labour's achievement in government.[109] Yet he also cautioned that the 'forces of change driving the future do not stop at any national boundaries today: they do not respect tradition.'[110] A report in the *Independent* described how Blair's 'speech did not touch delegates as Gordon Brown's had done on Monday, but that was because it was less respectful of the collective nostalgia of the party, more determined to think about what, exactly, it had become.'[111]

New Labour became stuck between its hostility to nostalgia and a party identity that remained overtly nostalgic. Writing in the *Independent*, Thomas Sutcliffe reported that an event held at the Old Vic in London in February 2000 'mixed nostalgia with a deferential apologia to the activists for having delivered the largest majority ever delivered by their party'.

He noted that Blair's record in government seemed underappreciated: speaking to an audience of party members, 'Mr Blair knew that he couldn't rely on the current affection – he had to evoke past struggles or predict future ones.'[112] The strength of the party's nostalgia forced New Labour to become defensive. Writing in a special commemorative edition of the *New Statesman*, Brown stated that New Labour's commitment to 'modernisation' did not represent either a betrayal or 'retreat' from the principles held by the party's founders.[113]

The centenary literature that originated from the party displayed a conflicted relationship with the past. Writing in the party's *Centennial Report*, Margaret McDonagh stated that Labour needed 'to celebrate our achievements but also to reflect on our mistakes' and she outlined how the party had only been in power for twenty three of its one hundred years.[114] The *Centennial Report* attempted to maintain a forward-looking perspective: only four of the twelve pages on Labour's 'Values and achievements' focused on the period before 1997.[115] The report declared that 'Labour's greatest successes have been achieved when the party has been modern and forward-looking and while we are proud of our history we are not bound to it.'[116]

The literature that was targeted at the party's members and activists was more celebratory in nature. The February 2000 edition of the party's magazine reflected the party's wider nostalgic culture. It contained a graphic that illustrated the numerous centenary events that were taking place across Britain and it gave the dates and locations for a travelling exhibition on Labour's history entitled 'The Builders and the Dreamers'.[117] An extensive centenary quiz appeared in the party's annual conference magazine. It declared 'So you think you know your Lansburys from your Kinnocks? Check out your party history quotient with our multiple choice political trivia quiz.' Amongst other trivia, the quiz asked questions about Keir Hardie and contained a 'fill-in-the-blank' replica of the original Clause IV.[118]

Six years later, in order to mark the 2006 centennial, a photograph of the Parliamentary Labour Party was taken in the chamber of House of Commons. According to Chris Mullin, the event 'was dressed up as an Adjournment debate in the name of Ann Clwyd, whose seat was once represented by Keir Hardie'. Mullin wrote in his diary that 'Ann made a speech extolling our achievements over the last hundred years, the mention of Ramsay MacDonald's name provoking some good-natured cheers from the Tories and jeers from our side.' The gathering concluded with the singing of the *Red Flag*.[119] A book entitled *Men Who Made Labour* was published that contained biographies of Labour's first 29 MPs that had been written by their modern PLP equivalents (or near equivalents). In the foreword to this book, in order to justify New Labour's overriding contemporary commitment to electoral success, Blair deployed nostalgia for Labour's history of parliamentarianism. His analysis echoed the manner in which he had engaged with the fiftieth anniversary of the 1945 election victory. Looking back at the original MPs from 1906, Blair stated that 'Today, 100 years later, we can see the results of their pioneering endeavours. Labour for the first time in its history, has won three successive election victories.'[120]

This recasting of the 1906 parliamentary party in terms conducive to New Labour's trajectory was not received particularly positively by party members and commentators. One article in *Chartist* compared Blair (a privately educated Barrister) unfavourably to Hardie (a self-educated ex-miner) and it stated that

> Considering the two greatest achievements of the Labour Party were masterminded by ex-coal miners – its Parliamentary formation by Keir Hardie, and the NHS by Aneurin Bevan – one begins to think the party has been truer to its cause when in the hands of those from the class that it traditionally purports to represent.[121]

In a similar fashion, a letter published in *Tribune* argued that the Government's record would leave Labour's parliamentary pioneers 'spinning in their graves' and it proclaimed that 'We owe it to those pioneers to reclaim the Labour Party and cleanse it of the virus which has affected it for the past decade.'[122]

The end of New Labour

Although the party would go on to win a historic third General Election victory in 2005, New Labour's political capital was greatly diminished by the onset of the Iraq War in March 2003. Amongst Labour members, the conflict exacerbated the idea that the party had moved too far away from its historical roots. An article that was published in *Chartist* drew comparisons between the protests that had taken place against the invasion of Iraq and the 1936 Jarrow marches.[123] At a press conference following George Galloway's disciplinary meeting with Labour's National Constitutional Committee in October 2003 (Galloway was expelled from the party the following day), Benn 'reminded' the press 'of the peace tradition in the Labour Party'. In an attempt to support Galloway, he provided historical examples of Labour's tradition of non-interventionism that included the fact that 'Keir Hardie had opposed the First World War.'[124] Reflecting on the overall situation in Iraq in 2004, Clare Short, who had resigned from her Cabinet position in protest against the conflict, concluded her book with the declaration that 'It took 100 years for British history to build the

Labour Party. We cannot allow its values to be trampled on when they are desperately needed to find a way through the crises we currently face.'[125] At a time when they were faced with widespread hostility, it appears that the Labour leadership made at least one nostalgic concession to the party's activists: having been absent since 2000, the traditional singing of the *Red Flag* at the end of the party's annual conference was, after an NEC vote, reinstated in 2003.[126]

Despite New Labour's anti-nostalgic proclamations, a positively idealised attachment to the past continued to shape the party's identity at a grassroots level. Visitors to the party's annual conference understood that this nostalgia could provide a mechanism with which to validate their own arguments. When Bono promoted the 'Make Poverty History' campaign at the 2004 Labour Party Conference, he stated, in a rather tongue-in-cheek manner, 'let me make the other, more muscular argument, I think you can take it, you're Labour, aren't you? You're tough aren't you? Keir Hardy [sic] is tough, right, you know, down the pits at the age of 11. Clement Attlee was tough right, fought in the Great War, worked in the slums. (Applause) Even the reddest of roses has some thorns, I believe.'[127] More generally, amongst party members, disillusionment with New Labour was increasingly framed in an overtly nostalgic manner. Tim Luckhurst, a former Labour staff member and election candidate, wrote an article in the *Daily Mail* that described how 'I used to be embarrassed by the party's fondness for socialist traditions such as singing the Red Flag. Now I recall the words "Tho' cowards flinch and traitors sneer, we'll keep the red flag flying here" with nostalgia and sadness.'[128]

Peter Mandelson has implied that nostalgia played a role in the internecine political struggles between Blair and Brown. He has written that, with Blair away at a funeral, Brown used his speech at the party's annual conference in 2003 'to deliver a *crie de coeur* directed at all those in the party who were unsettled by Tony's policies, and by Iraq. His refrain was the need for the party to be truly Labour: "I believe that at every point in our history, Labour needs not just a political programme – but a soul."'[129] Certainly, amongst Labour politicians, there was a belief that Brown was less hostile to the party's past than Blair.[130] Yet, due to his association with New Labour's hyper-modernity, Brown's nostalgic appeal was limited. Party members were highly critical of both Blair and Brown. In 2006, one letter to *Tribune* declared that

> There must be somebody in the Labour Party who is a proper Left-winger – Jeremy Corbyn and John McDonnell spring to mind. One of these fine MPs could restore the Labour Party to how it was set up by Keir Hardie as a working-class socialist party, not a lapdog for Mr Bush and a Tory Party in disguise.[131]

Brown became leader of the Labour Party in 2007. His 'honeymoon period' was short-lived and his time as Prime Minister was shaped by a global financial crisis. His speeches as leader differed little from the ones that he had delivered as Chancellor of the Exchequer during the Blair era.[132] With a General Election on the horizon, the backlash against New Labour's trajectory found expression in the Left's desire for the trade unions to 'do their utmost to influence the [parliamentary] selection of truly labour movement candidates ... They owe it to James Loveless [one of the Tolpuddle Martyrs] and his comrades.'[133] A broader call was made for members with 'traditional Labour ideals' to 're-take the party'.[134] Writing in his diary, Benn noted how a resilient party culture that had continued to manifest itself at commemorative events like the Durham Miners' Gala and the Tolpuddle Martyrs' Festival indicated that 'when we are defeated, there is a core support we can go to.'[135]

With its domestic agenda curtailed by the adverse economic environment in which it found itself, Labour stagnated politically. The party sought refuge in its nostalgia. According to one journalist, the annual Labour Party Conference remained an arena in which party activists could come 'together to talk about their heritage and tradition' and the gathering resembled 'an exercise in collective nostalgia'.[136] In 2009, a campaign was mounted by a labour activist called Ellie Gellard to get a nostalgic film entitled 'Fighters and Believers' released as a party political broadcast. In an email to party members, Gellard noted that, when it was originally shown at the 2009 Labour Party Conference, the film had 'made me cry. It reminded me why I joined this Party, why I campaign for this Party and why I will always fight for this Party.' [137] Gellard's campaign was successful. The video was broadcasted on 18 November 2009. Against a backdrop of footage that included grainy black-and-white images of figures and episodes from Labour's heroic traditional industrial past, the video's narrator declared that 'It's the fighters and believers who change our world.'[138] The success of this video campaign suggested that, after almost thirteen years of New Labour in government, the party's nostalgia-identity remained largely intact.

Conclusion

As this book has shown, New Labour exhibited a high level of hostility towards nostalgia. Influential figures within the New Labour project believed that, in the past, nostalgia had held back Labour's political development and that it had left the party out of touch with the changing nature of British society. The reform of Clause IV in 1995 represented a symbolic statement that was explicitly designed to send out a signal to the electorate that New Labour had broken with the party's past. Throughout the period 1992 to 2010, nostalgia remained separated from Labour's programmatic commitments. In this respect, New Labour continued on the same trajectory as had been initiated by Kinnock in 1986.

There is little evidence to suggest that, in the wider party, a broader emotional break with the past occurred. In 2010, the party's identity still remained rooted in nostalgia. Throughout New Labour's period in government, the historically orientated nature of the party's collective identity continued to represent a source of political capital. In order to legitimise and gain support for their political agenda, New Labour elites frequently drew upon the party's nostalgia. These instrumental deployments were the product of political necessity: they were indicative of the unrelenting grip that nostalgia still held on the party. In turn, these mnemonic mobilisations served to reinforce mutually the nostalgic dimensions of the party's identity in a self-perpetuating cycle. Taken as a whole, this process shaped the options that were available to elites and dictated the extent to which the party could modernise. New Labour's anti-nostalgic impetus was also restrained by events. In particular, the centennial anniversaries that took place in 2000 and 2006 served to focus Labour's attention on its history in a way that limited New Labour's capacity to overturn the party's attachment to the past.

Tony Blair viewed nostalgia as problematic but, in order to secure goals and objectives, he often deployed positively idealised memories of the past. This chapter has highlighted the four main variants of nostalgia that were used by Blair during the New Labour era. The first variant fell within the established parameters of Labour's nostalgia-identity. Blair mobilised nostalgia for heroic figures from the party's traditional industrial past, including Keir Hardie and the party's 'pioneers', when he was either running short of political capital or needed to legitimise a contentious political position. The second variant focused on Labour's history of parliamentarianism. Most notably, this nostalgia came to the fore on the fiftieth anniversary of the Attlee Government in 1995 and on the one hundredth anniversary of the parliamentary 'Labour Party' in 2006. On these historic occasions, Blair deployed selective memories in order to justify New Labour's overarching commitment to electoral success. The third variant centred on New Liberalism and the idea of a lost progressive coalition between Liberals and Social Democrats. This chapter has argued that this nostalgia was more limited and more overtly strategic than other academic studies have suggested. The fourth variant was broadly 'communitarian'. It focused on idealised notions of post-war British communities. There was a brief engagement with this type of nostalgia during the period before the 1997 General Election. Above all, when coupled with the anti-nostalgic pronouncements that he made in both public and private, Blair's tendency to shift between different types of nostalgia suggests that a high level of instrumentalism underpinned these deployments.

Overall, New Labour failed in its stated aim to reorient the party away from the past in a fundamental way. This failure was to have dramatic repercussions for the Labour Party during the period in which it returned to political opposition.

Notes

1. Cronin, *New Labour's Pasts*, 14.
2. See R. Heffernan, *New Labour and Thatcherism: Political Change in Britain* (Basingstoke: MacMillan, 2000).
3. N. Randall, 'Time and British Politics: Memory, the Present and Teleology in the Politics of New Labour', *British Politics*, 4:2 (2009), 194.
4. R. Toye, 'The Smallest Party in History? New Labour in Historical Perspective', *Labour History Review*, 69:1 (2004), 85; D. Marquand, *The Progressive Dilemma: From Lloyd George to Blair* (London: Heinemann, 1991).
5. Robinson, *History, Heritage and Tradition*, 134–135.
6. *Ibid.*, 147.
7. In particular, by southern voters: see G. Radice, *Southern Discomfort*, Fabian Pamphlet 555 (London: The Fabian Society, 1992), 10.
8. P. Derrick, 'Towards Common Ownership', Letter to *Chartist*, Summer 1992, 4.
9. A. Davies, quoted in The Labour Party, *Conference Report: Ninety-First Annual Conference of the Labour Party* (London: The Labour Party, 1992), 208; S. Bailey, quoted in *LPACR 1992*, 210.
10. M. McLurg, quoted in *LPACR 1992*, 66.
11. S. Bailey, quoted in *LPACR 1992*, 210.
12. T. Pearce, quoted in *LPACR 1992*, 68.
13. H. Young, 'Thinking or Sinking Together', *The Guardian*, 14 January 1993, 20.
14. G. Warner, 'Crystal Gazers with Distorted Vision', *The Sunday Times*, 15 August 1993.
15. G. Mulgan, 'Desperately Seeking Strategy', *The Guardian*, 27 September 1993, 20.
16. T. Benn, diary entry for 29 June 1992 in T. Benn (R. Winstone ed.), *Free at Last: Diaries, 1991–2001* (London: Arrow Books, 2003), 119.
17. D. Skinner, quoted in The Labour Party, *Conference Report: Ninety-Second Annual Conference of the Labour Party* (London: The Labour Party, 1993), 85.
18. T. Benn, diary entry for 14 November 1992 in Benn, *Free at Last*, 148.
19. See. J. Smith, quoted in *LPACR 1992*, 103.
20. J. Straw, Policy and Ideology (Blackburn: Blackburn Labour Party, 1993), 2.
21. *Ibid.*, 10.
22. *Ibid.*, 188.
23. *Ibid.*
24. M. Jacques, 'Smith Faces the Big One', *The Sunday Times*, 13 June 1993.

25 See J. Smith, quoted in *LPACR 1993*, 133; J. Knapp, quoted in *LPACR 1995*, 135.
26 F. Williams, quoted in *LPACR 1993*, 139.
27 See L. Davies, quoted in *LPACR 1993*, 139.
28 H. Scadding, quoted in *LPACR 1993*, 155.
29 J. Prescott, quoted in *LPACR 1993*, 162.
30 Bagehot, 'The Same Old Beast?', *The Economist*, 2 October 1993, 34.
31 Editorial, 'The Next Steps' *The Guardian*, 13 May 1994, 23.
32 See A. Seldon, *Blair* (London: The Free Press, 2005), 184–195
33 Editorial, 'Blair's Utopian Vision is Not Enough', *The Independent*, 25 May 1994, 15.
34 G. F. Mills, 'Lacking in Soul', letter to *Labour Party News*, April/May 1994, 3.
35 F. Roberts, 'Back to Basics', letter to *Labour Party News*, September/October 1994, 3.
36 The Labour Party, 'The Labour Party Leadership Elections' (London: The Labour Party, 1994), FAULDS/4/7/19, Andrew Faulds Papers, LSE, 4.
37 T. Benn, diary entry for 21 July 1994 in Benn, *Free at Last*, 258; C. Benn, *Keir Hardie* (London: Hutchinson, 1992); T. Blair, 'Lost Leader', *The Sunday Times*, 25 October 1992.
38 T. Blair, *Socialism*, Fabian Pamphlet 565 (London: Fabian Society, 1994), 2.
39 T. Blair, quoted in Labour Party, *LPACR 1994/Special Conference 1995*, 100.
40 For example, see S. Goodwin, 'The Labour Party in Blackpool', *The Independent*, 5 October 1994, 6.
41 A. Scargill, quoted in *LPACR 1994/Special Conference 1995*, 43.
42 A. Campbell, diary entry for 30 September 1994 in A. Campbell and R. Stott (eds), *The Blair Years: Extracts from the Alastair Campbell Diaries* (London: Hutchinson), 16.
43 Campbell, diary entry for 30 September 1994 in Campbell, *The Blair Years*, 16.
44 Mandelson, *The Third Man*, 184.
45 J. Mearns, quoted in *LPACR 1994/Special Conference 1995*, 193.
46 J. Carroll, quoted in *LPACR 1994/Special Conference 1995*, 193.
47 L. Whitty, quoted in *LPACR 1994/Special Conference 1995*, 198.
48 A. Johnson, 'Labour's Objects', *Labour Party News*, January 1995, 13.
49 T. Blair, 'Leader's Column', *Labour Party News*, January 1995, 2.
50 J. Prescott, 'Labour's Objects: Points of View', *Labour Party News*, January 1995, 7.
51 See Robinson, *History, Heritage and Tradition*, 141–144.
52 Submission 7978 and 7989, Labour Party Clause IV Consultation, Labour History Archive, Manchester.
53 Submission 3335, Clause IV Consultation.
54 Submission 1810, Clause IV Consultation.
55 Submission 1662, Clause IV Consultation.
56 Submission 6369, Clause IV Consultation.
57 Submission 7579, Clause IV Consultation.
58 Submission 2142, Clause IV Consultation.

59 V. Derer, 'Vote to Keep Clause 4 on 29 April', *Socialist Campaign Group News*, April 1995, 7.
60 T. Benn, 'Why Labour Must Keep Clause IV', *Socialist Campaign Group News*, January 1995, 3; T. Benn, 'Labour's Objects', *Labour Party News*, January 1995, 13.
61 B. Wilson, quoted in P. Wintour and S. Bates, 'Benn Urges the Left to Rebel on Clause 4', *The Guardian*, 22 February 1995, 6.
62 D. Abbott, 'Labour Needs Clause 4', *Socialist Campaign Group News*, March 1995, 1.
63 K. Coates, *Common Ownership: Clause IV and the Labour Party* (Nottingham: Spokesman, 1995), 100.
64 P. Smith, 'Much Ado about Nothing', *Chartist*, November-December 1994, 19.
65 T. Benn, diary entry for 1 December 1994 in Benn, *Free at Last*, 288.
66 M. Mowlam, quoted in *LPACR 1994/Special Conference 1995*, 302.
67 T. Blair, quoted in *LPACR 1994/Special Conference 1995*, 291.
68 L. Adams, quoted in *LPACR 1994/Special Conference 1995*, 303.
69 T. Blair, quoted in The Labour Party, *Conference Report: Ninety-Fourth Annual Conference of the Labour Party* (London: The Labour Party, 1995), 101.
70 R. Cook, 'Goodbye to Nostalgia', *The Observer*, 13 October 1996.
71 See D. Blunkett, quoted in J. Meikle, 'Blunkett Back on the Attack', *The Guardian*, 6 January 1995, 6.
72 T. Blair, foreword to The Labour Party, *Manifesto: New Labour because Britain Deserves Better* (London: The Labour Party, 1997), www.politicsresources.net/area/uk/man/lab97.htm.
73 T. Blair, 'Speech to the Annual Conference of the CBI – 13 November 1995' quoted in Blair, *New Britain*, 107.
74 T. Blair, 'Speech to Keidanren – 5 January 1996' quoted in Blair, *New Britain*, 129.
75 For example, see Campbell, diary entry for 30 August 2000 in Campbell, *The Blair Years*, 467.
76 J. Prescott (with H. Davies), *Prezza: My Story: Pulling No Punches* (London: Headline Publishing, 2008), 204.
77 T. Blair, 'Let Us Face the Future', *Labour Party News*, July/August 1995, 8.
78 T. Blair, *Let Us Face the Future – The 1945 Anniversary Lecture*, Fabian Pamphlet 571 (London: The Fabian Society, 1995), 12.
79 Blair, *Let Us Face the Future*, 14.
80 T. Blair, quoted in The Labour Party, *The Labour Party Conference Verbatim Report 1997* (London: The Labour Party, 1997), 72.
81 'The Politics of Restoration', *The Economist*, 24 December 1994, 65.
82 T. Blair, 'Leader's Speech, Blackpool, 1996', www.britishpoliticalspeech.org/speech-archive.htm?speech=202.
83 Editorial, 'A Triumph of Decent Middle-Class Radicalism', *The Independent*, 2 October 1996, 13.
84 T. Blair, 'From the Spectator Lecture, London, 22 March 1995' quoted in Blair, *New Britain*, 238.
85 T. Blair, 'Introduction' in T. Wright and M. Carter, *The People's Party: The History of the Labour Party* (London: Thames and Hudson, 1997), 8.

86 T. Wright, *Why Vote Labour?* (London: Penguin, 1997), 26.
87 T. Blair, 'General Election Victory Speech, 1997', delivered at 10 Downing Street, London on 2 May 1997, www.britishpoliticalspeech.org/speech-archive.htm?speech=222.
88 Benn, diary entry for 26 March 1997 in Benn, *Free at Last*, 401.
89 T. Heath, '"S" Word Strikes a Chord on May Day in Wales', *The Independent*, 6 May 1997, 8.
90 B. Williams, 'Personal and Political', letter to *Socialist Campaign Group News*, March 1998, 11.
91 P. Roberts, 'Review of Unfinished Revolution – How the Modernisers Saved the Labour Party by Philip Gould', *Socialist Campaign Group News*, February 1999, 7.
92 G. Young, 'The Stirrer', *The Guardian*, 20 July 2002, 37.
93 J. Freedland, 'What a Swell Party This Is. But Not All of Us Seem to Have an Invitation', *The Guardian*, 30 September 1998, 20.
94 R. Hattersley, 'Why I'm No Longer Loyal to Labour', *The Guardian*, 26 July 1997, 21.
95 R. Stock, 'The Campaign for Real Labour', *Chartist*, September-October 2001, 9.
96 D. Macintyre, 'Blair Embraces Morgan and Spirit of Keir Hardie', *The Independent*, 6 April 2000, www.independent.co.uk/news/uk/politics/blair-embraces-morgan-and-spirit-of-keir-hardie-281864.html.
97 T. Blair, quoted in The Labour Party, *Verbatim Report of the One Hundreth Conference of the Labour Party* (London: The Labour Party, 2001), 94.
98 For example, see E. Macaskill, 'Stage Directions', *The Guardian*, 21 September 1998, 2.
99 G. Brown, quoted in *LPACR 1997*, 31.
100 *Ibid.*; H. Blears, quoted in *LPACR 1997*, 24; J. Prescott, quoted in *LPACR 1997*, 107.
101 C. Mullin, diary entry 10 March 1998 in C. Mullin (R. Winstone ed.), *A Walk on Part: Diaries 1994–99* (London: Penguin Books, 2012), 327.
102 P. Hain, *Outside In* (London: Biteback, 2012), 386.
103 Prescott, *Prezza*, 332.
104 'Blame it on the Boogie', *The Economist*, 30 May 1998, 20.
105 M. Foot, 'Preface' in B. Brivati and R. Heffernan (eds), *The Labour Party: A Centenary History* (Basingstoke: MacMillan, 2000), xi.
106 B. Etchells, quoted in The Labour Party, *Verbatim Report of the Ninety-Eighth Conference of the Labour Party* (London: The Labour Party, 1999), 1.
107 M. McDonagh, quoted in *LPACR 1999*, 3.
108 G. Brown, quoted in *LPACR 1999*, 28.
109 T. Blair, quoted in *LPACR 1999*, 61.
110 *Ibid.*, 58.
111 T. Sutcliffe, 'Labour Party Conference: Master of the Labour Hounds', *The Independent*, 29 September 1999, 8.
112 T. Sutcliffe, 'Labour's Centenary: The Royalty and the Rabble, the Winners and the Losers', *The Independent*, 28 February 2000, 3.

113 G. Brown, 'Why the Party Still Needs its Soul', *New Statesman*, 28 February 2000, 22.
114 The Labour Party, *Centennial Report 1999* (London: The Labour Party, 1999), 5.
115 *Ibid.*, 8–19.
116 *Ibid.*, 16.
117 The Labour Party, *Inside: The New Labour Magazine*, 1:4 (February, 2000), 10–11.
118 The Labour Party, *Conference 2000: The Magazine* (London: The Labour Party, 2000), 53.
119 C. Mullin, diary entry for 8 February 2006 in C. Mullin (R. Winstone ed.), *Decline and Fall: Diaries 2005–10* (London: Profile Books, 2010), 78.
120 T. Blair, 'Foreword' in A. Haworth and D. Hayter (eds), *Men Who Made Labour: The PLP of 1906 – The Personalities and the Politics* (London: Routledge, 2006), xvii–xviii.
121 A. Morrison, 'A Scowling Class Apart', *Chartist*, March–April 2006, 22.
122 M. Le Cornu, 'Rotating Pioneers would be Embarrassed by Blairism', letter to *Tribune*, 5 May 2006, 19.
123 J. Legg, 'The Last Crusade', *Chartist*, January/February 2004, 23.
124 T. Benn, diary entry for 22 October 2003 in T. Benn (R. Winstone ed.), *More Time for Politics: Diaries 2001–07* (London: Arrow Books, 2008), 149.
125 C. Short, *An Honourable Deception? New Labour, Iraq and the Misuse of Power* (London: Free Press, 2004), 282.
126 See M. Wheeler, quoted in The Labour Party, *Verbatim Report of the 102nd Conference of the Labour Party* (London: The Labour Party, 2003), 4.
127 Bono, quoted in The Labour Party, *Verbatim Report 2004* (London: The Labour Party, 2004), 130.
128 T. Luckhurst, 'Betrayed by Money: How Labour's Craven Behaviour Towards the Wealthy has Betrayed the Party's Roots', *The Daily Mail*, 24 April 2006, 12.
129 Mandelson, *The Third Man*, 370.
130 See Short, *An Honourable Deception*, 43.
131 S. Kelly, 'Brown is No Better', letter to *Tribune* 10 March 2006, 22.
132 For example, see G. Brown, 'Leader's Speech, Bournemouth 2007', www.britishpoliticalspeech.org/speech-archive.htm?speech=179.
133 Editorial, 'Debt Still Owed to Union Martyrs', *Tribune*, 13 July 2007, 18.
134 E. Dougall, 'Give Us Back Our Party, Please', letter to *Tribune*, 20 May 2008, 18.
135 T. Benn, diary entry for 20 July 2008 in T. Benn (R. Winstone ed.), *A Blaze of Autumn Sunshine: The Last Diaries* (London: Arrow Books, 2014), 155.
136 M. Bright, 'The History Boys', *New Statesman*, 20 September 2009, www.newstatesman.com/blogs/martin-bright/2007/09/conference-brown-party.
137 E. Gellard, 'When We Fight We Win', email to Labour party members, 18 November 2009.
138 The Labour Party, 'Fighters and Believers' Party Political Broadcast, 18 November 2009, www.youtube.com/watch?v=iOYlDmVB3tM.

6

Back to the past? Labour's return to opposition, 2010 to the present

Following the party's defeat at the 2010 General Election, Labour found itself in opposition for the first time in thirteen years. Although the party had suffered a significant electoral setback, this return to opposition offered an opportunity for ideational and programmatic renewal. Freed from the restraints and considerations of government, the party had the time and space that was needed to address the intellectual stagnation that many perceived had characterised the end of the New Labour era. Recent studies have described how, under Ed Miliband's leadership, an attempt was made to refashion Labour in line with modern developments and in a manner that took account of the economic considerations of the post-2008 financial crisis world. Academics have suggested that Miliband was only partially successful in achieving these objectives. Eunice Goes has argued that 'under Ed Miliband the Labour Party has sought to re-imagine social democracy by rejecting the main tenets of New Labour, but was only marginally successful in this enterprise.'[1] Similarly, Tim Bale has portrayed Miliband as a figure who wanted to enact 'radical' changes but was restrained by his own sense of caution.[2] Significantly, the existing literature has, almost uniformly, highlighted the way in which the party's trajectory during the Miliband era was shaped by modern and contemporary concerns, issues and events.[3]

Recent biographical accounts of the rise of Jeremy Corbyn have declared that his victory in the 2015 Labour leadership contest marked a fundamental rupture with the party's past.[4] 'Corbynism' has been described as a response to recent developments in British politics. Rosa Prince has stated that 'Those drawn to Corbyn were people, often but by no means exclusively young, who were disgusted by the 2009 expenses scandal and attracted by the anti-austerity Occupy movement.'[5] The modern dimensions of Corbyn's 2015 leadership campaign have been emphasised. The campaign harnessed new social media and supporter-mobilisation techniques.[6] Corbyn advocated 'a new way of doing politics'.[7] Yet, simultaneously, Corbynism has been portrayed as an ideological throwback to a bygone era. Furthermore, the attachment of Corbyn and his allies to historic traditions and rituals has also been noted.[8]

This chapter will outline the ways in which nostalgia has shaped Labour's political development since its return to opposition in 2010. In contrast to the existing literature's emphasis on modernity, the first half of this chapter will examine the nostalgic contours and parameters of Miliband's Labour Party. In order to provide a greater understanding of Corbynism, the second half of this chapter will offer a detailed and systematic analysis of the role played by nostalgia during both Corbyn's rise to political prominence and his time as party leader.

2010 Labour leadership contest

Throughout the summer of 2010, five candidates competed to replace Gordon Brown as leader of the Labour Party. Diane Abbott, Ed Balls, Andy Burnham, David Miliband and Ed Miliband all received the required number of parliamentary nominations to make the final ballot paper. Discussions of this leadership contest have tended to focus on the fratricidal nature of the competition that took place between the two Miliband brothers.[9] However, the manner in which the candidates attempted to frame their individual campaigns reveals a great deal about the party's relationship to its past at this point in its political development.

All of the candidates displayed an awareness of the undesirability of being either perceived or characterised as nostalgic. This awareness was often coupled with the desire to be seen as a modern 'change' candidate. Ed Miliband, the contest's eventual winner, appeared to be particularly keen to distance his campaign from any sentimental attachment to the preceding New Labour era. He proclaimed that it was his 'rejection of this New Labour nostalgia' that made him 'the modernising candidate at this election' and he decried 'the belittling of any attempt to move on from past verities'.[10] On another occasion, he accused both New Labour and Old Labour of 'clinging to old truths that had served their time: we got stuck with old certainties, bad policies and became out of touch.'[11] David Miliband, Ed's brother and main rival for the leadership, also seemed to be wary of the problematic nature of nostalgia. In his Keir Hardie Memorial Lecture in July 2010, he explicitly rejected 'a nostalgia that is hopeless'. Ostensibly, he seemed to challenge nostalgia for a bygone industrial era that encouraged people 'to ignore the poverty, the exploitation, the insanitary housing, the illiteracy, the dangerous pits, the precariousness of the lives of working people at that time.'[12]

Elsewhere, in a letter that was sent to the parliamentary party, Andy Burnham argued that 'we need to rebuild our Party for new times. We must become a more modern, open and campaigning force for good.'[13] In an interview with the *Left Foot Forward* Blogsite, Ed Balls indicated that he believed that the Miliband brothers had not managed 'to move beyond the new Labour/old Labour debates of the past … I worry that they're rerunning the debates of the past.'[14] During an interview that was posted on *LabourList*, Diane Abbott was faced with the question 'someone told me they would vote for you because they wanted to remind Labour of its socialist roots … how important is it to remind Labour of this heritage?' Abbott responded unequivocally: 'I don't think it's about a heritage issue. I think it's about a 21st century issue of what the Labour Party is for.'[15]

Nevertheless, in a rather contradictory manner and in contrast to their aforementioned rhetorical hostility towards the past, all of the candidates attempted to locate themselves within the emotional parameters of the party's nostalgia. Ed Miliband regularly made references to the party's industrial working-class past. In a speech in Leeds in June 2010, Ed Miliband described the 1984–85 Miners' Strike as a formative moment in his personal political development.[16] He joined the crowd in Govan at the funeral of the veteran trade union leader Jimmy Reid and he stated that 'I thought it was right to come and pay my respects with all the men who work here. It's party of the legacy of these yards.'[17] In order to justify his political priorities, he also evoked memories of the achievements of the 1945 Labour Government.[18] Speaking towards the end of the contest, Ed Miliband declared that 'While certainly I don't consider myself Old Labour – I can sort of understand the tradition.'[19] This nostalgic orientation was noted by onlookers. The journalist Matthew d'Ancona suggested that Ed Miliband was speaking to those party members who wanted a return to 'Old Labour' commitments and beliefs: 'I am sure he believes he is the spokesman of the future, but what he offers is little more than a nostalgia tour.'[20]

In a similar manner, wary of being framed as the continuity New Labour candidate, David Miliband deployed nostalgic memories in order both to demonstrate his sensitivity to the party's past and to define his own political agenda. Despite its stated aim to chart a course between nostalgia and 'a contemptuous modernism', his Keir Hardie Memorial Lecture was orientated very much towards the former rather than the latter. In this speech, he reimagined and reconceptualised Hardie, a heroic figure deeply engrained in the party's traditional working-class nostalgia-identity, in terms congruent with his own political orientation:

> Hardie was a socialist not a statist … [he] helped build a transformational movement in hard times, and we need to reconnect with that mission and

recognise the importance of the Labour tradition as a means through which we protect each other from the market storms that are upon us once more.[21]

In August 2010, David Miliband also used memories of Hardie and the party's founding 'pioneers' to legitimise his candidacy and ideas in a lecture entitled 'The Change Britain Needs'.[22] In this way, in a crowded leadership contest, he attempted to indicate to the party that he was the candidate who was the rightful heir to Hardie's legacy and not a historically rootless 'moderniser'.

In order to gain a strategic mnemonic advantage over their opponents, the other candidates in the contest also evoked the party's past. In August 2010, Ed Balls used his widely reported Bloomberg speech to draw parallels between the 1930s and the current economic crisis. Drawing on Labour's history, he compared the Conservative and Liberal Democrat Coalition's attempts to cut public spending to the actions of Ramsay MacDonald and his National Government in 1931.[23] Furthermore, his campaign communications to party members attempted to position his family's history within positively charged memories of the 1945 Labour Government and he talked about continuing Labour's 'historic mission to build a more just society'.[24] Andy Burnham framed his campaign as a way to 'reconnect' the party with its traditional supporters and as a mechanism for 'bringing forward big ideas in the best traditions of the Labour Party'.[25] One sympathetic commentator wrote in *Tribune* that Burnham's working-class background located him within Labour's political heritage and that 'In a party whose very conception inherited much from Chartism – the original working person's voice – the question of one's route to power should be essential.'[26] In her speech at the Policy Exchange think tank in September 2010, Diane Abbott described how 'New Labour regarded mutual organisation and co-ops as dusty and old fashioned' but she argued that 'maybe it is time to rediscover some of those old models.' She concluded her speech by stressing that 'A movement born out of the best of working-class self-help and self-organisation should be leading the debate on these issues.'[27]

Blue Labour

In the aftermath of Ed Miliband's 2010 Labour leadership victory, the communitarian 'Blue Labour' movement emerged as a significant intellectual force within the Labour Party.[28] During Miliband's period as Labour leader, figures associated with Blue Labour went on to hold positions of power and influence: Maurice Glasman was made a member of the House of Lords, the MP Jon Cruddas headed Labour's Policy Review,

Jonathan Rutherford worked on the Policy Review and Marc Stears acted as a close political adviser to the Labour leader. In July 2011, following some controversial comments made by Glasman on immigration, Blue Labour appeared to dissolve itself.[29] Nevertheless, many of the ideas that informed the Blue Labour project continued to exert an influence on the politics of the Labour Party and, in particular, its leadership.[30]

Blue Labour referred frequently to a perceived need to return to the values of the early twentieth-century Guild Socialists.[31] Glasman also regularly mobilised memories of Labour's founding moments and made references to heroic struggles from the past, such as the London Dock Strike of 1889.[32] He declared that the British labour movement had lost touch with the values that had sustained it during it its formative years.[33] In this way, he mobilised nostalgic tropes that were recognisably congruent with the party's long-held nostalgia-identity. These tropes reached back further into Labour's past than discussions of Blue Labour's 'Austerity Nostalgia' have suggested.[34] Jon Cruddas exhibited a similar type of nostalgia to Glasman. Speaking at the Aneurin Bevan Memorial Lecture in 2010, Cruddas noted that traditional working-class communities, cultures and identities were in decline, but he proclaimed that 'there is hope for Labour precisely because we have a powerful tradition; a collective memory built in previous periods of dispossession.'[35] The following year, Cruddas wrote that 'Labour should democratise its own dead to conserve what it fought for.'[36] More generally, Blue Labour appeared to be preoccupied with male traditional industrial workers. In particular, Rutherford seemed to lament the fact that 'Labour's patrimony, the party loyalty and culture of work that fathers handed down to their sons – and daughters too, but Labour has been a deeply patriarchal movement – is dying out.'[37]

Blue Labour's historical orientation represented a direct response to the perceived modernity of the New Labour era. In early 2011, in a highly significant move, one of the leading figures behind Blue Labour publicly embraced the politics of nostalgia. In a lecture that focused on Robert Tressell's book *The Ragged-Trousered Philanthropists*, Cruddas argued that 'people "on the left" tend to scorn tradition ... Labour is in trouble today because of this lack of tradition.'[38] New Labour was attacked as a 'blank "progressive" wall' and an 'empty "radical" desk'. Cruddas's speech revolved around the idea that 'The future for Labour lies in the past.' He declared that nostalgia needed to be reclaimed as a mechanism by which to resist the negative effects of modern capitalistic change: 'A "radical nostalgia" can create a popular culture that is less open to manipulation.'[39] This nostalgic impetus was supported in the media by the columnist Madeleine Bunting. Bunting suggested that

'Nostalgia has to be recognised as legitimate; it's a powerful emotional current in the electorate with which politicians need to connect.'[40]

Cruddas's lecture in Liverpool exposed a significant fault line within the Blue Labour project. Divisions centred on the perceived desirability of the promotion of an agenda that was presented as explicitly nostalgic. The following month, Glasman emphasised that the forgotten past that Blue Labour referred to represented a fundamental historical truth rather than a nostalgic fiction: 'This is not a politics of nostalgia … It is a claim that practices and values crucial to what Labour is and stands for have been forgotten.'[41] Likewise, Stears argued that '"What people see as nostalgia is actually just an insight from the past, buried in Labour's own intellectual tradition."'[42] In contrast to Cruddas's speech in Liverpool, such statements represented a return to the binary discourse between historical truth and fiction that had previously characterised intraparty debates within the party under New Labour: nostalgia reassumed negative, rather than positive, normative dimensions.

Political sensitivities regarding the word 'nostalgia' itself clearly played a role in this rhetorical shift. Members of Ed Miliband's team seemed wary of the negative connotations of the word 'nostalgia'. In his speech to Progress's annual conference in May 2011, Miliband declared that it was important for Labour to

> understand what really matters to people. It goes to the heart of what Maurice Glasman calls Blue Labour. Some have presented this as a nostalgic vision of the past – the Labour equivalent of warm beer, leather on willow and bicycling maidens. I think this is to wholly misunderstand what this is about.[43]

In the event, therefore, Blue Labour's explicit promotion of 'nostalgia' as a means by which to direct Labour's politics was short-lived.

Due to the manner in which Blue Labour tapped into the party's nostalgia for its traditional working-class past, the Labour Left's response to Blue Labour's evocations of the party's working-class past seemed unclear. The singer Billy Bragg wrongly associated Blue Labour with an 'economically liberal agenda'. Bragg declared that 'tradition does, nonetheless, have an important role to play in helping Labour reconnect with its lost support, not by making us feel nostalgic, but by helping us to recognise that we have been here before.'[44] Writing in the *New Statesman*, Mehdi Hasan described Bragg's intervention as 'bizarre' and suggested that 'There was no golden age and the party must not idealise the working class.'[45] Articles that were broadly supportive of Blue Labour appeared in *Tribune* and one writer suggested that Blue Labour 'is intriguing and, for some, a quite appealing attempt to undo the damage caused by New Labour's aversion to the party's former bedrock – the working class.'[46]

The Labour Right responded to the rise of Blue Labour in a similarly confused manner. In an interview with *The Times*, Blair expressed his wariness of '"indulging a nostalgia which suggests a great emotional empathy with someone when you don't have a policy to deal with it ... [Labour] won't win by a Labour equivalent of warm beer and old maids bicycling."'[47] In a similar manner, the journalist Mary Riddell warned that 'The risk for Blue Labourites lies in a neverland inhabited by superannuated pigeon-fanciers who like Woodbines and Watneys and don't think much of foreigners. Britain is not a museum of nostalgia but a forward-looking country that became so sickened by new Labour's techno-cant that it now risks overdosing on the past.'[48] Robert Philpot (director of the New Labour think tank 'Progress') declared that 'blue Labour all too often appears fundamentally backward-looking.'[49] However, he then proceeded to urge the party to 'rediscover an old [decentralist] tradition rooted deep in Labour's history which is right for new times' and to refer to significant socialist figures from Britain's past like William Morris and Robert Owen.[50] The similarities with Blue Labour's historical narrative were striking.

A more resolutely coherent anti-nostalgic discourse originated from feminists who noted the heavily gendered vision of the past that Blue Labour promoted. The left-wing journalist Laurie Penny described how 'at its heart, social conservatism responds to the problems of modernity with a frantic nostalgia for the comforts of the past, even if that past was less than pleasant for those who were actually obliged to live there.' Penny then proceeded to dismiss Blue Labour's version of 'radicalism': 'Rather than challenging the status quo ... Blue Labour responds with a paranoid hankering for a time when workers didn't leave their country of origin and women didn't leave the kitchen.'[51] Inside the Parliamentary Labour Party, Helen Goodman was the most vocal advocate of the feminist anti-nostalgic position: '"If Glasman thinks we will all greet this with an ironic post-feminist smile, he is wrong ... He seems to be harking back to a Janet and John Fifties era."'[52] The anti-nostalgic attacks that were made by feminists clearly impacted on Blue Labour's historical narrative. In an interview with Ivana Bartoletti for Fabian Women's Network e-magazine in the autumn of 2011, Glasman emphasised that women 'are completely central to BL [Blue Labour]. BL is fundamentally a relational politics in which people resist their domination. BL rejects domination, it comes out of feminism and this is the most neglected aspect of it all.'[53] Such rhetoric contrasted markedly with an earlier historical narrative which had both emphasised and located the project's origins in nostalgia for a male working-class past.

One Nation Labour

During Ed Miliband's period as party leader, the political narrative that received the most attention from media commentators and academics was 'One Nation Labour'. At the party's annual conference in 2012, Miliband attempted to present himself as the heir to Benjamin Disraeli's 'One Nation' approach to politics. Appropriating nostalgia for a nineteenth-century Conservative Prime Minister represented a bold political move, albeit one that was not as original as commentators believed at the time.[54] Capitalising on the sense of national pride that had been generated by the 2012 London Olympics, Miliband's Leader's speech tied Disraeli's idea of 'One Nation' in with the Labour leader's personal background as the son of Jewish immigrants.[55]

Writing for the *Guardian*, Patrick Wintour described the speech as 'high risk' and he argued that it represented 'an audacious raid deep into Conservative heritage'.[56] Yet, despite the repeated references to Disraeli, Miliband's 'One Nation' speech was not completely devoid of interactions with Labour's past. A link was made between Disraeli and the 1945 Attlee Government and Miliband concluded his speech by talking about how 'it falls to us, the Labour Party. As it has fallen to previous generations of Labour Party pioneers to leave our country a better place than we found it.'[57] Similarly, when Miliband added depth to his 'One Nation' analysis at a speech in Bedford in February 2013, he mobilised memories of Britain's Industrial Revolution and he declared that 'it wasn't just the mill owners and the factory bosses who drove our economy forward. It was the people who went down the mines, spun the cotton, built the ships and constructed the bridges.'[58] In this way, Miliband tried to temper the elements of his 'One Nation' narrative that were alien to the party's historically orientated identity with a type of nostalgia that was more recognisable to his party.

Parallels were drawn between the 'One Nation Labour' and Blue Labour movements.[59] Writing for *Progress*, Anthony Giddens argued that both movements contained 'more than a hint of nostalgia for a world that has disappeared, never to return.'[60] Certainly, Labour politicians like Owen Smith, who advocated a 'One Nation' approach, attempted to reframe the idea in a manner that located its origins in the party's industrial past. Smith argued that One Nation Labour's 'roots lie deep in our heritage, and in that of the wider movement of which we are a part' and he referred to the 'friendly societies and the co-op, miners' lodges and the Fed, unions and the Labour Party' of early twentieth-century Pontypridd.[61] Nevertheless, despite these attempts, Miliband's One Nation Labour narrative gained little traction within the wider party.

The appropriation of Conservative Party traditions and historical figures clearly held little appeal for party members, activists and writers who, at around the time of the launch of One Nation Labour, were framing their arguments with a more established nostalgia: 'The challenge for Labour politicians today, as it was in Hardie's time, is to present a clear alternative and the promise of real change.'[62]

Reviewing Miliband's 'One Nation' speech, one article on the *Left Futures* website urged the party to be cautious about adopting a 'Tory term'.[63] Responding to an article by Tristram Hunt MP, another article criticised the use of Disraeli in Labour's 'One Nation' narrative: 'Disraeli was many things but "working class champion" was certainly not one of them.'[64] Writing for *Tribune* almost a year after Miliband's 2012 conference speech, Joe Haines (Harold Wilson's former press secretary) deemed the Labour leader's deployment of Disraeli as 'absurd' and he stated that he would have 'done better to read [Charles] Dickens and [Henry] Mayhew for his inspiration.'[65]

In the face of Miliband's 'One Nation' nostalgic mobilisations, party members sought to re-establish Labour's true nostalgia-identity. After Miliband had delivered another 'One Nation' speech at the TUC Congress in September 2013,[66] Scottish Labour's 'Campaign for Socialism' group criticised the way that the Labour leader had 'looked back to Edward Stanley and Disraeli for inspiration for his peculiar "One nation" approach and neglected the thoughts of Keir Hardie.'[67] Elsewhere, the left-wing 'Red Labour' movement gained support 'in the face of a Blairite retrenchment in [the form of] *One Nation Labour*'.[68] Red Labour's appeal was explicitly nostalgic and far-reaching. Ben Sellars, who was involved in the project from an early stage, has recalled how the group had a 'particular penchant for Nye Bevan memes'.[69] In August 2013, Sellars claimed that one post on its Facebook page 'quoting Keir Hardie on the arrival of the royal baby in 1894 [had] reached 181,568 people and attracted 14,970 likes, comments or shares.'[70]

Red Labour successfully channelled the type of nostalgia that, at this point, appeared to onlookers to be flourishing within the party. Increasingly, under Miliband's leadership, media commentators noted that having 'gone through the painful process of modernisation in the Nineties', the party 'now seems gripped by nostalgia'.[71] Indeed, in a discussion with Ed Balls at the *Mirror's* party at the 2014 Labour Party Conference (held on the set of Coronation Street), one journalist talked about the 'collective nostalgia the Labour party has for being the party of the working man' and she suggested that Labour 'seems to rely too much on the folk memory of being the party of coal miners and the kind of machinists who worked in Mike Baldwin's factory'.[72]

Academics have shown how the idea of 'One Nation' rhetoric became closely tied to Miliband's individual political persona.[73] Nevertheless, in reality, due to its lack of resonance within the wider party, Labour's adoption of the 'One Nation' moniker was sporadic and short-lived.[74] Towards the end of his period as leader, Miliband's attempts to adopt Conservative nostalgia did not extend very far beyond the very limited reference to Disraeli that was made in the 'One Nation Society' document that originated from the party's Policy Review.[75] There were no references to Disraeli in the foreword that Miliband co-authored with Ed Balls for the 'One Nation Economy' report.[76] Furthermore, the twenty-two page *One Nation* magazine that was sent to party members in 2014 contained no mention of the nineteenth-century Conservative Party politician.[77] At the same time, in contrast to Miliband's 2012 speech, documents produced by Labour politicians stressed the relationship between the idea of 'One Nation' and figures from Labour's past like Nye Bevan.[78]

It was also noticeable that Cruddas and Rutherford's quasi-official 2014 policy report emphasised the role that the question posed by Thomas Carlyle in his 1839 essay 'Chartism' ('"What is the condition of the working classes in their houses and in their hearts?"') had played in shaping Disraeli's concept of 'One Nation'. In this reworked narrative of Miliband's 2012 conference speech, the Labour leader had thus 'once again raised Carlyle's question and called on the Labour Party to Rebuild Britain as One Nation'.[79] In his sympathetic review of Cruddas and Rutherford's E-book, Nick Forbes (leader of Newcastle Council) positioned Ed Miliband and his policies within a historical Labour lineage that dated from the time of Keir Hardie.[80] Disraeli was conspicuous by his absence.

Towards the 2015 General Election

Aside from his evocations of Disraeli, Miliband's relationship with Labour's nostalgia was fairly routine and straightforward. In a similar manner to previous leaders of the Labour Party, when he found himself either short of political capital or needed to generate support for contentious changes and policies, Miliband deployed memories that were more congruent with the party's nostalgia. A number of democratic issues had surrounded the operation of Labour's Electoral College during the 2010 Leadership contest.[81] Amongst other recommendations, the 2014 Collins Review suggested that the existing system for Labour's leadership elections should be abolished in favour of the implementation of a more genuinely one member, one vote process that weighted the individual votes of party members, affiliated supporters and registered supporters equally.[82] The Collins Review emphasised the way in which the pioneers who had conceived and implemented Labour's 1918 Constitution had always 'believed the new structures would evolve over time'.[83]

On 1 March 2014, in order for the party to vote on the proposed changes, a special conference was convened in London. Although Miliband's centrepiece speech at this conference touched on the idea of One Nation Labour briefly (there was no mention of Disraeli), it cited a more recognisable figure from the party's past. Miliband proclaimed 'Keir Hardie used to call our party a movement. Think about that word. It's movements that change things.'[84] In this way, he suggested that the implementation of the changes that were advocated by the Collins Review would simply return the party to the ideals that had been pursued by Hardie during Labour's founding moments. At the end of his speech, Miliband reinforced this mnemonic construction of the present with the phrase 'Let's build a movement.'[85] The changes were passed.

Miliband fell back on a similar type of nostalgia when his party found itself in difficulties in Scotland. When it appeared that the votes of Labour supporters might shape the outcome of the 2014 Scottish Referendum in a decisive way, he headed north of the border to give a speech in Blantyre. Delivered on 4 September 2014, the speech's location was significant: the *Guardian* noted that 'Miliband urged party activists to remember the traditions of Labour party founder Keir Hardie, who was born eight miles away.'[86] The *Independent* described how

> Mr Miliband told supporters that Scotland would only be made fairer if the country voted No and then elected a Labour government. 'We can build a more just Scotland within a more just United Kingdom. True to the traditions of our pioneers, true to the traditions of the heroes of Scotland' he said.[87]

Both of these reports indicated that the speech was received in an unfavourable manner by the wider Scottish electorate. In a sense, on this occasion, Miliband misinterpreted the nature of his audience. He deployed a Labour nostalgia that had little emotional purchase beyond his own party's members. In any case, as one commentator for a Scottish paper noted, the mobilisation of memories of Hardie was problematic because of the Labour founder's historic support for 'home rule'.[88] In contrast, Gordon Brown's 'Better Together' campaign intervention, delivered the day before Scottish polling stations opened, evoked a more inclusive and nationally orientated nostalgia that drew broadly on Scotland's past achievements and successes.[89] Brown's speech was 'widely hailed as one of the best of all time'.[90]

The Scottish public's lukewarm reaction to Miliband's Blantyre speech did not deter him from making similar appeals to the past during the General Election campaign of 2015. In Glasgow on 1 May 2015, with

Labour looking like it was going to haemorrhage votes to the Scottish National Party, he made nostalgic references to previous generations of Scottish Labour. The speech was pre-briefed to journalists. Both the *Independent* and the *Guardian* stated that Miliband was expected to talk about the people who had 'built Labour in Scotland' and 'fought for their rights in the shipyards and mines across this country'. [91] It was also noted that he intended to cite significant Scottish figures from Labour's history, including Jennie Lee and Keir Hardie.[92] However, once again, these nostalgic mobilisations seem to have been unsuccessful. At the 2015 General Election, Labour lost all but one of its Scottish MPs.

The 2015 Labour leadership contest

In May 2015, after Labour had suffered a largely unexpected election defeat, Ed Miliband resigned from his position as leader of the party. A leadership contest was triggered (following Harriet Harman's resignation, a deputy leadership also took place). The four candidates who received enough nominations from the Parliamentary Labour Party to make the final ballot paper for Labour's 2015 leadership election were Andy Burnham, Yvette Cooper, Jeremy Corbyn and Liz Kendall.

I began this book by outlining the overtly nostalgic appeals that Jeremy Corbyn made to the party's internal electorate during the summer of 2015. Despite his claims that he represented a 'new kind of politics',[93] Corbyn articulated memories associated with Labour's nostalgia-identity with an unrelenting vigour and enthusiasm. Media commentators noted that his success was rooted in nostalgia.[94] An editorial in the *Daily Telegraph* described Corbyn as 'a nostalgia addict'.[95] At the first of his one hundred campaign rallies, Corbyn declared that

> The Labour Party was founded by people who had a fantastic vision of a different world. I was reading a lot about the works of Keir Hardie, and he sounds like he was a really awkward guy – he was probably very nice underneath it all – but he had this absolute steely determination that he was going to build a political party that would represent the working class.

In this speech, Corbyn contrasted the heroism and vision of Labour's founders with the way that 'New Labour didn't follow any of those traditions.'[96] Delivering another speech at the 'End Austerity Now' demonstration on 20 June 2015, he compared the anti-austerity movement to the Chartists and he also declared that 'I want us to stand up, as brave people did in the 1920s and 1930s, and said "we want a state that takes responsibility."'[97] One Corbyn supporter noted that this section of his speech was particular well-received by his audience.[98]

Yet Corbyn was not the only candidate in this contest who deployed rhetoric that displayed an attachment to the past. If Corbyn's candidacy and subsequent popularity drew the other candidates to the left, then it also pulled the language that they used towards the nostalgic. A *Guardian* editorial, written in late July, declared that 'Too much of the campaigning sounds nostalgic and backward-looking. Labour needs answers for the future, not the past.'[99] This advice was not heeded. Speaking at the People's History Museum in Manchester in August 2015, Andy Burnham proclaimed that 'as well as listening to voices of the present, we must also hear from those from our past. So this is the right place to be on a morning as important as this.' He went on to describe how 'Upstairs here, there is a wonderful collection of banners. If you walk through, you will quickly notice how one motto runs through them all. Unity is strength. If our forefathers and mothers could ask us to bear in mind one piece of advice right now, then surely it would be that.'[100] Burnham's campaign communications to party members stated that 'The time has come for Labour to recapture the "spirit of 45."'[101]

In a widely reported speech in August 2015, Yvette Cooper argued that Corbyn was 'offering old solutions to old problems, not new answers to the problems of today'. She attacked his desire to reopen Britain's coalmines: 'I'm not going to make people false promises on the coalfield communities that we can turn the clock back to the middle of the 20th century.' However, at the same time, Cooper also referenced Labour's founding moments to legitimise her calls for unity in the present.[102] One pamphlet sent to Labour members stressed that 'My politics comes from two Labour traditions – the solidarity of the coalfield communities and the fight for equality.'[103] Elsewhere, in a fairly undisguised critique of Corbyn's elevated rhetoric, Cooper argued that 'As Labour's first leader Keir Hardie told us a century ago, "Socialism does not come by shouting."'[104] On another occasion, Cooper stated that Labour needed a female leader and she suggested that 'Keir Hardie who campaigned with suffragettes would be shocked that it's taken us more than 100 years.'[105]

Alan Johnson MP wrote a commentary piece that was widely interpreted as implying that, if he were still alive, Hardie would be backing Cooper and not Corbyn.[106] In response, an article on the *Left Futures* blog site declared that Johnson's 'references to policy matters are as reliable as his reference to the views of Keir Hardie.'[107] Similarly, Melissa Benn (Tony Benn's daughter) contested Johnson's historical analysis and she outlined how 'When it comes to the politics of agitation, Jeremy Corbyn is Hardie's clear heir.'[108] In general, this debate was indicative of the way that Labour's nostalgia for Hardie became amplified by the leadership contest's historical proximity to the one hundredth anniversary of his death on 26 September 1915.[109]

Liz Kendall, who was widely seen as the candidate of the party's 'modernising' wing, also mobilised memories of the party's past. In one campaign statement in June 2015, she mentioned that 'I owe our party – and those great pioneers who came before us so much.'[110] In a speech to the Reuters news agency about the economy, in order to support a historically orientated narrative that suggested that 'Fiscal responsibility is part of a proud Labour tradition', Kendall quoted from Labour's 1923 manifesto.[111] In another widely reported speech that commentators suggested was influenced by Blue Labour, Kendall outlined her support for an English Labour Party and she cited England's long history of radicalism. Her rhetoric appeared simultaneously to be both dismissive of and reliant upon nostalgia: 'We shouldn't be nostalgic. Industrial Britain was a world of rigid hierarchies, gender stereotypes, and often accepted prejudices too. Yet, many people had a sense of being part of something.'[112] In one of her campaign interviews, Kendall attempted to frame her campaign within a Labour tradition of self-help and mutualism that ran from Keir Hardie and the party's founders.[113] A supportive article that was written for *Progress* suggested that, by reconciling New and Blue Labour, Kendall was the true 'inheritor' of Hardie's political legacy.[114]

Above all, Corbyn's successful nostalgic articulation of the party's past forced his opponents to campaign in a more backward-looking manner. In turn, this historical emphasis created the mnemonic environment in which Corbyn, the candidate who had the ideas and rhetoric with the greatest nostalgic resonance, could flourish. As this book has shown, within the wider party, Labour remained characterised by its nostalgia-imbued identity. In the 2015 Labour leadership contest, a new electoral system that delivered more power to a nostalgic rank-and-file delivered a decisive victory for Corbyn on the first round of voting.

Jeremy Corbyn as leader

During the relatively short period in which Jeremy Corbyn has been Labour Leader, very few concrete policy proposals have originated from the party.[115] This limits any assessment of the extent to which nostalgia has shaped Labour's programmatic commitments. Yet, it is clear that, at least at an abstract level, the trajectory that has been initiated by the party's current leader is less hostile to nostalgia than the approach that his predecessors adopted from the mid-1980s onwards.

Corbyn's speeches have indicated that nostalgia for a bygone era of traditional industrial working-class struggle continues to influence his politics in a significant way. Speaking to the Scottish Labour Conference in October 2015, Corbyn argued that 'Our history is proud and can inform how we should react now, and what we could do in the future.' He outlined a very static model of politics that appeared to be rooted in the past: 'Our mission now is the same as that which he [Keir Hardie] laid out just 21 years into the Labour Party's life [Corbyn was placing the party's origins in the formation of the Independent Labour Party in 1893] when he said that the movement would not rest until "the sunshine of Socialism and human freedom break forth upon our land."'[116] Delivering the annual Keir Hardie Memorial Lecture in the Cynon Valley in March 2016, Corbyn reiterated his belief that Hardie's life and actions should provide inspiration and shape the party's current trajectory.[117] Corbyn's constant references to Hardie have not gone unnoticed by commentators. In December 2015, an article for the *Big Issue* declared that 'Thanks to Corbynmania, Hardie hasn't been this hot – nor has Labour ruffled this many feathers – since the start of the last century.'[118] The party's current leader has also referred to other figures from Labour's industrial past. Specifically, Corbyn has evoked Nye Bevan's memory in order to urge people to stand up for the National Health Service.[119]

In a similar manner, the economic analysis that has been offered by John McDonnell – Corbyn's main political ally and Labour's Shadow Chancellor – has routinely been historically orientated. Talking to the Co-operative Conference in January 2016, McDonnell noted that any understandings of the present and future should be rooted in the past: 'We learn from the past. As anti-fascist writer Carlo Levi put it, the future has an ancient heart.' He outlined how the labour movement's 'radical tradition has deep roots in our collective history. From RH Tawney, GDH Cole and the guild socialists, back to the Rochdale Pioneers, the Society of Weavers in Fenwick, Ayrshire, and even further back to the radicals of the English Civil War.' Moreover, McDonnell argued that this tradition had shaped Bevan's views on the Welfare State and could provide economic guidance in the present.[120] At the 'New Economy' conference in May 2016, McDonnell restated his belief that historical examples of 'grassroots ownership' could illuminate the way forward for the British economy and he reemphasised how (this time without any reference to Levi) the 'future has an ancient heart'.[121]

Increasingly, the party's interactions and communications with its membership have been characterised by nostalgia. In April 2015, in what seemed like an attempt to capitalise financially on the party's historical attachments, three consecutive emails were sent from Labour's headquarters to members selling postcards with 'vintage designs and iconic quotes' that included retro images of historic Labour campaign posters and pictures of Nye Bevan. Blurring the past and the present, one postcard appeared to state the post-1995 wording of Clause IV of the party's constitution in an old-fashioned typeface.[122] On this occasion, Labour's strategy seems to have worked: the third and final communication stated that 'We can't believe how many of you have donated to snap up our amazing sets of postcards. It looks like we'll be sending thousands of our vintage designs and iconic quotes out next week!'[123]

Throughout Jeremy Corbyn's tenure as party leader, Labour has been defined by factionalism, dissent and divisions. During the parliamentary debate on airstrikes in Syria, Hilary Benn MP (Shadow Foreign Secretary) martialled support against his leader's position of non-interventionism with a highly regarded speech that cited Labour's historic role in fighting Fascism and the way in which 'socialists, trade unionists and others joined the International Brigade in the 1930s to fight against Franco.'[124] Interestingly, the issue on which the party has appeared to have been the most united has been the future of the British steel industry. As we have seen in previous chapters, this particular industry has, historically, been central to Labour's traditional industrial nostalgia-identity. In March 2016, faced with the potential closure of the Tata steel works in Port Talbot, an email was sent out to party members requesting that they sign a petition for the recall of Parliament.[125] Writing in the *Daily Telegraph*, Tim Stanley questioned why job losses in the steel industry merited a petition when Labour had, in the past, been quiet about closures in other employment sectors. Stanley noted that 'Perhaps the answer is nostalgia, that heavy industry reminds us of when Britain was the "workshop of the world". A period dominated by the Left's leadership of the working-class, Labour can't shake off good memories of that time, and this week has reasserted its claim to be the authentic voice of men and women who work with their hands.'[126]

The challenge to Corbyn's leadership

In a referendum on 23 June 2016, Britain voted to leave the European Union. This decision amplified pre-existing tensions and divisions within the party. Corbyn's opponents believed that he lacked leadership skills and that he had not argued either convincingly or effectively for Britain to stay in the EU.[127] On the day after the referendum, in an attempt to maintain party unity, Corbyn sent an email to party members that declared that 'Labour was created to serve people in their communities and workplaces. We need to put that historic purpose into action now and campaign and protect the people we serve.'[128] Evidently, this request was superseded by events.

Following some internal manoeuvrings against the party's leader, Hilary Benn was sacked from his role as Shadow Foreign Secretary. Mass resignations from the Shadow Cabinet followed. Pressure was put on Corbyn to resign and a successful vote of no confidence was held at a meeting of the PLP on 27 June 2016. Outside the PLP meeting, a rally in support of Corbyn contained overtly nostalgic dimensions: one speaker reportedly advocated renationalising Britain's non-existent coal mines.[129] Historically orientated rhetoric was also directed at Corbyn by his opponents. Following his refusal to resign as Labour Leader, Chris Bryant MP compared Corbyn to Ramsay MacDonald.[130] In response to his detractors, Corbyn sent out an email to party members that proclaimed 'United we stand, divided we fall is one of the oldest and truest slogans of the Labour movement.'[131]

In a rambunctious speech to the PLP, Neil Kinnock attempted to portray Corbynism and, in particular, the conflict between Corbyn's extra-parliamentary support and the parliamentary party as alien to Labour's traditions and heritage. Kinnock proclaimed that 'In 1906 and then in the constitution of 1918, in Clause I they lay down that it would be the purpose of the Labour party to establish and retain in parliament and in the country a political Labour party.'[132] On 11 July 2016, a leadership contest was formally triggered by Angela Eagle. She attempted to position herself as the candidate who was 'rooted in and proud of our party' and she described how 'Labour was founded to be the voice of working people in Parliament. We have never just been a parliamentary party or just a movement.'[133]

A debate ensued about whether or not, as party leader, Corbyn should automatically make the ballot paper without accruing nominations. Len McCluskey (General Secretary of the Unite union) argued that excluding Corbyn from the ballot paper would be 'alien to the traditions of the Labour party.'[134] In the event, the NEC voted that Corbyn did not need to gather nominations. Having also announced his intention to run for leader, Owen Smith MP became the rebels' 'unity candidate' to take on Corbyn after he gained more nominations than Eagle. The same day, Red Labour's Facebook site posted an image of Corbyn and a strikingly similar photograph of Keir Hardie alongside some text that stated 'Keir Hardie & Jeremy Corbyn: socialist, republican, Anti-war & internationalist: Real Labour Leaders.' The post read 'Not saying Jezza is the reincarnation of Keir Hardie, however, how else do you explain this ....'[135]

The 2016 Labour leadership contest

The second half of this chapter has outlined how much of Jeremy Corbyn's appeal has lain in his ability to articulate Labour's nostalgia and to locate himself within the party's nostalgically imbued identity. During the 2016 leadership contest, Corbyn exhibited little inclination to move away from the type of backward-looking emphasis that had previously characterised his time as party leader. His campaign launch echoed the language of William Beveridge's five 'giant evils' and the establishment of the post-war welfare state.[136] At the contest's final televised debate, in response to Smith's accusation that his view of politics was overly idealistic, Corbyn reminded both his audience and his challenger that Labour 'was created by brave people in order to bring about a fairer and more just society, and we have made great achievements.'[137] On another occasion, when addressing the issue of a potential party split, he paid a similar homage to the 'brave' pioneers who founded Labour.[138] In this context, his campaign communications that declared that 'Labour should always be the party that looks to the future' felt rather anomalous.[139] However, these interjections of modernity also reflected the security of Corbyn's status as a candidate who was in tune with Labour's past. Reflecting after Corbyn's victory in the 2016 contest, the journalist James Bloodworth described how the Labour leader's popularity remained 'bound up with all the worm-eaten and musty nostalgia floating around on the left'.[140] At around the same time, writing for *The Times*, Rachel Sylvester commented on 'how old-fashioned [Corbyn's] Labour now seems.'[141]

In many ways, the 2016 Labour leadership contest was defined by the unrelenting manner in which Owen Smith, the challenger, sought to exhibit his sensitivity towards the party's past. The strength of Labour's historical identity forced Smith to fight a leadership battle on Corbyn's nostalgic terrain. Smith's campaign communications and statements referred to the impact of the 1984–85 Miners' Strike on his formative years.[142] In an interview with the *Daily Record*, Smith described his upbringing as having been so steeped in Labour's traditions and heritage that he spent his early years believing that Keir Hardie and Nye Bevan were party of his family. During the same conversation, he stressed the continued relevance of Hardie's political ideas.[143] Similarly, at one of the contest's leadership hustings, Smith referred to the need to return to 'good old-fashioned socialist policies'.[144] Elsewhere, he promised to 'work tirelessly to deliver the proud traditions of our labour movement.'[145] Smith's campaign also released a nostalgically charged video that combined extracts from speeches by Nye Bevan, Clement Attlee and Barbara Castle with images of Britain's industrial past. In this video, Smith emerged, speaking firstly in black and white and then in colour, from the historical montage.[146]

During the contest, Smith and his allies regularly argued that Corbynism's perceived extra-parliamentary emphasis was anathema to Labour's history.[147] On other occasions, whilst attacking what he believed to be Corbyn's failure to offer effective leadership and direction, Smith praised his opponent for having 'reconnected our party with its radical principles'.[148] To this end, Smith's leadership bid appeared to be stuck between two conflicting and contradictory strategic positions. On the one hand, Smith attempted to portray Corbynism as alien to the party's parliamentary past. On the other hand, he seemed to acknowledge that Corbyn had successfully located his leadership within the parameters of Labour's historical identity. Ultimately, this approach might have had a degree of success in so far as it presented Smith as a candidate willing to engage with the party's history. Yet, at the same time, it also served to legitimise Corbynism's historical orientation. In such a nostalgically charged environment, Corbyn's second leadership election victory was all but assured.

Conclusion

Within the party, the years after Labour's return to opposition have heralded something akin to a nostalgic resurgence. Whereas nostalgia had previously been suppressed and pushed underground by New Labour, it now appears to be flourishing. All of the candidates who participated in the 2010 leadership election mobilised positively charged idealised memories of the past. This contest represented an important precursor to the overtly nostalgic period that would follow. Indeed, when compared to the anti-nostalgic rhetoric of the New Labour era, the period after 2010 has been characterised by elite political discourses that have routinely been much less hostile to the party's historical identity. These discourses have served to legitimise the type of nostalgia that exists amongst the party's rank-and-file members, but they have also been made possible and facilitated by the nostalgic impetus of the wider party. In this way, the nostalgic emphasis of party elites has been both the product and the cause of the continued significance of Labour's collective nostalgia-identity.

If Ed Miliband had a vision of a new radical agenda and of an approach to politics that responded to the economic and social concerns of a post-financial crash world, the party's members, on the whole, did not. During the period in which Miliband led the party, groups and movements that exhibited a sentimental attachment to the past grew in strength. Blue Labour, which was the most notable of these groups, even briefly endorsed the politics of nostalgia in an explicit and overt manner. Other groups, including the Red Labour movement that would go on to play an important role in the rise of Jeremy Corbyn, also achieved high levels of popularity by appealing to the party's historically informed understanding of itself.

Aided by new leadership election rules that placed more power in the hands of the party's members, Corbyn's ascension to Labour Leader should be viewed as less surprising than political commentators have suggested. During the 2015 Labour leadership contest, Corbyn's candidacy and the expressive manner in which he deployed and engaged with memories of a bygone era of industrial working-class struggle connected with Labour Party members at an emotional level. The other candidates were forced onto Corbyn's nostalgic terrain. In turn, a nostalgic climate was generated that served to benefit a candidate who seemed to be completely at ease with Labour's history and traditions. In a similar manner, the 2016 leadership election was an overtly backward-looking contest that legitimised the Labour leader's largely historically orientated approach to politics. 'Corbynism' does not signify a break with Labour's past; it represents a celebration of it. Its origins lie in the stability and continuities of the nostalgia that has shaped the party's identity throughout the post-war era. Underneath its shiny veneer of grassroots movements and social media campaigns, the 'new kind of politics' appears to be rather old.

Notes

1 E. Goes, *The Labour Party under Ed Miliband: Trying but Failing to Renew Social Democracy* (Manchester: Manchester University Press, 2016), 3.
2 T. Bale, *Five Year Mission: The Labour Party under Ed Miliband* (Oxford: Oxford University Press, 2015), 264.
3 The two exceptions are the articles upon which this chapter draws. R. Jobson and M. Wickham-Jones, 'Gripped by the Past: Nostalgia and the 2010 Labour Party Leadership Contest', *British Politics*, 5:2 (2010), 525–548; R. Jobson, 'Blue Labour and Nostalgia: The Politics of Tradition', *Renewal*, 22:1–2 (2014), 102–117.
4 See R. Seymour, *Corbyn: The Strange Rebirth of Radical Politics* (London: Verso, 2016), 2.
5 R. Prince, *Comrade Corbyn: A Very Unlikely Coup: How Jeremy Corbyn Stormed to the Labour Leadership* (London: Biteback, 2016), 354.
6 See I. Watson, *Five Million Conversations: How Labour Lost an Election and Rediscovered Its Roots* (Glasgow: Luath Press, 2015), 33–34.
7 Watson, *Five Million Conversations*, 35.

8   For example, see Prince, *Comrade Corbyn*, xiv.
9   See M. Hasan and J. Macintyre, *Ed: The Milibands and the Making of a Labour Leader* (London: Biteback, 2011), 191–232.
10 The Fabian Society, *The Labour Leadership* (London: The Fabian Society, 2010), 55–56, https://www.fabians.org.uk/publications/the-labour-leadership/.
11 E. Miliband, 'A Mandate for Change', Speech, 27 August 2010, *Labourlist*, http://labourlist.org/2010/08/a-mandate-for-change-ed-milibands-speech/.
12 D. Miliband, 'Keir Hardie Memorial Lecture', Mountain Ash, Cynon Valley, 9 July 2010, LabourList, http://labourlist.org/2010/07/david-milibands-keir-hardie-lecture-full-speech/.
13 A. Burnham, 'Letter to the Parliamentary Labour Party', 22 May 2010, http://labour-uncut.co.uk/2010/05/22/andy-burnhams-letter-to-the-parliamentary-labour-party/.
14 W. Straw, 'Balls Accuses Milibands of "Rerunning Debates of the Past"', *Left Foot Forward*, 26 August 2010. http://leftfootforward.org/2010/08/balls-accuses-milibands-of-rerunning-debates-of-the-past/.
15 K. McCrory, '"The Most Dangerous Thing is to Elect the Anointed Heir": The Diane Abbott interview', *LabourList*, 7 September 2010, http://labourlist.org/2010/09/the-most-dangerous-thing-is-to-elect-the-anointed-heir-the-diane-abbott-interview/.
16 E. Miliband, 'Why I'm Standing', Speech, Leeds, 10 June 2010.
17 E. Roy, 'Ed's Govan Moment', *NewsnetScotland*, 29 September 2010. http://newsnetscotland.com/speakers/706-eds-govan-moment.
18 M. Ferguson, '"Do We Have the Courage to Change?": The Ed Miliband interview', *LabourList*, 26 August 2010, http://labourlist.org/2010/08/do-we-have-the-courage-to-change-the-ed-miliband-interview/.
19 T. Adams, 'When Politics is in the Blood', *The Observer*, 5 October 2010, 8.
20 M. d'Ancona, 'His Brother's Jealousy Could Make a Leader of Miliband', *The Sunday Telegraph*, 29 August 2010, 18.
21 Miliband, 'Keir Hardie Memorial Lecture'.
22 D. Miliband, 'The Change Britain Needs – Full Speech', *LabourList*, 25 August 2010, http://labourlist.org/2010/08/david-miliband-the-change-britain-needs-full-speech/.
23 E. Balls, 'There is an Alternative – My Bloomberg Speech', 27 August 2010, www.edballs.co.uk/blog/speeches-articles/there-is-an-alternative-my-bloomberg-speech-august-2010/.
24 E. Balls, 'Defending Our Values, Fighting for Fairness', letter to Labour party members, 2010; E. Balls, 'Ed Balls for Leader', letter to Labour party members, 2010.
25 A. Burnham, 'Why I Can Reconnect Labour – Leadership 2010', email to Labour party members, 11 June 2010; A. Burnham, 'Leadership 2010', Uploaded by the Labour Party on 14 July 2010, www.youtube.com/watch?v=EHwaRjuz3DI.
26 B. Webb, 'Whither Labour's Working Class Heritage', *Tribune*, 7 August 2010, www.tribunemagazine.org/2010/08/working-class-labou/.

27 D. Abbott, 'The Big Society: A Big Con: Diane Abbott's full speech', Speech to Policy Exchange, *LabourList*, 2 September 2010, http://labourlist.org/2010/09/the-big-society-a-big-con-diane-abbotts-full-speech/.
28 For more on the rise of Blue Labour, see R. Davis, *Tangled Up in Blue: Blue Labour and the Struggle for Labour's Soul* (London: Ruskin, 2011).
29 D. Hodges, 'Exclusive: The End of Blue Labour', *New Statesman*, 20 July 2011, www.newstatesman.com/blogs/dan-hodges/2011/07/blue-labour-maurice-glasman.
30 R. Davis, 'What Became of Blue Labour?', *New Statesman*, 30 September 2012, www.newstatesman.com/blogs/politics/2012/09/what-became-blue-labour.
31 BBC Radio 4, 'Analysis: Blue Labour'. Broadcast between 20.30 and 21.00 on 21 March 2011.
32 M. Glasman, 'Labour as a Radical Tradition' in M. Glasman, J. Rutherford, M. Stears and S. White (eds), *The Labour Tradition and the Politics of Paradox* (The Oxford London Seminars: E-book, 2011), 19.
33 Glasman, 'Labour as a Radical Tradition', 29.
34 See O. Hatherley, *The Ministry of Nostalgia: Consuming Austerity* (London: Verso, 2016), 45–46.
35 J. Cruddas, 'Taking Back the Big Society', Aneurin Bevan Memorial Lecture, 19 October 2010, www.nyebevan.org.uk/bevan-lectures/jon-cruddas/.
36 J. Cruddas, 'Democracy of the Dead' in Glasman et al., *The Labour Tradition*, 142.
37 J. Rutherford, 'The Future is Conservative' in Glasman et al., *The Labour Tradition*, 88.
38 R. Tressell, *The Ragged-Trousered Philanthropists* (London: Grant Richards, 1918); J. Cruddas, 'LJMU Roscoe Lecture: Liverpool', *New Statesman*, 3 March 2011, www.newstatesman.com/2011/03/labour-book-noonan-tradition. This lecture was clearly inspired by Bonnett, *Left in the Past*.
39 Cruddas, 'LJMU Roscoe Lecture'.
40 M. Bunting, 'New Labour Insisted that the Past be Left Behind. What a Mistake that Was', *The Guardian*, 4 April 2011, 27.
41 M. Glasman, 'My Blue Labour Vision Can Defeat the Coalition', *The Observer*, 14 April 2011.
42 P. Wintour and A. Stratton, 'Blue Labour: A Vision of the Future, or In Thrall to the Past?', *The Guardian*, 22 April 2011, 21.
43 E. Miliband, 'Speech to Progress Conference', *LabourList*, 21 May 2011, http://labourlist.org/2011/05/ed-miliband-let-me-tell-you-today-how-we-are-going-to-win-the-next-election/.
44 B. Bragg, 'Labour is Already Too Blue', *The Guardian: Comment is Free*, 7 April 2011, www.guardian.co.uk/commentisfree/2011/apr/07/blue-labour-globalised-capitalism.
45 M. Hasan, 'Memo to Blue Labourites: Tone Down the Nostalgia', *New Statesman*, 20 April 2011, www.newstatesman.com/uk-politics/2011/04/blue-labour-party-glasman.
46 T. Rainsborough, 'Is Ed's Head Already on the Chopping Block?', *Tribune*, 23 May 2011, www.tribunemagazine.co.uk/2011/05/12336/.

47 D. Aaronovitch and J. Harding, 'Blue Labour? I'd be Worried about Nostalgia: The Party Wins at the Cutting Edge', *The Times*, 9 June 2011, 6–7.
48 M. Riddell, 'Labour Must Not be Airbrushed from History', *The Daily Telegraph*, 3 May 2011, 25.
49 R. Philpot, 'Introduction' in R. Philpot (ed.), *The Purple Book* (London: Biteback Publishing, 2011), 15.
50 Philpot, 'Introduction', 17.
51 L. Penny, 'Why Seek Power if You Have to Turn on Your Own to Get It?', *The Independent*, 21 July 2011, www.independent.co.uk/voices/commentators/laurie-penny-why-seek-power-if-you-have-to-turn-on-your-own-to-get-it-2318303.html.
52 G. Owen, 'Miliband's Policy Guru is Accused of Sexism', *The Daily Mail*, 26 June 2011.
53 I. Bartoletti, 'Sparring with Maurice Glasman', *Fabiana*, 1 (2011), 10, https://fabianwomensnetwork.files.wordpress.com/2013/03/fabiana-september-2011.pdf.
54 See M. Wickham-Jones, 'The Modernising Antecedents and Historical Origins of One Nation Labour', *The Political Quarterly*, 84:3 (2013), 321–329.
55 E. Miliband, 'Leader's Speech, Manchester 2012', www.britishpoliticalspeech.org/speech-archive.htm?speech=323.
56 P. Wintour, 'Ed Miliband Moves to Claim Disraeli's "One Nation" Mantle', *The Guardian*, 2 October 2012.
57 Miliband, 'Leader's Speech, Manchester 2012'.
58 E. Miliband, 'Rebuilding Britain with a One Nation Economy', Speech in Bedford, 14 February 2013, https://www.youtube.com/watch?v=hzXK4nRvbpY.
59 M. Ferguson, 'One Nation Labour? It's Blue Labour 2.0', *LabourList*, 3 October 2012, http://labourlist.org/2012/10/one-nation-labour-its-blue-labour-2-0/; C. Umunna, 'Left Foot Forward: my vision for One Nation Labour', www.chuka.org.uk/my_vision_for_one_nation_labour.
60 A. Giddens, 'The Future's European', *Progress*, 13 November 2013, www.progressonline.org.uk/2013/11/13/the-futures-european/.
61 O. Smith, 'Our Common Aim' in O. Smith and R. Reeves (eds), *One Nation: Power, Hope and Community* (London: One Nation Register E-book, 2013), 21–22.
62 K. Meagher, 'Keir Hardie and the Realist's Dilemma', *LabourList*, 15 August 2012, http://labourlist.org/2012/08/keir-hardie-and-the-realists-dilemma/.
63 C. Landin, 'A Powerful, Forward-Thinking Speech: But "One Nation"?', *Left Futures*, 2 October 2012, www.leftfutures.org/2012/10/a-forward-thinking-speech-but-%e2%80%98one-nation%e2%80%99/.
64 D. Pavett, 'One Nation: A Smokescreen or a Curb on the Power of Wealth', *Left Futures*, 18 February 2013, www.leftfutures.org/2013/02/one-nation-a-smokescreen-or-a-curb-on-the-power-of-wealth/. This article was quoting from T. Hunt, 'In Extreme Social Contexts it is Possible to be both Radical and Conservative' in J. Cruddas (ed.), *One Nation Labour – Debating the Future* (LabourList E-book, 2013), 9.
65 J. Haines, 'Brutal Questions Can't Be Dodged', *Tribune*, 21 September 2013, www.tribunemagazine.org/2013/09/brutal-question-cant-be-dodged/.

66 See The Trades Union Congress 'Ed Miliband Speech to Congress 2013', Speech, 10 September 2013, https://www.tuc.org.uk/about-tuc/congress/congress-2013/ed-miliband-speech-congress-2013.
67 The Citizen, 'Editorial', 5 December 2013, www.thecitizen.org.uk/2013/12/editorial-5/.
68 B. Sellers, 'Why We Need a Red Labour Alternative' *Left Futures*, 5 August 2013, www.leftfutures.org/2013/08/why-we-need-a-red-labour-alternative/.
69 B. Sellers. '#JezWeDid' in T. Unterrainer (ed.) *Corbyn's Campaign* (Spokesman: Nottingham, 2016), 29
70 Sellers, 'Why We Need a Red Labour Alternative'.
71 F. Nelson, 'Low-Rent Labour is Positioning Itself as the UKIP of the Left', *The Daily Telegraph*, 2 May 2014, 24.
72 C. Cadwalladr, 'How Passion Has Been Purged from Politics – Along with Ordinary People', *The Observer*, 28 September 2014, 16.
73 J. Gaffney and A. Lahel, 'The Morphology of the Labour Party's One Nation Narrative: Story Plot and Authorship', *The Political Quarterly*, 84:3 (2013), 339.
74 See A. Chakelian, 'So Long, Slogan: Whatever Happened to One Nation?', *New Statesman*, 23 September 2014, www.newstatesman.com/politics/2014/09/so-long-slogan-whatever-happened-one-nation.
75 The Labour Party, *Labour's Policy Review: One Nation Society* (London: The Labour Party, 2014), 5, www.yourbritain.org.uk/uploads/editor/files/SOCIETY_one_nation.pdf.
76 The Labour Party, *Labour's Policy Review: One Nation Economy* (London: The Labour Party, 2014), 5–6, www.yourbritain.org.uk/uploads/editor/files/ONE_NATION_ECONOMY.pdf.
77 The Labour Party, *One Nation: The Labour Party Membership Magazine* (London: The Labour Party, 2014).
78 See A. Gwynne, 'A One Nation Health Service Fit for the Twenty-First Century' in R. Blackman-Woods, D. Johnson and B. Keeley (eds), *One Nation Fizz* (Fiz Publications E-book, 2014), 20–21, www.yourbritain.org.uk/uploads/editor/files/One_Nation_Fizz.pdf.
79 J. Cruddas and J. Rutherford, *One Nation: Labour's Political Renewal* (One Nation Register E-book, 2014), 30, http://joncruddas.org.uk/sites/joncruddas.org.uk/files/OneNation%20by%20Jon.pdf. The backward-looking nature of this report and other texts that originated from Labour politicians at roughly the same time were highlighted by Alan Finlayson in A. Finlayson, 'Labour's New Identity Politics', *Renewal*, 23:1/2 (2015), 141–151.
80 N. Forbes, 'Review: One Nation: Labour's Political Renewal by Jon Cruddas', *Left Foot Forward*, 11 September 2014, http://leftfootforward.org/2014/09/review-one-nation-labours-political-renewal-by-jon-cruddas/.
81 See R. Jobson and M. Wickham-Jones, 'Reinventing the Block Vote? Trade Unions and the 2010 Labour Party Leadership Election', *British Politics*, 6:3 (2011), 317–344.
82 R. Collins, *The Collins Review into Labour Party Reform* (London: The Labour Party, 2014).

83 Collins, *The Collins Review*, 12.
84 E. Miliband, 'Speech to Labour's Special Conference: Full Text', *New Statesman*, 1 March 2014, www.newstatesman.com/politics/2014/03/ed-milibands-speech-labours-special-conference-full-text.
85 Miliband, 'Speech to Labour's Special Conference'.
86 S. Carrell, 'Ed Miliband Arrives in Scotland to Rally No Voters for Referendum', *The Guardian*, 4 September 2014, www.theguardian.com/politics/2014/sep/04/ed-miliband-scotland-referendum-voters.
87 C. Green, 'Scottish Independence: Ed Miliband Fails to Impress the People of Labour-Founder Keir Hardie's Home Town', *The Independent*, 4 September 2014, www.independent.co.uk/news/uk/scottish-independence/scottish-independence-ed-miliband-fails-to-impress-the-people-of-labour-founder-keir-hardies-home-9712564.html.
88 B. Holman, 'Why Ed Miliband Should Learn the Lessons of Keir Hardie', *Herald Scotland*, 12 September 2014, www.heraldscotland.com/opinion/13179495.Bob_Holman__why_Ed_Miliband_should_learn_the_lessons_of_Keir_Hardie/.
89 See G. Brown, 'Better Together Speech', uploaded by *LabourList* on 17 September 2014, https://www.youtube.com/watch?v=J39bBV7CBJk.
90 K. Mudie, 'Gordon Brown Scottish Referendum Speech', *The Mirror*, 17 September 2014, www.mirror.co.uk/news/uk-news/gordon-brown-scottish-referendum-speech-4276089.
91 C. Green, 'Think of the Values Your Ancestors Fought For Before Abandoning Labour For the SNP, says Ed Miliband', *The Independent*, 30 April 2015, www.independent.co.uk/news/uk/politics/generalelection/general-election-2015-think-of-the-values-your-ancestors-fought-for-before-abandoning-labour-for-snp-10217263.html; S. Carrell and R. Mason, 'Ed Miliband to Summon up Ghosts of Labour's Past to Avoid SNP Rout', *The Guardian* 1 May 2015, www.theguardian.com/politics/2015/may/01/ed-miliband-summons-up-ghosts-of-labours-past-in-bid-to-avoid-rout-by-snp.
92 Green, 'Think of the Values Your Ancestors Fought For'; Carrell and Mason, 'Ed Miliband to Summon up Ghosts of Labour's Past'.
93 See J. Corbyn, 'Straight Talking, Honest Politics', campaign communication to Labour members, 2015.
94 H. Jacobson, 'Only the Foolish would Allow Themselves to be Swayed Solely by Jeremy Corbyn's Sincerity', *The Independent*, 15 August 2015, 39.
95 Editorial, 'Victory for the Left would be a Disaster', *The Daily Telegraph*, 22 August 2015, 23.
96 J. Corbyn, 'Building a Social Movement', speech at Nottingham on 28 June 2015, in Unterrainer (ed.), *Corbyn's Campaign*, 17.
97 J. Corbyn, 'End Austerity Now', speech in London on 20 June 2015. https://www.youtube.com/watch?v=DK36ps3L-aU
98 A. Rhodes, 'The "Unelectable" Elected Man' in Unterrainer (ed.), *Corbyn's Campaign*, 74.
99 Editorial, 'The Guardian View on the Labour Leadership', *The Guardian*, 27 July 2015.

100 S. Whale, 'Andy Burnham Speech in Manchester: Full Transcript', *PoliticsHome*, 17 August 2015, https://www.politicshome.com/news/uk/social-affairs/politics/news/61787/andy-burnham-speech-manchester.
101 A. Burnham, 'Be Part of the Change', campaign communication to Labour members, 2015.
102 Y. Cooper, 'I'm In It to Win It. The Labour Party Must be Too', *New Statesman*, 13 August 2015, www.newstatesman.com/politics/2015/08/yvette-coopers-manchester-speech-i-m-it-win-it-labour-party-must-be-too.
103 Y. Cooper, 'Yvette: Proud of Our Values: The Strength to Win', campaign communication to Labour members, 2015.
104 A. Burnham, Y. Cooper, J. Corbyn and L. Kendall, 'The Labour Leadership: Who'll Get Your Support?', *The Guardian*, 14 August 2015, https://www.theguardian.com/commentisfree/2015/aug/14/labour-leadership-vote.
105 D. Bloom, 'Labour Leadership Hustings Recap: Follow Updates as Four Candidates Clash in BBC Radio 5 Live Debate', *The Mirror*, 25 August 2015, www.mirror.co.uk/news/uk-news/labour-leadership-hustings-live-follow-6314152.
106 A. Johnson, 'Why Labour Should End the Madness and Elect Yvette Cooper', *The Guardian*, 4 August 2015, https://www.theguardian.com/commentisfree/2015/aug/04/labour-yvette-cooper-jeremy-corbyn-alan-johnson.
107 D. Pavett, 'On the Madness of Alan Johnson Invoking Keir Hardie to Attack Jeremy Corbyn', *Left Futures*, 5 August 2015, www.leftfutures.org/2015/08/on-the-madness-of-alan-johnson-invoking-keir-hardie-to-attack-jeremy-corbyn/.
108 M. Benn, 'Labour Should Ask Itself: What Would Keir Hardie Do?', *The Guardian*, 31st August 2015, www.theguardian.com/commentisfree/2015/aug/31/labour-party-keir-hardie.
109 For other examples, see P. Bryan (ed), *What Would Keir Hardie Say? Exploring Hardie's Vision and Relevance to 21st Century Politics* (Edinburgh: Luath Press, 2016).
110 L. Kendall, 'The Country Comes First', blog for Labour's website dated 19 June 2015, www.labour.org.uk/blog/entry/the-country-comes-first.
111 J. Smith, 'What the Labour Leadership Candidates Say on Macroeconomic Policy', *openDemocracy*, 26 August 2015, https://www.opendemocracy.net/ourkingdom/jeremy-smith/what-labour-leadership-candidates-say-on-macroeconomic-policy.
112 'Liz Kendall Announces Support for Creation of an English Labour Party', *LabourList*, 20 July 2015, http://labourlist.org/2015/07/liz-kendall-announces-support-for-creation-of-an-english-labour-party/.
113 See D. Williamson, 'Liz Kendall Vows to Fight to the "Very End" as She Warns a Corbyn Victory would be a "Disaster" not just for Labour but for Britain', *WalesOnline*, 13 August 2015, www.walesonline.co.uk/news/wales-news/liz-kendall-vows-fight-very-9849096.
114 R. Anjeh, 'Hardie's Inheritor', *Progress Online*, 19 August 2015, www.progressonline.org.uk/2015/08/19/hardies-inheritor/.
115 More policies appeared during his 2016 leadership campaign. See J. Corbyn, 'Winning Values', communication to Labour Party members (2016).

116　J. Corbyn, 'Speech to Scottish Labour Conference', 30 October 2015, http://jeremycorbyn.org.uk/articles/jeremy-corbyns-speech-to-scottish-labour-conference/.
117　J. Corbyn, 'Keir Hardie Memorial Lecture', 5 March 2015, http://jeremycorbyn.org.uk/articles/jeremy-corbyn-keir-hardie-memorial-lecture/.
118　'What Does Keir Hardie Think of Jeremy Corbyn? The Big Issue Finds Out', *The Big Issue*, 26 December 2015, www.bigissue.com/features/6084/what-does-keir-hardie-think-of-jeremy-corbyn-the-big-issue-finds-out.
119　See J. Corbyn, 'Speech to the Welsh Labour Conference', 20 February 2016, http://press.labour.org.uk/post/139654275374/jeremy-corbyns-speech-to-the-welsh-labour.
120　J. McDonnell, 'Speech to the Co-operative Conference', 21 January 2016, http://press.labour.org.uk/post/137744360189/john-mcdonnell-speech-to-the-co-operative.
121　J. McDonnell, 'Speech to the New Economy conference', 21 May 2015, http://press.labour.org.uk/post/144695186849/shadow-chancellor-john-mcdonnell-mps-speech-to.
122　The Labour Party, 'Our Vintage Designs and Iconic Quotes', email to party members, 4 April 2016.
123　The Labour Party, 'Did You Get These Limited Edition Prints Yet?', email to party members, 8 April 2016.
124　H. Benn, 'Speech on Syria Air Strikes', House of Commons, 2 December 2015, www.hilarybennmp.com/hilary_s_speech_on_syria_air_strikes.
125　See J. Corbyn, 'David Cameron's Failed Leadership on Steel', email to party members, 30 March 2016.
126　T. Stanley, 'Labour is a Useless, Fair Weather Friend of the Industrial Working Class', *The Daily Telegraph*, 1 April 2016.
127　See A. McSmith, 'Hilary Benn: Jeremy Corbyn "Is a Good and Decent Man, But he is Not a Leader', *The Independent*, 26 June 2016, www.independent.co.uk/news/uk/politics/hilary-benn-jeremy-corbyn-labour-leadership-brexit-eu-referendum-latest-news-shadow-cabinet-a7104031.html.
128　J. Corbyn, 'Yesterday's European Referendum', email to party members, 24 June 2016.
129　N. Woolf, C. Phipps, A. Sparrow and M. Weaver, 'Brexit: Labour MPs to Hold No-Confidence Vote in Jeremy Corbyn – As it Happened', *The Guardian*, 28 June 2015, www.theguardian.com/politics/live/2016/jun/27/brexit-live-george-osborne-economy-corbyn-shadow-cabinet.
130　C. Bryant, 'If Jeremy Corbyn Doesn't Resign Right Now, He'll Destroy Our Party. That's the Awful Truth', *The Daily Telegraph*, 28 June 2016, www.telegraph.co.uk/news/2016/06/28/if-jeremy-corbyn-doesnt-resign-right-now-hell-destroy-our-party/.
131　J. Corbyn, 'United We Stand', email to party members, 30 June 2016.
132　J. May, '"Remember History": Neil Kinnock's Speech to the PLP – Full Transcript and Recording', *PoliticsHome*, 8 July 2016, https://www.politicshome.com/news/uk/political-parties/labour-party/news/77082/remember-history-neil-kinnocks-speech-plp-full.

133 B. Riley Smith and M. Wilkinson, 'Labour "Could Lose 100 MPs" as Jeremy Corbyn Calls for a Snap General Election while Angela Eagle Launches Bid for Leadership', *The Daily Telegraph*, 11 July 2016, www.telegraph.co.uk/news/2016/07/11/angela-eagle-jeremy-corbyn-labour-leadership-theresa-may/.

134 P. Walker and R. Syal, 'Corbyn's Exclusion from Labour Leadership Vote would be "Sordid Fix"', *The Guardian*, 12 July 2016, www.theguardian.com/politics/2016/jul/12/labour-leadership-vote-without-jeremy-corbyn-would-be-sordid-fix.

135 Red Labour, post on Facebook dated 19 July 2016, https://www.facebook.com/RedLabour2016/.

136 Editorial, 'When Will Labour be a Decent Opposition?', *The Evening Standard*, 21 July 2016, 14.

137 J. Corbyn, 'The Battle for Labour', *Sky News*, broadcast on 14 September 2016.

138 Press Association, 'Jeremy Corbyn Urges MPs to Rethink "Bizarre" Attempts to Split Labour', *The Guardian*, 30 July 2016, https://www.theguardian.com/politics/2016/jul/30/owen-smith-should-condemn-attempts-to-split-labour-says-john-mcdonnell.

139 J. Corbyn, 'No Community Left Behind', email to Labour Party members, 1 August 2016.

140 J. Bloodworth, 'From Corbyn to Trump: Welcome to the Politics of Nostalgia', *International Business Times*, 26 September 2016, www.ibtimes.co.uk/corbyn-trump-welcome-politics-nostalgia-1583383.

141 R. Sylvester, 'Labour Remains Stuck as the World Moves On', *The* Times, 27 September 2016, 25.

142 For example, see The Labour Party, *Candidate Booklet: Candidates for Leader of the Labour Party* (London: The Labour Party, 2016), 8.

143 M. Aitken, '"Keir Hardie would be Spinning in his Grave": Labour Leadership Challenger Owen Smith Slams State of the Party', *Daily Record*, 24 July 2016, www.dailyrecord.co.uk/news/politics/keir-hardie-would-spinning-grave-8480934.

144 A. Ross and R. Mason, 'Jeremy Corbyn and Owen Smith Face Off in Tense Labour Leadership Hustings', *The Guardian*, 5 August 2016, https://www.theguardian.com/politics/2016/aug/04/corbyn-and-smith-face-off-in-tense-labour-leadership-hustings.

145 O. Smith, 'Our Greatest Achievements', email to Labour Party members, 29 August 2016.

146 Owen 2016, 'We Weren't Born with Liberty, We Had to Win It – Nye Bevan', uploaded on 29 August 2016, https://www.youtube.com/watch?v=1dMonAp1_yA.

147 For example, see J. Blanchard, 'Owen Smith Says Labour Should Consider Banning Pro-Corbyn Campaign Group "Momentum"', *The Mirror*, 16 September 2016, www.mirror.co.uk/news/uk-news/owen-smith-says-labour-should-8849208.

148 O. Smith, 'Labour's Future: Radical Politics', email to Labour Party members, 26 June 2016.

Conclusion

Labour's nostalgia has provided the emotional adhesive that has held the party together. Yet it has also served to constrain the party's political development and restrict Labour's ability to communicate effectively with the modern demands of British voters. Memories of Keir Hardie and an era of male traditional industrial working-class struggle might resonate within the party. Outside the confines of Labour's unique group identity, they are largely met with indifference. Given the continued strength of its historical attachments, there remains a possibility that Labour could follow in the footsteps of its 1970 to 1983 Alternative Economic Strategy and pursue programmatic commitments that are interpreted and pursued through the lens of the party's nostalgia. This would be a mistake. If the socioeconomic nature of Britain has changed significantly since 1983, it has altered immeasurably from the industrial vision of Britain that the party revered at this point in its development and which, even then, seemed to contemporary onlookers to be outdated and backward-looking.

This book has argued that New Labour's belief, albeit often ill-defined and lacking in analytical content, that the post-war party's trajectory had been shaped by nostalgia contained substantial merit. It did so regardless of the views that we might hold about the desirability or success of the remedies that were employed by New Labour in order to address this historically informed impetus. More broadly, throughout the entire period that this book has examined, nostalgia has been integral to Labour's shared understanding of the past. In turn, this collective nostalgic memory has sustained the party's distinctive identity. Despite the attempts of anti-nostalgic modernisers to reorient Labour away from the past, the contours of the party's nostalgia-identity have remained well-defined and the core mnemonic idealisations that have underpinned it have been characterised by uniformity, stability and coherence. Above all, Labour's nostalgia has revolved around positively charged memories of a late nineteenth and early twentieth-century male traditional industrial working class. The dominant historical narrative that has been associated with this particular social group has been one of strength and solidarity or 'heroism' in the face of adversity. Subsidiary and tangential memories (for example, memories of pre-industrial struggles) have often been reworked and reimagined in terms conducive to this nostalgia.[1]

Viewed in this way, Labour's nostalgia-identity has remained largely isolated from the wider external cultural forces (nostalgic or otherwise) that have shaped British politics.[2] Instead, the particular characteristics of the two-way relationship between nostalgia and identity that has defined Labour might be better understood as a product of the party's own parochial origins and early experiences. From the point of its foundation, Labour self-identified as (and primarily took the form of) a male industrial working-class party. Since 1951, the sustenance and preservation of this identity appears to have both driven and been informed by much of the nostalgia that this book has highlighted. In this sense, it is possible to interpret Labour's nostalgia as a species of 'Labourism'.[3] In itself, the name 'Labour' contains connotations of the party's founding moments and early political development. Psychologically, 'Labour' has remained a vessel for an emotionally charged conceptualisation of worthy, noble and heroic male manual work. It is highly significant that, during Labour's recent internecine struggles and disputes, there has been much discussion about which group, if the party splits, would get to retain the name.[4] It would seem that, in the event of such a fundamental rupture taking place, Labour's attachment to the past would be one notable survivor.

Throughout the post-war era, the party's historically inclined discursive emphasis has generated the mnemonic environment in which nostalgia has been able to flourish. Certainly, negative memories, particularly of the hardships of the 1930s, have coexisted and interacted with nostalgia; for example, Labour members have frequently expressed their fears of a 'return to the 1930s'. These fears have become heightened at times of economic crisis and dislocation. However, whilst negative memories of the hardships of the past have served to frame contemporary problems, nostalgia, often for the heroic traditional male industrial working-class struggles of the same era, has influenced the nature of the political solutions that have been pursued. Negative memories have defined the problem and positive idealised memories have provided the solution. In this way, nostalgia has dictated the way forward.

In a socioeconomic sense, Britain has changed dramatically since 1951. Whilst the number of workers employed in Britain's traditional industries has declined, there has been a simultaneous expansion of white-collar and service sector employment.[5] There has also been an important rise in the number of women in the British workforce.[6] Despite these changes, Labour has remained wedded to a political identity characterised by nostalgia for a bygone male-dominated industrial era. At times, Labour's emotional attachment to this particular vision of the past has left the party unable to engage with the changing nature of Britain in either a constructive or a rational manner. Increasingly, it has left the party out of sync with its surrounding social and economic environment.

When compared to its continental social democratic counterparts, Labour appears to have been less inclined to theoretical and ideational revision and more resistant to renewing itself in response to socioeconomic developments.[7] In a domestic political sense, Labour's nostalgic orientation has also, on significant occasions, allowed a party, with an explicit nominative aim to 'conserve' traditional values and an implied aversion to change, to present itself as more in tune with the modern concerns and demands of voters. The intriguing prospect arises that the British Conservative Party, comparatively unencumbered by such a specific and time limited socio-structural understanding, has been able to respond to the shifting desires of the electorate with greater efficiency and conviction than Labour.

Forgoing the nostalgic potentiality of any contemporary situation in which the party might find itself, Labour's AES represented the political zenith or apotheosis of the party's nostalgia. The AES had startlingly little to say about either women or the new white-collar occupations. Instead, it prioritised and focused on the male-dominated traditional industries of the past. These industries had been in terminal decline since 1951 and their economic significance had been greatly diminished by the 1970s. The AES talked to a vision of a traditional and industrial Britain that no longer existed. Nostalgia left the party out of touch with the modern world and directed Labour to its disastrous 1983 General Election defeat.

One particularly interesting aspect of Labour's nostalgia-identity is that it appears to have transcended social and gender differences within the party. During the post-war period, it is true that a number of the nostalgic deployments that I have discussed originated from men who worked in Britain's traditional industries. Understandably, these men were eager to return to an era in which their industries played a more substantive role at the heart of the British economy. They also understood that, in a party that identified emotionally with the traditional industries in which they worked, they could legitimise their arguments by referring to the history of their industries in an instrumental manner. Yet women and workers from white-collar industries have also been inclined to make spontaneous nostalgic references to the party's industrial past. The pervasiveness of this nostalgia has been indicative of the uniformity and coherence of Labour's nostalgia-identity. Moreover, it has highlighted the extent to which, within the party, Labour's nostalgia has operated as an omnipotent force that has crossed gender and socioeconomic boundaries.

Certain policies have gained a symbolic nostalgic significance that has far outweighed their contemporary political worth or merit. Indeed, Labour's nostalgia has often decisively shaped the way in which the party's programmatic commitments have been understood and pursued. In particular, Labour's attachment to Clause IV of its 1918 constitution was (and to a certain extent still remains) inseparable from the party's emotional conceptualisation of its past. To this end, Labour's programmatic commitments have not always been based upon ideological or theoretical reasoning. Rather, policies have often been formulated and supported in an overtly nostalgic manner. On occasions, as in the case of industrial democracy during the 1970s and early 1980s, the nostalgic understanding of the policy became inseparable from the policy itself: nostalgia became the policy.

In this book's introduction, I engaged with Svetlana Boym's conceptualisation of reflective and restorative nostalgia. Both of these types of nostalgia have impacted upon Labour's post-war development in different ways and at different stages. Reflective nostalgia can frustrate change and modernisation. It shapes the options that are available; for example, Gaitskell's attempts to reform Clause IV in 1959 and 1960 were obstructed by the party's poorly understood and ill-defined reflective nostalgic attachment to public ownership. Similarly, reflective nostalgia defined the parameters within which Harold Wilson's 1964 to 1970 Governments could operate and limited the extent to which a modernising agenda could be pursued. In both of these cases, this particular variant of nostalgia took the form of an active rather than a passive force. To this extent, Boym's concept of reflective nostalgia might be understood to be limited by the passivity and lack of agency that she assigned to it.[8]

At other stages in the party's post-war development, Labour has pursued an overtly restoratively nostalgic agenda. In particular, the party's AES quickly became interpreted as a means by which to restore a positively charged mnemonic understanding of Britain's past in the present. This strategy was understood as a means by which the male traditional industrial worker could be reinstated at the forefront of the British economy. In a way that was not directly envisaged by those who conceptualised the AES in the early 1970s, the policies that were contained within the strategy gained actively restorative qualities. To this extent, nostalgia was aided by the ambiguous and often contradictory approach towards Britain's traditional and industrial occupations that was contained within earlier versions of the strategy. As the 1970s progressed, rather than being understood as a modern and dynamic strategy for developing the economy of the future, the AES became reinterpreted as a mechanism by which to reinstate a particular vision of the past.

The deployment of nostalgia by Labour members has frequently been spontaneous, expressive and genuine. However, this book has also highlighted the significant role that instrumental nostalgia has played in the party's development. Senior party figures have deployed nostalgia in order to facilitate the obtainment of their objectives. To take one example, during the early period, the party's Croslandite/Gaitskellite revisionists seemed to channel the party's nostalgia in a manner that they hoped would enable them to achieve their modernising political goals. They displayed an awareness of the powerful (and often negative) grip that nostalgia had on the party. Yet, simultaneously, they also deployed the very same nostalgia to placate and persuade party members and to legitimise their own arguments. In adopting this kind of approach to the party's internal debates, Labour's post-war revisionists have not been alone. Even Tony Blair, the most ardent of Labour modernisers, appeared to recognise the potential political capital that lay in the party's nostalgia. Despite his anti-nostalgic proclamations, Blair, at the very least, seemed to exhibit an understanding of the way in which the past could be mobilised in order to legitimise and ease the political passage of certain changes and reforms.

Significantly, such instrumental deployments of the past appear to have had fairly limited success. Regardless of whether or not modernisers have attempted to couch their reforms within a historically orientated discourse, most attempts to reform and change the party have met with nostalgic resistance. Within the context of Labour's internal politics, it is worth highlighting the limitations of instrumental nostalgia. Nostalgic references might endear a speaker to the party, but this endearment will be, more often than not, cancelled out if the same speaker is perceived to be challenging something that is fundamental to Labour's core nostalgia-identity. Furthermore, for modernisers, these type of mobilisations of the past can have unintended and unwanted consequences. Specifically, the relationship between instrumental mnemonic deployments and the party's nostalgia-identity should be understood to be mutually reinforcing: the mobilisation of positively charged memories inadvertently serves to legitimise and bolster existing nostalgia. This cyclical process of nostalgic self-perpetuation has, in the past, helped to sustain Labour's historical impetus.

By highlighting the manner in which intraparty disputes have invariably followed the direct contestation and challenging of the party's nostalgia-identity, this book has placed the role that Labour's nostalgia has played in its internal politics in a somewhat complex and irreconcilable position. On the one hand, nostalgia has acted as a form of emotional glue that has held Labour's shared identification with the past together and has given the party its coherence and a sense of uniformity. On the other hand, nostalgia has been the source of many of the virulent and disruptive arguments and disputes that have threatened to tear the party apart. Labour's nostalgia has thus acted, simultaneously, as both a constructive and destructive force within the party.

Ultimately, regardless of the language that has been deployed or the approach that has been taken, it has been extremely hard for modernisers to overturn, contest or shape the contours of the party's attachment to the past. Labour's nostalgia needs to be seen as a significant and important factor that has shaped the party's trajectory precisely because it has been so resilient to a wide range of contestations and attacks. Whilst both Neil Kinnock and New Labour attempted, to varying degrees, to overturn the party's nostalgia, they were largely unable to do so. Important changes to Labour's programmatic commitments did not equate to wholesale reform of the party's identity. Moreover, given the weight of historical evidence to the contrary, we need to question the extent to which such a reorientation away from nostalgia might even be possible. Without replacing Labour's existing attachment to the past with an emotionally charged equivalent, it is likely that the disintegration of the mnemonic bonds that have held the party together would lead to the party becoming even more fractious and divided than is currently the case.

It is also necessary to pose the counter-question 'What might a non-nostalgic and modern social democratic party look like?' Here, there is no single answer that it is either totally satisfactory or complete. Modernity can take a variety of forms. Wilson's vision of the scientific and technological revolution was, in many ways, as forward-looking and forward-thinking as Blair's New Labour project. Even the manner in which Holland's initial vision of the AES (not the party's subsequent interpretation of the strategy as a mechanism for preservation and restoration) engaged with the challenges of a new globalised economic environment contained elements of modernity that might have functioned as a useful guideline for programmatic renewal.

In a non-nostalgic party, the past would be engaged with in a manner that would exhibit a wariness of historical complexity, contradictions, tensions and paradoxes. There would be no sense that this party was reliant on the type of over-simplified and often idealised historical narrative that has shaped Labour's political development. Furthermore, this party would be characterised by a greater awareness of the problematic nature of directly applying mnemonic images and narratives to current events and situations. The analytical starting point would frequently be the dissimilarities, rather than the similarities, that exist between the past and the present. More generally, in order to achieve its social democratic goals, a thoroughly modern party would be able to disentangle its emotional attachments and commitments to the past from its response to current realities.

In many ways, the mid-to-late Kinnock era represented the point at which the party's leadership pursued the most forward-looking agenda that has been adopted since 1951. Aided by a lengthy period in opposition, the policy discussions that occurred at this stage in Labour's political development were far more complex, complete and modern in orientation than most academic studies of the period have suggested. The policies that emerged from the 1986 Jobs and Industry campaign and the post-1987 policy review were preoccupied with future social and economic changes. They were intended to shape the Britain of the 1990s and beyond in a manner that was conducive to the obtainment of social democratic objectives. In this respect, Kinnock's team offered a vision of the future that was perhaps even more forward-looking (and, in some ways, less reactive) than the New Labour era that followed. Yet this historical example should only be used to generate a sense of the type of temporal policy orientation and process that might be beneficial to the contemporary Labour Party. If they were to be applied today, the programmatic structures and commitments devised in the mid to late 1980s would almost certainly find themselves out of sync with the modern world.

In the Brexit era, there remains a strong possibility that Labour either measures voters in its traditional heartlands against an unobtainable ideal drawn from the past or attempts to reimagine the needs and aspirations of these people in line with a self-comforting and illusory societal vision informed by outdated mnemonic attachments. More broadly, a continued nostalgic trajectory is likely to neglect and repel the vast swathes of the electorate for whom Labour's core historical identity engenders no more of an emotional connection than a sepia-tinted photograph of unfamiliar faces in a time long forgotten. If Labour has reached the point at which it is either unwilling or unable to reform or suppress a nostalgically imbued identity that has held less and less political purchase, then, consigned to a period in which its attachment to an era of male traditional industrial working-class struggle might have contained a functional (albeit rapidly decreasing) value, the party could potentially become a historical aberration. Imprisoned by a particular vision of the past, Labour could find itself outmoded as the British political system readjusts to contemporary developments and realignments.

Regardless of the nature of the political programme that is pursued, without a potentially destructive overhaul of the party's collective nostalgia-identity, tensions between Labour's past and future will continue. In the absence of any new and distinctive social democratic political formation with a significantly different understanding of itself and its political role, nostalgia is here to stay. Therefore, we are left with something akin to a double paradox. Nostalgia has been a positive force that has given Labour its coherence and mobilised party members. Yet, as socioeconomic changes have served to open up a gap between the idealised past and present realities, nostalgia has also been a negative force that has served to alienate potential voters. This fundamental tension shows no sign of abating. Furthermore, the continued nostalgic dimensions of Labour Party politics mean that any aspiring leader or political figure who wishes to gain influence and status within the modern party must establish an empathetic relationship with its historically defined emotional identity. Paradoxically, any politician who seeks to reorient Labour towards the future must, firstly, engage with the significant relationship that the party holds with its past.

Notes

1 For a study of how memories of the heroic struggles of rural workers were shaped by the industrial based inter-war labour movement in Britain, see Griffiths, 'Remembering Tolpuddle', 145–169.
2 For a different perspective that highlights how nostalgia is a broader cultural feature of British politics, see Robinson, *History, Heritage and Tradition*.
3 For more on 'Labourism', see Foote, *Labour Party's Political Thought*, 6–8; Miliband, *Parliamentary Socialism*, 272–349; T. Nairn, 'The Nature of the Labour Party' in P. Anderson and R. Blackburn (eds), *Towards Socialism* (London: The Fontana Library, 1965), 159–217; Marquand, *Progressive Dilemma*, 17. Elsewhere, Steven Fielding has challenged 'those accounts of Labourism which have emphasized its social foundations': S. Fielding, 'Labourism in the 1940s', *Twentieth Century British History*, 3:2 (1992), 153.
4 See H. Stewart, '"Saving Labour": Anti-Corbyn MPs Investigate Party Name Ownership', *The Guardian*, 29 June 2016, www.theguardian.com/politics/2016/jun/29/anti-corbyn-labour-mps-plan-breakaway-group-in-parliament.

5 As well as the texts cited in earlier chapters, see S. N. Broadberry, *The Productivity Race: British Manufacturing in International Perspective, 1850–1990* (Cambridge: Cambridge University Press, 1997), 64; For a discussion of the surges in the growth of the service sector after 1945, see R. Millward, 'The Rise of the Service Economy' in R. Floud and P. Johnson (eds), *The Cambridge Economic History of Modern Britain: Volume 3, Structural Change and Growth, 1939–2000* (Cambridge: Cambridge University Press, 2004), 265.
6 See also A. Cairncross, *The British Economy since 1945: Economic Policy and Performance, 1945–90* (Oxford: Blackwell, 1992), 299.
7 There is clearly scope for more comparative research into the influence of nostalgia on other social democratic parties. Mark Wickham-Jones has argued that between 1951 and 1964, when compared to the Swedish Social Democratic Party, Labour lacked political imagination and was characterised by insularity: M. Wickham-Jones, 'Missed Opportunities: British Social Democracy and the Rehn Model, 1951–1964' in H. Milner and E. Wadensjö (eds), *Gösta Rehn, the Swedish Model and Labour Market Politics* (Aldershot: Ashgate, 2001), 277–296. It is significant that, around the same time that Gaitskell unsuccessfully attempted to revise Clause IV of Labour's constitution, the Social Democratic Party of Germany adopted its Godesberg programme. Stefan Berger has stressed the similarities between the political development of Labour and its Western European equivalents. In particular, see S. Berger, *The British Labour Party and German Social Democrats, 1900–1931* (Oxford: Clarendon Press, 1994). However, despite questioning the longer-term significance of Gaitskell's Clause IV defeat, Berger has noted that 'in contrast to the German SPD, Gaitskell was not successful in abandoning key symbolic features connected to the old class party, notably Clause IV. Such failure had much to do with the Gaitskellites' complete disregard for the party's sense of tradition and history': S. Berger, 'Labour in Comparative Perspective' in Tanner, Thane and Tiratsoo (eds), *Labour's First Century*, 325–326.
8 However, her study still offers an important conceptual exploration of nostalgia. See Boym, *Future of Nostalgia*.

Select bibliography

Archives:

The Churchill Archives Centre, University of Cambridge
Neil Kinnock Papers

Labour History Archive and Study Centre, Manchester
The Labour Party National Executive Committee Minutes and Papers
The Labour Party Clause IV Consultation

The London School of Economics
Charles Anthony Raven Crosland Papers
Andrew Faulds Papers
Hector Alastair Hetherington Papers
Stanley Orme Papers
Peter Shore Papers

The Modern Records Centre, University of Warwick
Coventry Borough Labour Party Records
Frank Cousins Papers
Richard Crossman Papers
Geoffrey Goodman Papers
Socialist Vanguard/Socialist Commentary: Correspondence and Papers

University College London
Hugh Gaitskell Papers

Newspapers and periodicals (excluding internet sources):

Chartist
The Daily Mail
The Economist
Fabian Journal
Forward

The Guardian (Formerly *The Manchester Guardian*)
The Independent
Inside: The New Labour Magazine
Labour Briefing
Labour Party News
Labour Weekly
Marxism Today
New Left Review
New Statesman
New Socialist
The Observer
The Scotsman
Socialist Campaign Group News
Socialist Commentary
Socialist Organiser
The Sunday Telegraph
The Sunday Times
The Times
Tribune
Workers' Control Bulletin

Publications:

Abrams, M., Hinden, R. and Rose, R., *Must Labour Lose?* (Harmondsworth: Penguin, 1960).

Atkinson, M., *Our Master's Voices: The Language and Body Language of Politics* (London: Methuen, 1984).

Bale, T., *Five Year Mission: The Labour Party under Ed Miliband* (Oxford: Oxford University Press, 2015).

Bazen, S. and Thirlwall, T., *UK Industrialisation and Deindustrialisation* (Oxford: Heinemann, 1997).

Bealey, F., Blondel, J. and McCann, W., *Constituency Politics: A Study of Newcastle-under-Lyme* (London: Faber and Faber, 1965).

Beer, S., *Modern British Politics: Parties and Pressure Groups in the Collectivist Age* (London: Faber, 1982).

Bell, P., *The Labour Party in Opposition, 1970–1974* (London: Routledge, 2004).

Benn, C., *Keir Hardie* (London: Hutchinson, 1992).

Benn, T., *Speeches* (Nottingham: Spokesman Books, 1974).

Benn, T. (Mullin, C. ed.), *Arguments for Socialism* (London: Cape, 1979).

Benn, T. (Mullin, C. ed.), *Arguments for Democracy* (London: Cape, 1981).

Benn, T. (Winstone, R. ed.), *Office Without Power: Diaries 1968–72* (London: Arrow, 1988).

Benn, T. (Winstone, R. ed.), *The End of an Era: Diaries 1980–90* (London: Hutchinson, 1992).

Benn, T. (Winstone, R. ed.), *Free at Last: Diaries, 1991–2001* (London: Arrow Books, 2003).

Benn, T. (Winstone, R. ed.), *More Time for Politics: Diaries 2001–2007* (London: Arrow Books, 2008).

Benn, T. (Winstone, R. ed.), *A Blaze of Autumn Sunshine: The Last Diaries* (London: Arrow Books, 2014).

Benney, M., Gray, A. P. and Pear, R. H., *How People Vote: A Study of Electoral Behaviour in Greenwich* (London: Routledge and Kegan Paul, 1956).

Berger, S., *The British Labour Party and German Social Democrats, 1900–1931* (Oxford: Clarendon Press, 1994).

Berger, S., 'Labour in Comparative Perspective' in D. Tanner, P. Thane and N. Tiratsoo (eds), *Labour's First Century* (Cambridge: Cambridge University Press, 2000), 309–340.

Bevan, A., *In Place of Fear* (London: Heinemann, 1952).

Birch, A. H., *Small-Town Politics* (Oxford: Oxford University Press, 1959).

Black, L., *The Political Culture of the Left in Affluent Britain, 1951–64: Old Labour, New Britain* (Basingstoke: Palgrave, 2003).

Blackaby, F. T., 'Narrative, 1960–74' in F. T. Blackaby (ed.), *British Economic Policy 1960–74* (Cambridge: Cambridge University Press, 1978), 11–76.

Blackman-Woods, R., Johnson, D. and Keeley, B. (eds), *One Nation Fizz* (Fizz Publications E-book, 2014).

Blair, T., *Socialism*, Fabian Pamphlet 565 (London: Fabian Society, 1994).

Blair, T., *Let Us Face the Future – The 1945 Anniversary Lecture*, Fabian Pamphlet 571 (London: The Fabian Society, 1995).

Blair, T., *New Britain: My Vision of a Young Country* (Boulder, CO: Westview Press, 1997).

Blair, T., *A Journey* (London: Arrow Books, 2011).

Bodington, S., Eaton, J., Barratt-Brown, M. and Coates, K., *An Alternative Strategy for the Labour Movement* (Nottingham: Spokesman for the Institute of Workers' Control, 1975).

Bonnett, A., *Left in the Past: Radicalism and the Politics of Nostalgia* (London: Bloomsbury, 2010).

Booth, W. J., *Communities of Memory: On Witness, Identity, and Justice* (New York: Cornell University Press, 2006).

Boym, S., *The Future of Nostalgia* (New York: Basic Books, 2001).

Brivati, B. and Heffernan, R. (eds), *The Labour Party: A Centenary History* (Basingstoke: MacMillan, 2000).

Broadberry, S. N., *The Productivity Race: British Manufacturing in International Perspective, 1850–1990* (Cambridge: Cambridge University Press, 1997).

Brown, G., *In My Way: The Political Memoirs of Lord George Brown* (London: Gollancz, 1971).

Bryan, P. (ed.), *What Would Keir Hardie Say? Exploring Hardie's Vision and Relevance to 21st Century Politics* (Edinburgh: Luath Press, 2016).

Butler, D. and King, A., *The British General Election of 1964* (London: Macmillan, 1965).

Butler, D. and Kavanagh, D., *The British General Election of 1983* (London: Macmillan, 1984).

Butler, D., *British General Elections since 1945* (Oxford: Blackwell, 1995).
Butler, D. and Butler, G., *Twentieth Century British Political Facts 1900–2000* (Basingstoke: Macmillan, 2000).
Cairncross, A., *The British Economy since 1945: Economic Policy and Performance, 1945–90* (Oxford: Blackwell, 1992).
Cairncross, A., *Managing the British Economy in the 1960s: A Treasury Perspective* (Basingstoke: Macmillan, 1996).
Calder, A., *The Myth of the Blitz* (London: Pimlico, 1992).
Campbell, A. and Stott, R. (eds), *The Blair Years: Extracts from the Alastair Campbell Diaries* (London: Hutchinson, 2007).
Castle, B., 'The Socialist Alternative' in The Fabian Society, *Fabian Journal*, 6 (London: The Fabian Society, 1952), 13–17.
Castle, B., *The Castle Diaries 1964–70* (London: Weidenfeld and Nicolson, 1984).
Castle, B., *Fighting all the Way* (London: Macmillan, 1993).
Coates, K. and Topham, T., *The New Unionism: The Case for Workers' Control* (Harmondsworth: Penguin Books, 1974).
Coates, K. and Topham, T., *The Shop Steward's Guide to the Bullock Report* (Nottingham: Spokesman Books, 1977).
Coates, K., *Common Ownership: Clause IV and the Labour Party* (Nottingham: Spokesman, 1995).
Collins, R., *The Collins Review into Labour Party Reform* (London: The Labour Party, 2014).
Connerton, P., *How Societies Remember* (Cambridge: Cambridge University Press, 1989).
Cooke, P., *Representing East Germany since Unification: From Colonization to Nostalgia* (Oxford: Berg, 2005).
Crafts, N. F. R., 'The British Economy' in F. Carnevali and J. M. Strange (eds), *Twentieth-Century Britain, Economic, Cultural and Social Change* (Harlow: Pearson Longman, 2007), 7–25.
Crick, M., *The March of Militant* (London: Faber, 1986).
Crines, A. S. and Hickson, K. (eds), *Harold Wilson: The Unprincipled Prime Minister? Reappraising Harold Wilson* (London: Biteback, 2016).
Crosland, C. A. R., 'The Transition from Capitalism' in R. H. S. Crossman (ed.), *New Fabian Essays* (London: Turnstile Press, 1952), 33–68.
Crosland, C. A. R., *The Future of Socialism* (London: Cape, 1956).
Crosland, C. A. R., *The Conservative Enemy: A Programme of Radical Reform for the 1960s* (London: Cape, 1962).
Cronin, J., *Labour and Society in Britain, 1918–1979* (London: Batsford, 1984).
Cronin, J., *New Labour's Pasts: The Labour Party and its Discontents* (Harlow: Pearson, Longman, 2004).
Crossman, R. H. S. (Howard, A. ed.), *The Crossman Diaries: Selections from the Diaries of a Cabinet Minister, 1964–1970* (London: Cape, 1979).
Crossman, R. H. S. (Morgan, J. ed.), *The Backbench Diaries of Richard Crossman* (London: H. Hamilton, 1981).

Cruddas, J. (ed.), *One Nation Labour – Debating the Future* (LabourList E-book, 2013).

Cruddas, J. and Rutherford, J., *One Nation: Labour's Political Renewal* (One Nation Register E-book, 2014).

Dalton, H. (Pimlott, B. ed.), *The Political Diaries of Hugh Dalton, 1914–18, 1945–60* (London: Cape, 1986).

Davis, R., *Tangled Up in Blue: Blue Labour and the Struggle for Labour's Soul* (London: Ruskin, 2011).

The Department of Economic Affairs, *The National Plan* (London: Her Majesty's Stationery Office, 1965).

The Department of Economic Affairs, *Working for Prosperity: The National Plan in Brief* (London: Her Majesty's Stationery Office, 1965).

Drucker, H. M., *Doctrine and Ethos in the Labour Party* (London: Allen and Unwin, 1979).

Fairclough, N., *New Labour, New Language?* (London: Routledge, 2000).

Fielding, S., 'Labourism in the 1940s', *Twentieth Century British History*, 3:2 (1992), 138–153.

Fielding, S., Thompson, P. and Tiratsoo, N., *'England Arise!' The Labour Party and Popular Politics in 1940s Britain* (Manchester: Manchester University Press, 1995).

Fielding, S., 'New Labour and the Past' in D. Tanner, P. Thane and N. Tiratsoo (eds), *Labour's First Century* (Cambridge: Cambridge University Press, 2000), 367–392.

Fielding, S., *The Labour Governments 1964–1970: Vol. 1, Labour and Cultural Change* (Manchester: Manchester University Press, 2003).

Finlayson, A., 'Labour's New Identity Politics', *Renewal*, 23:1/2 (2015), 141–151.

Foot, M., *Aneurin Bevan: A Biography, Volume 2, 1945–1960* (London: Davis-Poynter, 1973).

Foot, P., *The Politics of Harold Wilson* (Harmondsworth: Penguin, 1968).

Foote, G., *The Labour Party's Political Thought: A History* (Basingstoke: Macmillan, 1997).

Fraser, W. H., *A History of British Trade Unionism: 1700–1998* (London: Macmillan, 1998).

Fussell, P., *The Great War and Modern Memory* (London: Oxford University Press, 1975).

Gaffney, J. and Lahel, A., 'The Morphology of the Labour Party's One Nation Narrative: Story Plot and Authorship', *The Political Quarterly*, 84:3 (2013), 330–341.

Gallie, D., 'The Labour Force' in A. H. Halsey and J. Webb (eds), *Twentieth-Century British Social Trends* (Basingstoke: Macmillan, 2000), 281–323.

Ginzburg, C., '"Your Country Needs You": A Case Study in Political Iconography', *History Workshop Journal*, 52 (Autumn, 2001), 1–22.

Glasman, M., Rutherford, J., Stears, M. and White, S. (eds), *The Labour Tradition and the Politics of Paradox* (The Oxford London Seminars: E-book, 2011).

Goes, E., *The Labour Party under Ed Miliband: Trying but Failing to Renew Social Democracy* (Manchester: Manchester University Press, 2016).
Goodman, G., *The Awkward Warrior – Frank Cousins: His Life and Times* (London: Davis-Poynter, 1979).
Gormley, J., *Battered Cherub* (London: Hamish Hamilton, 1982).
Gould, P., *The Unfinished Revolution: How Modernisation Saved the Labour Party* (London: Little, Brown, 1998).
Goydor, M., *Socialism Tomorrow: Fresh Thinking for the Labour Party*, Young Fabian Pamphlet 49 (London: Fabian Society, 1979).
Griffiths, C., 'Remembering Tolpuddle: Rural History and Commemoration in the Inter-War Labour Movement', *History Workshop Journal*, 44 (1997), 144–169.
Hain, P., *Outside In* (London: Biteback, 2012).
Hasan, M. and Macintyre, J., *Ed: The Milibands and the Making of a Labour Leader* (London: Biteback, 2011).
Haseler, S., *The Gaitskellites: Revisionism in the British Labour Party, 1951–64* (London: Macmillan, 1969).
Haseler, S., *The Tragedy of Labour* (Oxford: Blackwell, 1980).
Hatfield, M., *The House the Left Built: Inside Labour Policy-Making, 1970–75* (London: Gollancz, 1978).
Hatherley, O. *The Ministry of Nostalgia: Consuming Austerity* (London: Verso, 2016).
Haworth, A. and Hayter, D. (eds), *Men Who Made Labour: The PLP of 1906 – The Personalities and the Politics* (London: Routledge, 2006).
Hay, C., *The Political Economy of New Labour: Labouring Under False Pretences* (Manchester: Manchester University Press, 1999).
Heath, A., Jowell, R. and Curtice, J., *How Britain Votes* (Oxford: Pergamon, 1985).
Heffer, E., *Labour's Future: Socialist or SDP Mark 2?* (London: Verso, 1986).
Heffernan, R. and Marqusee, M., *Defeat from the Jaws of Victory: Inside Kinnock's Labour Party* (London: Verso, 1992).
Heffernan, R., *New Labour and Thatcherism: Political Change in Britain* (Basingstoke: MacMillan, 2000).
Hennessy, P., *Never Again: Britain 1945–51* (London: Penguin, 2006).
Hindess, B., *The Decline of Working-Class Politics* (London: Granada, 1971).
Hirsch, M. and Spitzer, L., '"We Would Not Have Come Without You": Generations of Nostalgia' in K. Hodgkin and S. Radstone (eds), *Contested Pasts: The Politics of Memory* (London: Routledge, 2003), 79–96.
Hobsbawm, E., 'Introduction: Inventing Traditions' in E. Hobsbawm and T. Ranger (eds), *The Invention of Tradition* (Cambridge: Cambridge University Press, 1983), 1–14.
Hobsbawm, E., 'Mass-Producing Traditions: Europe, 1870–1914' in E. Hobsbawm and T. Ranger (eds), *The Invention of Tradition* (Cambridge: Cambridge University Press, 1983), 263–308.
Hodgkin, K. and Radstone, S., 'Introduction: Contested Pasts' in K. Hodgkin and S. Radstone (eds), *Contested Pasts: The Politics of Memory* (London: Routledge, 2003), 23–28.

Holland, S., *Strategy for Socialism: The Challenge of Labour's Programme* (Nottingham: Spokesman Books, 1975).
Holland, S., *The Socialist Challenge* (London: Quartet Books, 1975).
Holland, S., *Capital Versus the Regions* (London: Macmillan, 1976).
Holland, S., *The Regional Problem* (London: Macmillan, 1976).
Howell, S., *British Social Democracy: A Study in Development and Decay* (London: Croom Helm, 1976).
Jackson, B., *Equality and the British Left: A Study in Progressive Political Thought, 1900–64* (Manchester: Manchester University Press, 2007).
Jay, D., *Change and Fortune: A Political Record* (London: Hutchinson, 1980).
Jefferys, K., *The Attlee Governments, 1945–51* (Harlow: Longman, 1992).
Jenkins, M., *Bevanism: Labour's High Tide. The Cold War and the Democratic Mass Movement* (Nottingham: Spokesman, 1979).
Jobson, R. and Wickham-Jones, M., 'Gripped by the Past: Nostalgia and the 2010 Labour Party Leadership Contest', *British Politics*, 5:4 (December 2010), 525–548.
Jobson, R. and Wickham-Jones, M., 'Reinventing the Block Vote? Trade Unions and the 2010 Labour Party Leadership Election', *British Politics*, 6:3 (2011), 317–444.
Jobson, R., '"Waving the Banners of a Bygone Age", Nostalgia and Labour's Clause IV Controversy, 1959–60', *Contemporary British History*, 27:2 (2013), 123–144.
Jobson, R., 'Blue Labour and Nostalgia: The Politics of Tradition', *Renewal*, 22:1–2 (2014), 102–117.
Jobson, R., 'A New Hope for an Old Britain? Nostalgia and the British Labour Party's Alternative Economic Strategy, 1970–83', *The Journal of Policy History*, 27:4 (2015), 670–694.
Johnson, R., McLennan, G., Schwarz, B. and Sutton, D. (eds), *Making Histories: Studies in History-Writing and Politics* (London: Hutchinson in association with the Centre for Contemporary Cultural Studies, 1982).
Jones, J., *Union Man: The Autobiography of Jack Jones* (London: Collins, 1986).
Jones, T., 'Neil Kinnock's Socialist journey: From Clause Four to the Policy Review', *Contemporary Record*, 8:3 (1994), 567–588.
Jones, T., '"Taking Genesis out of the Bible": Hugh Gaitskell, Clause IV and Labour's Socialist Myth', *Contemporary British History*, 11:2 (1997), 1–23.
Kansteiner, W., 'Finding Meaning in Memory: A Methodological Critique of Collective Memory Studies', *History and Theory*, 41:2 (May, 2002), 179–197.
Kelly, J., *Ethical Socialism and the Trade Unions: Allan Flanders and British Industrial Relations Reform* (London: Routledge, 2010).
Kenny, M., *The First New Left: British Intellectuals after Stalin* (London: Lawrence and Wishart, 1995).
Kenny, M. and Smith, M. J., 'Discourses of Modernization: Gaitskell, Blair and the Reform of Clause IV', *British Elections and Parties Review*, 7:1 (1997), 110–126.
Kinnock, N., *The Future of Socialism*, Fabian Society 509 (London: Fabian Society, 1986).

Kinnock, N., *Making Our Way: Investing in Britain's Future* (Oxford; London: Basil Blackwell; Fabian Society, 1986).
Kinnock, N., 'Reforming the Labour Party 1983–92', *Contemporary Record*, 8:3 (1994), 535–554.
Klein, K. L., 'On the Emergence of Memory in Historical Discourse', *Representations*, 69, Special Issue: Grounds for Remembering (Winter, 2000), 127–150.
The Labour Party, *Constitution: Adopted at the London Conference, February 26, 1918, and Amended at Subsequent Conferences to October, 1924* (London: The Labour Party, 1925).
The Labour Party, *Report of the 50th Annual Conference held in Spa, Grand Hall, Scarborough, October 1st to October 3rd, 1951* (London: The Labour Party, 1951).
The Labour Party, *Report of the 51st Annual Conference held in Winter Gardens, Morecambe, September 29th to October 3rd, 1952* (London: The Labour Party, 1952).
The Labour Party, *Report of the 54th Annual Conference held in Winter Gardens, Margate, October 10th to October 14th, 1955* (London: The Labour Party, 1955).
The Labour Party, *Report of the 55th Annual Conference held in the Empress Ballroom, Winter Gardens, Blackpool, October 1st to October 5th, 1956* (London: The Labour Party, 1956).
The Labour Party, *Industry and Society: Labour's Policy on Future Public Ownership* (London: The Labour Party, 1957).
The Labour Party, *Report of the 56th Annual Conference held in the Sports Stadium, West Street, Brighton, September 30th to October 4th, 1957* (London: The Labour Party, 1957).
The Labour Party, *Report of the 58th Annual Conference held in the Opera House, Winter Gardens, Blackpool, November 28th and November 29th, 1959* (London: The Labour Party, 1959).
The Labour Party, *Report of the 59th Annual Conference held in the SPA Grand Hall, Scarborough, October 3rd to October 7th, 1960* (London: The Labour Party, 1960).
The Labour Party, *Signposts for the Sixties* (London: Labour Party, 1961).
The Labour Party, *Report of the 62nd Annual Conference held in the Spa, Grand Hall, Scarborough, September 30th to October 4th, 1963* (London: The Labour Party, 1963).
The Labour Party, *The New Britain* (London: The Labour Party, 1964).
The Labour Party, *Report of the 63rd Annual Conference held in the Sports Stadium, West Street, Brighton, December 12th and 13th, 1964* (London: The Labour Party, 1964).
The Labour Party, *Report of the 64th Annual Conference held in the Empress Ballroom, Winter Gardens, Blackpool, September 27th to October 1st, 1965* (London: The Labour Party, 1965).
The Labour Party, *Report of the 65th Annual Conference held in the Top Rank Entertainments Centre, Brighton, October 3rd to October 7th, 1966* (London: The Labour Party, 1966).

The Labour Party, *Report of the Sixty-Sixth Annual Conference of the Labour Party, Scarborough, 1967, October 2nd to 6th* (London: The Labour Party, 1967).
The Labour Party, *Report of the Sixty-Seventh Annual Conference of the Labour Party, Blackpool, 1968, September 30th to October 4th* (London: The Labour Party, 1968).
The Labour Party, *Report of the Sixty-Eighth Annual Conference of the Labour Party, Brighton, 1969, September 29th to October 3rd* (London: The Labour Party, 1969).
The Labour Party, *Report of the Seventieth Annual Conference of the Labour Party, Brighton, 1971, October 4th to 8th* (London: The Labour Party, 1971).
The Labour Party, *Report of the Seventy-First Annual Conference of the Labour Party, Blackpool, 1972, October 2nd to 6th* (London: The Labour Party, 1972).
The Labour Party, *Labour's Programme 1973* (London: The Labour Party, 1973).
The Labour Party, *Labour's Programme: Campaign Document 1974* (London: The Labour Party, 1974).
The Labour Party, *Let Us Work Together – Labour's Way Out of the Crisis* (London: The Labour Party, 1974).
The Labour Party, *The Archives of the British Labour Party, Series 1, National Executive Committee: Minutes of the Labour Representation Committee 1900–06 and the Labour Party since 1906, 1900–1967* (Brighton: Harvester Press, 1974–79).
The Labour Party, *Report of the Seventy-Fourth Annual Conference of the Labour Party, Blackpool, 1975, September 29th to October 3rd* (London: The Labour Party, 1975).
The Labour Party, *The Archives of the British Labour Party, Series 2, Pamphlets and Leaflets of the Labour Representation Committee 1900–06 and the Labour Party since 1906, 1900–1969* (Brighton: Harvester Press, 1976–83).
The Labour Party, *Report of the Seventy-Sixth Annual Conference of the Labour Party, Brighton, 1977, October 3rd to 7th* (London: The Labour Party, 1977).
The Labour Party, *Labour's Draft Manifesto: Issued on the Authority of the National Executive Committee* (London: The Labour Party, 1980).
The Labour Party, *Report of the Annual Conference and Special Conference of the Labour Party 1980* (London: The Labour Party, 1980).
The Labour Party, *Labour's Programme 1982* (London: The Labour Party, 1982).
The Labour Party, *Report of the Annual Conference of the Labour Party 1982* (London: The Labour Party, 1982).
The Labour Party, *The New Hope for Britain: Labour's Manifesto 1983* (London: The Labour Party, 1983).
The Labour Party, *Report of the Annual Conference of the Labour Party 1983* (London: The Labour Party, 1983).
The Labour Party, *Report of the Annual Conference of the Labour Party 1984* (London: The Labour Party, 1984).

Select bibliography 203

The Labour Party, *Report of the Annual Conference of the Labour Party 1985* (London: The Labour Party, 1985).
The Labour Party, *Report of the Annual Conference of the Labour Party 1986* (London: The Labour Party, 1986).
The Labour Party, *The Future We Offer: Neil Kinnock's Speeches in the 1987 General Election* (London: The Labour Party, 1987).
The Labour Party, *Manifesto: Britain Will Win with Labour* (London: The Labour Party, 1987).
The Labour Party, *New Industrial Strength for Britain* (London: The Labour Party, 1987).
The Labour Party, *New Skills for Britain* (London: The Labour Party, 1987).
The Labour Party, *Report of the Eighty-Sixth Annual Conference of the Labour Party 1987* (London: The Labour Party, 1987).
The Labour Party, *Democratic and Socialist Aims and Values* (London: The Labour Party, 1988).
The Labour Party, *Report of the Eighty-Seventh Annual Conference of the Labour Party 1988* (London: The Labour Party, 1988).
The Labour Party, *Social Justice and Economic Efficiency: First Report of Labour's Policy Review for the 1990s* (London: The Labour Party, 1988).
The Labour Party, *Meet the Challenge, Make the Change: A New Agenda for Britain* (London: the Labour Party, 1989).
The Labour Party, *Report of the Eighty-Eighth Annual Conference of the Labour Party 1989* (London: The Labour Party, 1989).
The Labour Party, *Conference Report: Eighty-Ninth Annual Conference of the Labour Party* (London: The Labour party, 1990).
The Labour Party, *Looking to the Future: A Dynamic Economy, A Decent Society, Strong in Europe* (London: The Labour Party, 1990).
The Labour Party, *Building a World Class Economy: Modern Manufacturing Strength* (London: The Labour Party, 1991).
The Labour Party, *Conference Report: Ninetieth Annual Conference of the Labour Party* (London: The Labour Party, 1991).
The Labour Party, *Opportunity Britain: Labour's Better Way for the 1990s* (London: The Labour Party, 1991).
The Labour Party, *Conference Report: Ninety-First Annual Conference of the Labour Party* (London: The Labour Party, 1992).
The Labour Party, *Manifesto: It's Time to Get Britain Working Again* (London: The Labour Party, 1992).
The Labour Party, *British Labour Party Research Department Memoranda and Information Papers, 1941–1979* (Marlborough: Adam Matthew, 1993).
The Labour Party, *Conference Report: Ninety-Second Annual Conference of the Labour Party* (London: The Labour Party, 1993).
The Labour Party, *Conference Report: Ninety-Fourth Annual Conference of the Labour Party* (London: The Labour Party, 1995).
The Labour Party, *Report of Conference: Annual Conference 1994/Special Conference 1995* (London: The Labour Party, 1995).

The Labour Party, *New Labour, New Life for Britain* (London: The Labour Party, 1996).
The Labour Party, *The Labour Party Conference Verbatim Report 1997* (London: The Labour Party, 1997).
The Labour Party, *Manifesto: New Labour because Britain Deserves Better* (London: The Labour Party, 1997).
The Labour Party (S. Bird ed.), *The Archives of the British Labour Party, Pamphlets and Leaflets: Part 6: 1970–1979* (Reading: Primary Source Media, 1999).
The Labour Party, *Centennial Report 1999* (London: The Labour Party, 1999).
The Labour Party, *Verbatim Report of the Ninety-Eighth Conference of the Labour Party* (London: The Labour Party, 1999).
The Labour Party, *Conference 2000: The Magazine* (London: The Labour Party, 2000).
The Labour Party, *Verbatim Report of the One Hundredth Conference of the Labour Party* (London: The Labour Party, 2001).
The Labour Party, *Verbatim Report of the 102nd Conference of the Labour Party* (London: The Labour Party, 2003).
The Labour Party, *Verbatim Report 2004* (London: The Labour Party, 2004).
The Labour Party, *Labour's Policy Review: One Nation Society* (London: The Labour Party, 2014).
Labour's Policy Review: One Nation Economy (London: The Labour Party, 2014).
The Labour Party, *One Nation: The Labour Party Membership Magazine* (London: The Labour Party, 2014).
The Labour Party, *Candidate Booklet: Candidates for Leader of the Labour Party*(London: The Labour Party, 2016).
Lawrence, J., 'Labour – The Myths it has Lived By' in D. Tanner, P. Thane and N. Tiratsoo, *Labour's First Century* (Cambridge: Cambridge University Press, 2000), 341–366.
Lindsay, C., 'A Century of Market Change: An Overview of Labour Market Conditions in the Previous Century', *Labour Market Trends*, 111 (March, 2003), 133–144.
Lloyd, J., *Understanding the Miners' Strike*, Fabian Tract 504 (London: Fabian Society, 1985).
Lukes, S., *Power: A Radical View* (London: Macmillan, 1974).
Mandelson, P., *The Blair Revolution Revisited* (London: Politicos, 2002).
Mandelson, P., *The Third Man* (London: Harper Press, 2011).
McIroy, J., *Trade Unions in Britain Today* (Manchester: Manchester University Press, 1995).
McKenzie, R. T., *British Political Parties: The Distribution of Power within the Conservative and Labour Parties* (London: Heinemann, 1963).
McKibbin, R., *Parties and People: England 1914–1951* (Oxford: Oxford University Press, 2010).
Mikardo, I., *Back-Bencher* (London: Weidenfeld and Nicolson, 1988).

Miliband, R., *Parliamentary Socialism: A Study in the Politics of Labour* (London: Merlin Press, 1972).
Millward, R., 'The Rise of the Service Economy' in R. Floud and P. Johnson (eds), *The Cambridge Economic History of Modern Britain: Volume 3, Structural Change and Growth, 1939–2000* (Cambridge: Cambridge University Press, 2004), 238–266.
Milne, R. S. and Mackenzie, H. C., *Straight Fight: A Study of Voting Behaviour in the Constituency of Bristol North-East at the General Election of 1951* (London: The Hansard Society, 1954).
Minkin, L., *The Labour Party Conference: A Study in the Politics of Intra-party Democracy* (Manchester: Manchester University Press, 1980).
Minkin, L., *The Contentious Alliance: Trade Unions and the Labour Party* (Edinburgh: Edinburgh University Press, 1991).
Misztal, B. A., *Theories of Social Remembering* (Maidenhead: Open University Press, 2003).
Mitchell, A., 'Rebuilding the coalition', in The Fabian Society, *Labour's Next Moves Forward*, Fabian Tract 521 (London: Fabian Society, 1987), 24–28.
Morgan, K. O., *Labour in Power, 1945–1951* (Oxford: Clarendon Press, 1984).
Morgan, K. O., 'The Wilson Years' in N. Tiratsoo (ed.) *From Blitz to Blair: A New History of Britain since 1939* (London: Weidenfield and Nicolson, 1997), 132–162.
Mowlam, M., *Momentum: The Struggle for Peace, Politics and the People* (London: Hodder and Stoughton, 2002).
Mullin, C. (Winstone, R. ed.), *Decline and Fall: Diaries 2005–2010* (London: Profile Books, 2010).
Mullin, C. (Winstone, R. ed.), *A Walk on Part: Diaries 1994–1999* (London: Penguin Books, 2012).
Nairn, T., 'The Nature of the Labour Party' in P. Anderson and R. Blackburn (eds), *Towards Socialism* (London: The Fontana Library, 1965), 159–217.
Novick, P., *The Holocaust and Collective Memory: The American Experience* (London: Bloomsbury, 2000).
Nuttall, J., *Psychological Socialism: The Labour Party and Qualities of Mind and Character, 1931 to the Present* (Manchester: Manchester University Press, 2006).
O'Hara, G. and Parr, H. (eds), *The Wilson Governments 1964–1970 Reconsidered* (London: Routledge, 2006).
Panitch, L. and Leys, C., *The End of Parliamentary Socialism: From New Left to New Labour* (London: Verso, 1997).
Pearce, R., *Attlee's Labour Governments, 1945–51* (London: Routledge, 1994).
Pelling, H. and Reid, A. J., *A Short History of the Labour Party* (Basingstoke: Macmillan, 1996).
Phillips, M., *Labour in the Sixties* (London: Labour Party, 1960).
Philpot, R. (ed.), *The Purple Book* (London: Biteback Publishing, 2011).
Pimlott, B., *Harold Wilson* (London: Harper Collins, 1992).
Potter, D., *The Glittering Coffin* (London: Gollancz, 1960).

Powell, J., *The New Machiavelli: How to Wield Power in the Modern World* (London: Vintage Books, 2010).

Prescott, J. (with Davies, H.), *Prezza: My Story: Pulling No Punches* (London: Headline Publishing, 2008).

Prince, R., *Comrade Corbyn: A Very Unlikely Coup: How Jeremy Corbyn Stormed to the Labour Leadership* (London: Biteback, 2016).

Pugh, M., *Speak For Britain: A New History of the Labour Party* (London: The Bodley Head, 2010).

Radice, G., *Southern Discomfort*, Fabian Pamphlet 555 (London: The Fabian Society, 1992).

Randall, N., 'Time and British Politics: Memory, the Present and Teleology in the Politics of New Labour', *British Politics*, 4:2 (2009), 188–216.

Reid, A. J., *United We Stand: A History of Britain's Trade Unions* (London: Penguin, 2004)

Robinson, E., *History, Heritage, and Tradition in Contemporary British Politics: Past Politics and Present Histories* (Manchester: Manchester University Press, 2012).

Rosaldo, R., 'Imperialist Nostalgia', *Representations*, 26 (Spring, 1989), 107–122.

Samuel, R., *Theatres of Memory. Volume 1: Past and Present in Contemporary Culture* (London: Verso, 1994).

Santesso, A., *A Careful Longing: The Poetics and Problems of Nostalgia* (Newark: University of Delaware Press, 2006).

Seldon, A., *Blair* (London: The Free Press, 2005).

Seyd, P., *The Rise and Fall of the Labour Left* (Basingstoke: Macmillan, 1987).

Seyd, P. and Whiteley, P., *Labour's Grass Roots: The Politics of Party Membership* (Oxford: Clarendon Press, 1992).

Seymour, R., *Corbyn: The Strange Rebirth of Radical Politics* (London: Verso, 2016).

Shaw, E., *The Labour Party since 1945: Old Labour – New Labour* (Oxford: Blackwell, 1996).

Short, C., *An Honourable Deception? New Labour, Iraq and the Misuse of Power* (London: Free Press, 2004).

Short, E., *Whip to Wilson* (London: MacDonald, 1989).

Singleton, J., 'Labour, the Conservatives and Nationalisation' in R. Millward and J. Singleton (eds), *The Political Economy of Nationalisation in Britain, 1920–50* (Cambridge: Cambridge University Press, 1995), 13–36.

Smith, M. J., 'Neil Kinnock and the Modernisation of the Labour Party', *Contemporary Record*, 8:3 (1994), 555–566.

Smith, O. and Reeves, R. (eds), *One Nation: Power, Hope and Community* (London: One Nation Register E-book, 2013).

Socialist Union, *Twentieth Century Socialism: The Economy of Tomorrow* (Harmondsworth: Penguin, 1956).

Strangleman, T., 'The Nostalgia of Organisations and the Organisation of Nostalgia: Past and Present in the Contemporary Railway Industry', *Sociology*, 33:4 (November 1999), 725–746.

Straw, J., *Policy and Ideology* (Blackburn: Blackburn Labour Party, 1993).

Straw, J., *Last Man Standing* (London: Macmillan, 2012).
Tannock, S., 'Nostalgia Critique', *Cultural Studies*, 9:3 (1995), 453–464.
Thorpe, A., *A History of the British Labour Party* (Basingstoke: Macmillan, 1997).
Tiratsoo, N. (ed.), *The Attlee Years* (London: Pinter Publishers, 1991).
Tomlinson, J., *The Labour Governments 1964–70: Vol. 3, Economic Policy* (Manchester: Manchester University Press, 2004).
Topham, T. (ed.), *Report of the 5th National Conference on Workers' Control and Industrial Democracy held at Transport House, Coventry on June 10th and 11th, 1967* (Hull: The Centre for Socialist Education, 1967).
Toye, R., 'The Smallest Party in History? New Labour in Historical Perspective', *Labour History Review*, 69:1 (2004), 83–103.
The Trades Union Congress, *Report of Proceedings at the 92nd Annual Trades Union Congress held at the Villa Marina, Douglas, September 5th to 9th 1960* (London: TUC, 1960).
The Trades Union Congress, *TUC Report 1963, Report of the 95th Annual Trades Union Congress held in The Dome, Brighton, September 2nd to 6th 1963* (London: TUC, 1963).
The Trades Union Congress, *TUC Report 1964, Report of the 96th Annual Trades Union Congress held in the Opera House, Blackpool, September 7th to 11th 1964* (London: TUC, 1964).
The Trades Union Congress, *TUC Report 1965, Report of the 97th Annual Trades Union Congress held in The Dome, Brighton, September 6th to 10th 1965* (London: TUC, 1965).
The Trades Union Congress, *TUC Report 1966, Report of the 98th Annual Trades Union Congress held in the Opera House, Blackpool, September 5th to 9th 1966* (London: TUC, 1966).
The Trades Union Congress, *TUC Report 1967, Report of the 99th Annual Trades Union Congress held in The Dome, Brighton, September 4th to 8th 1967* (London: TUC, 1967).
The Trades Union Congress, *TUC Report 1968, Report of the 100th Annual Trades Union Congress held in the Opera House, Blackpool, September 2nd to 6th 1968* (London: TUC, 1968).
The Trades Union Congress, *TUC Report 1969, Report of the 101st Annual Trades Union Congress held in the Guildhall, Portsmouth, September 1st to 5th 1969* (London: TUC, 1969).
The Trades Union Congress, *TUC Report 1970: Report of the Proceedings of the 102nd Annual Trades Union Congress held in the Dome, Brighton, September 7th to 11th 1970* (London: TUC, 1970).
The Trades Union Congress, *TUC Report 1971: Report of the Proceedings of the 103rd Annual Trades Union Congress held in the Opera House, Blackpool, September 6th to 10th 1971* (London: TUC, 1971).
The Trades Union Congress, *Report of the 114th Annual Trades Union Congress held in the Conference Centre, Brighton, September 6th to 10th 1982* (London: TUC, 1982).

The Trades Union Congress, *Report of the 115th Annual Trades Union Congress held in the Opera House, Blackpool, September 5th to 9th 1983* (London: TUC, 1983).
The Trades Union Congress, *TUC Report 1984, Report of the 116th Annual Trades Union Congress held in Brighton Centre, Brighton, September 3rd to 7th 1984* (London: TUC, 1984).
Tressell, R., *The Ragged-Trousered Philanthropists* (London: Grant Richards, 1918).
Unterrainer, T. (ed.), *Corbyn's Campaign* (Spokesman: Nottingham, 2016).
Watson, I., *Five Million Conversations: How Labour Lost an Election and Rediscovered Its Roots* (Glasgow: Luath Press, 2015).
Wertheimer, E., *A Portrait of the Labour Party* (London: G. P. Putnam and Sons, 1930).
Westlake, M. (with St. John, I.), *Kinnock: The Biography* (London: Little, Brown and Company, 2001).
Wickham-Jones, M., *Economic Strategy and the Labour Party: Politics and Policy-making, 1970–83* (Basingstoke: Macmillan, 1996).
Wickham-Jones, M., 'Missed Opportunities: British social democracy and the Rehn model, 1951–1964' in H. Milner and E. Wadensjö (eds), *Gösta Rehn, the Swedish Model and Labour Market Politics* (Aldershot: Ashgate, 2001), 277–296.
Wickham-Jones, M., 'The Modernising Antecedents and Historical Origins of One Nation Labour', *The Political Quarterly*, 84:3 (2013), 321–329.
Williams, P. M., *Hugh Gaitskell: A Political Biography* (London: Cape, 1979).
Wilson, H., *Purpose in Power: Selected Speeches* (London: Weidenfeld and Nicolson, 1966).
Wilson, H., *The Labour Government 1964–1970: A Personal Record* (London: Weidenfeld and Nicolson, 1971).
Wright, T., *Why Vote Labour* (London: Penguin, 1997).
Wright, T. and Carter, M., *The People's Party: The History of the Labour Party* (London: Thames and Hudson, 1997).
Wrigley, C., *British Trade Unions, 1945–1995* (Manchester: Manchester University Press, 1997).
Young, H. (Trewin, I. ed.), *The Hugo Young Papers: Thirty Years of British Politics – Off the Record* (London: Penguin, 2008).

Index

Abbott, Diane 140, 158–160
Abrams, Mark 46
Adams, Lew 141
Alternative Economic Strategy (AES)
  academic analysis of 85–86, 101
  and European Economic Community (EEC) 86–87, 93–96, 101–102
  and import controls 86, 94–96
  and industrial democracy and workers' control 86, 96–101, 102, 188
  origins and formulation of 85–87
  party moves away from 110, 118, 122, 125, 127
  and public ownership 85–93, 96, 100–102
  and relationship to heritage boom 87
  situated in broader historical context 185, 187–190
Amalgamated Union of Engineering Workers 98
Andrew Marr Show 2
Aneurin Bevan Memorial Lecture (2010) 161
Arguments for Democracy 88–89, 101
Arguments for Socialism 88–89, 101
Associated Society of Locomotive Engineers and Firemen 141
Association of Scientific, Technical and Managerial Staff (ASTMS) 94, 99
Attlee, Clement 20, 89, 118, 122, 136, 141–142, 144–145, 149, 174
Attlee Governments (1945-51) 20, 63, 126, 142, 151, 159–160, 164, 169

Bacon, Alice 21
Balls, Ed 158–160, 165–166

Barratt-Brown, Michael 61
Bartoletti, Ivana 163
Beer, Samuel 16–17
'betrayal' of 1931 42, 67–70, 72, 74–76, 94, 123, 160
Benn, Hilary 172–173
Benn, Melissa 169
Benn, Tony 88–90, 93, 98, 101–102, 111, 115, 118, 123, 135–136, 138, 140, 144, 148, 150, 169
Better Together campaign 167
Bevan, Aneurin 17, 20, 22, 30, 31–33, 35, 61, 76, 89, 91, 111–112, 116–118, 124, 126, 142, 144–145, 148, 161, 165–166, 171–172, 174
Beveridge, William 142, 174
Bevin, Ernest 66, 142
Big Issue, The 171
Bish, Geoff 92, 122
Blair, Tony
  becomes Labour leader 137–138
  and 'Blairism' 134
  and centennial anniversary of 'Labour Party in Parliament' 148, 151–152
  centennial anniversary of LRC, speech at celebrations for 146–147
  and communitarianism 138, 142–143, 151–152, 162
  and criticisms of Kinnock era 109
  and fiftieth anniversary of Labour's 1945 General Election victory 142, 151–152
  and hostility towards the past 2–4, 126, 138, 141, 151–152, 163, 189–190

and modernisation 137–138, 141, 144, 151–152, 189
and political capital 145, 151–152, 189
and 'progressive alliance' narrative 134–135, 142, 151–152
and relationship with Gordon Brown 149
and revision of Clause IV 138–141, 150–151
Blake, William 90
Blatchford, Robert 34, 37–38, 41, 66
Blears, Hazel 145
block vote 21
Bloodworth, James 174
Blue Labour 160–163, 170, 176
Blumler, Jay 41
Blunkett, David 124
Bono 149
Boyd, John 72
Boym, Svetlana 7–9, 188
Bowman, Sir James 47
Bragg, Billy 162
Brassed Off 145
Brexit 172–173, 191–192
British Iron, Steel and Kindred Trades Association 22
British Empire 14
Brittan, Leon 115
Brown, George 37, 43, 61, 64, 66, 69, 74–76, 78
Brown, Gordon 137, 145–147, 149–150, 158, 167
Bryant, Chris 173
Bullock Report 100
Bunting, Madeleine 161–162
Burnham, Andy 158–160, 168, 169
Bush, George 149

Callaghan, James 72, 74, 122, 141
Campaign for Real Labour 144–145
Campaign for Socialism 165
Campbell, Alastair 121, 138
Carlyle, Thomas 166
Castle, Barbara 21, 32, 39, 46, 76–77, 126, 174
Catholic Herald 35
Centennial Report 147
'Change Britain Needs' 160
Chapple, Frank 92
Chartism 31, 71, 88–90, 101, 112–113, 115, 160, 166, 168
Chartist 148

Clause IV 2–3, 16, 30–31, 38–47, 49–52, 60, 62, 77, 88–89, 92, 102, 134–136, 138–141, 147, 150, 172, 188
Clause IV Consultation 139–140
Clerical and Administrative Workers' Union 22
Clwyd, Ann 147
Coal and Rail Transfer Bill 135
coal
  industry 2, 21, 47, 64, 68, 72, 74, 87–88, 91–93, 97, 110, 114, 135, 146, 169, 173
  miners 1, 21–22, 31, 36–38, 40, 42, 47, 61, 67, 72–74, 76, 97, 100–101, 110–116, 121, 125, 127, 135–136, 138, 145, 148, 150, 159, 164–165, 168, 174
Coalition 160
Coates, Ken 96–99, 140
Cole, George Douglas Howard 117, 171
Collins, Philip 1
Collins Review 166–167
Combination Laws 71, 76, 89
Confederation of British Industry 141
Connolly, James 74
Conservative Enemy, The 61
Conservative Party 6, 40, 42, 64–65, 67, 77, 91, 103, 111–112, 121, 125–126, 135, 149, 160, 164–166, 187
Cook, Arthur James 113–114
Cook, Robin 141
Co-operative movement 40, 160, 164, 171
Co-operative News 35
Cooper, Yvette 168–169
Corbyn, Jeremy
  advocated as future Labour leader 149
  becomes Labour leader 170–172
  and campaigning techniques 157–158, 176
  and 'Corbynism' 1, 157–158, 175–176
  and first annual conference speech as Labour leader 1–2
  and Labour leadership election (2015) 1, 2, 168–170, 176
  and Labour leadership election (2016) 173–176
  and opposition to leadership of 172–175
Corina, John 41

Index 211

Coronation Street 165
Cousins, Frank 39, 45–46, 69–70
Cripps, Stafford 118
Crosland, Anthony 20, 32–35, 61, 189
Crossman, Richard 50, 74
Cruddas, Jon 160–162, 166

Daily Mail, The 149
Daily Mirror, The 113, 165
Daily Record, The 174
Daily Telegraph, The 35, 121–122, 168, 172
Dalton, Hugh 38
d'Ancona, Matthew 159
Davies, Idris 91, 125
Day, Alan 95
definitions of nostalgia 4–5, 7–11
Democratic Socialist Aims and Values 122–123
Demos 135
Department of Economic Affairs (DEA) 66
devaluation (1967) 74–75
Dickens, Charles 121, 165
Diggers 112, 115
Disraeli, Benjamin 164–167
Dock Strike (1889) 88, 161
Donlon, Frank 73
Donovan Commission 75
Douglas-Home, Alec 64–65
Drucker, Henry 17–19
Durham Miners' Gala 1–2, 114, 145, 150

Eagle, Angela 173
Ebbw Vale 32
Economist, The 31, 35, 43, 47, 112, 137, 142–143, 145–146
Electrical, Electronic and Telecommunication Union – Plumbing Trades Union 77
Electrical Trades Union 45
English Civil War 112, 118, 171
Etchells, Brenda 146
European Union referendum 172

Fabian Society 32, 90, 110, 117, 122, 142, 163
Featherstone miners 115
Fenton, James 89
Fenwick Weavers' Society 171
Fields, Terry 118
'Fighters and Believers' 150
financial crisis (2008) 150, 157

Financial Times, The 35
Flanders, Allan 33–34
Flavius, Francis 94
Fletcher, Raymond 63
Foot, Michael 40, 90–91, 111, 118, 126, 144, 146
Foot, Paul 78
Forbes, Nick 166
Forward 36–38
founders and founding 1, 4, 48, 63, 64, 66, 75–76, 97, 111, 117, 119, 122, 126, 136, 138, 143, 145–147, 160–161, 167–170, 173–174, 186
free collective bargaining, labour movement's attachment to 19, 68–70, 75
Freedland, Jonathan 144
Freedom and Fairness Campaign 120
Fundamentalism 20, 30–31, 33, 39, 40–43, 46, 49, 51, 61, 67, 74
Future of Socialism, The 34–35
Future of the Party, The 47

Gaitskell, Dora 50
Gaitskell, Hugh
  academic analysis of 30–31, 51
  and attack on Clause IV 30, 38–41
  and compromise on Clause IV 43–44, 49, 188
  and death in 1963 50, 61
  and defeat on Clause IV 45–47, 49–52, 77
  and hostility towards the past 37, 39–40
  and *Industry and Society* 36
  and new statement of aims 44–47
  and response to Jay's *Forward* article 38
  and revisionism 30, 36, 89, 189
Galloway, George 148
Gas Workers' Union 48
Gellard, Ellie 150
General Election
  (1945) 63, 126, 142
  (1951) 22
  (1959) 30, 36, 40
  (1964) 60, 64–66
  (1966) 69
  (1970) 85
  (February 1974) 88
  (1979) 91
  (1983) 91–92, 99, 103, 110–111, 127, 187

(1987) 110, 121–122
(1992) 125–127, 135
(1997) 143–144, 151
(2001) 144
(2005) 148
(2010) 157
(2015) 167
General Strike 62, 88, 113
Giddens, Anthony 164
Gilhespy, Diana 99
Gill, Ken 114
Glasman, Maurice 160–163
Glittering Coffin, The 42–43
Goodman, Geoffrey 50, 113
Goodman, Helen 163
Gormley, Joe 100
Gould, Philip 4, 120, 122
Gothic Revival 8
Gracchi brothers 34
Grand National Consolidated Trades Union 97
Great War 6, 96, 148–149
Greenwood, Arthur 46
Griffiths, James 118
Guardian, The 38, 45, 50, 89–90, 117, 124, 137, 144, 164, 167–169
Guild Socialism 97, 161, 171
Gunter, Ray 48

Hain, Peter 145
Haines, Joe 165
Hammond, Barbara 34
Hammond, John 34
Hardie, Keir 1, 31, 33–35, 37–38, 41, 43, 48–49, 63, 65–68, 72, 76, 90, 98, 113, 119, 121–122, 126, 135, 138, 141, 145–149, 151, 158–160, 165–171, 173, 174, 185
Harman, Harriet 99, 142, 168
Hart, Judith 90
Hasan, Mehdi 162
Hatfield, Michael 94
Hattersley, Roy 89, 120, 144–145
Heath, Edward 127
Heffer, Eric 74, 112, 117, 119–120, 123
Henderson, Arthur 39
Hepburn, Stephen 145
Hetherington, Alastair 38, 47, 62
Hewitt, Patricia 99
Hinden, Rita 33–34, 41, 46
Hobsbawm, Eric 9, 11–12, 100, 110
Hoggart, Simon 90
Holland, Stuart 85–87, 93, 96, 102
Holocaust 9

Hunt, Tristram 165
Hyman, Peter 138
Hyndman, Henry 66

Independent Labour Party (ILP) 48, 71, 171
Independent, The 137, 143–144, 146, 167–168
Industry and Society 35–36, 50
In Place of Fear 20, 31, 76
In Place of Strife 76–77
Institute for Workers Control (IWC) 96–98
instrumental nostalgia, concept of 9–11, 34, 49–51, 116, 124, 142–143, 145, 151–152, 187–190
International Brigades 172
International Monetary Fund, loan from 90
Iraq War 148–149

Jacques, Martin 136
Jarrow 86 119–120
Jarrow March (1936) 32, 77, 88, 111, 119–120, 135, 148
Jay, Douglas 36–39
Jenkins, Clive 71, 94, 99
Jenkins, Peter 68
Jenkins, Roy 48, 74, 89–90, 94
Jobs and Industry Campaign 118–120, 127
Johnson, Alan 139–140, 169
July measures (1966) 69–70, 78

Keidanren 154
Keir Hardie Memorial Lecture
  (2010) 158–160
  (2016) 171
Kendall, Liz 168, 170
Keynesianism 85–86
Keynes, John Maynard 142
Kingsley, Charles 66
Kinnock, Neil
  academic analysis of 109–10, 127
  attacks Jeremy Corbyn's leadership 173
  and General Election (1987) 121
  and General Election (1992) 125–127
  and Jobs and Industry Campaign 118–120, 127, 151, 191
  and Labour leadership election (1983) 110–111
  and Labour leadership election (1988) 123–124

and letters of support to 110–111
and Militant Tendency 116–117, 127, 139
and 1984-5 Miners' Strike 112, 114–116
and modernisation 109–110, 112, 116–117, 119, 121–125, 127–128, 139, 190–191
New Labour's criticisms of 109, 127
oratorical skills of 111–112, 116, 121
personal background of 110, 114, 121, 124–125, 128
question in centennial magazine regarding 147
and Policy Review (1987) 122–124, 191
and response to Bullock Report 100
and Sheffield Rally 126–127
'Kinnock – The Movie' 121
Kitchener, Lord 12

Labour's Draft Manifesto 1980 91, 95
Labour in the Sixties 47–48
Labour Party
  annual conference (1951) 21–22
  annual conference (1956) 34
  annual conference (1957) 36
  annual conference (1959) 38–40
  annual conference (1960) 48–49
  annual conference (1963) 62–63
  annual conference (1964) 65–66
  annual conference (1965) 69
  annual conference (1966) 71
  annual conference (1967) 72
  annual conference (1968) 74, 76
  annual conference (1969) 77
  annual conference (1972) 98
  annual conference (1977) 100–101
  annual conference (1980) 86, 94
  annual conference (1982) 117–118
  annual conference (1983) 111–112
  annual conference (1984) 112–115
  annual conference (1985) 110, 115–116
  annual conference (1986) 120–121
  annual conference (1987) 122, 124
  annual conference (1988) 122–124
  annual conference (1989) 124
  annual conference (1990) 125–126
  annual conference (1991) 118, 125–126
  annual conference (1992) 135
  annual conference (1993) 135–137
  annual conference (1994) 3, 138–139
  annual conference (1995) 141, 143
  annual conference (1996) 143
  annual conference (1997) 142, 145
  annual conference (1999) 146
  annual conference (2003) 149
  annual conference (2004) 149
  annual conference (2009) 150
  annual conference (2012) 164, 166
  annual conference (2014) 165
  annual conference (2015) 1
  and 'Britishness' 13–14
  and 'class image of politics' 16–17
  and commitment to parliamentarianism 15–16, 18–19
  compared to its continental counterparts 187
  Constituency Labour Parties (CLPs) 21, 23, 31, 42, 48, 72, 111, 139
  emails to members 171–172
  and 'ethos' 17
  historical approaches to 13–20
  Home Policy Sub-Committee 50
  Industrial Policy Sub-Committee 87–88
  leadership election (1983) 110–111,
  leadership election (1988) 123–124
  leadership election (1994) 137
  leadership election (2010) 158–160, 166, 175
  leadership election (2015) 157, 168–170, 176
  leadership election (2016) 173–176
  membership, composition of 20–21, 23
  National Conference of Labour Women (1965) 67
  National Conference of Labour Women (1967) 71
  National Constitutional Committee 148
  National Executive Committee (NEC) 21, 44–48, 52, 64, 73, 76–77, 85, 98, 120, 122–123, 126, 149, 173
  Parliamentary Labour Party (PLP) 15, 23, 31, 68, 145–147, 163, 168, 173
  Policy Review (1987) 109–110, 122–124, 127, 191
  Policy Review (2010) 160–161, 166
  Policy Review Groups (PRGs) 122–123
  Scottish Labour Conference (2015) 171
  Scottish Labour Party 136, 165, 168
  Special Conference on Clause IV (1995) 140–141

Special Conference on Collins Review (2014) 167
Transport House 50
Welsh Labour Party Conference (1987) 121
Women's Committee 126
Labourism 186
LabourList 159
Labour Party News 126, 137, 139, 140
Labour's Programme 1973 85, 88
Labour's Programme 1976 85, 122
Labour's Programme 1982 91–92, 95, 122
Labour's Programme: Campaign Document 1974 88
Labour Representation Committee (LRC) 89, 146
Labour Solidarity Campaign 117
Labour Weekly 98, 113–114
Langham, Gladys 67
Lansbury, George 37, 89, 147
Lee, Jennie 17, 44–45, 76, 168
Left Foot Forward 159
Left Futures 165
Lenin 41
Let Us Work Together – Labour's Way Out of the Crisis 88
Levellers 89, 112, 115
Levi, Carlo 171
Liberal Democrats 142, 144, 160
Liberal Party 42, 134–135, 142
Livingstone, Ken 123
Lloyd George, David 142
Locke, John 33
London Olympics (2012) 164
Loveless, James 150
Luckhurst, Tim 149
Luddites 62

Maclean, John 100
Macpherson, Hugh 115
McCluskey, Len 173
McDonagh, Margaret 146–147
MacDonald, Ramsay 42, 67, 69, 74–76, 89, 94, 116–117, 123, 144, 147, 160, 173
McDonnell, John 149, 171
McGarvey, Danny 64, 70, 75
McKenzie, Robert 14–16, 18
McKie, David 90, 124
MacShane, Denis 121
Magee, Bryan 66–67
Major, John 10
Making Our Way 118–120, 127
Mandelson, Peter 2, 109, 120–121, 149

Manchester Guardian, The 31
Manifesto: Britain Will Win with Labour 119
Manifesto: New Labour because Britain Deserves Better 141
Marquand, David 89, 134, 142
Marris, Robin 40–41,
Marsh, Richard 70, 89
Marxism 90
Marx, Karl 33
May Day 42, 144
Mayhew, Henry 165
Maynard, Joan 115
Maxton, James 144
Meet the Challenge, Make the Change 109, 124
Men Who Made Labour 147–148
Mikardo, Ian 50
Miliband, David 140, 158–160
Miliband, Ed
   academic analysis of 157–158, 166
   becomes Labour leader 160
   and Blue Labour 162
   and Collins Review 167
   and General Election (2015) 167–168
   and Labour leadership contest (2010) 158–160
   and modernisation 157, 175
   and 'One Nation Labour' 164–166
   and resignation as Labour leader 168
   and Scottish independence referendum 167
Miliband, Ralph 15–16, 52
Militant Tendency 116–118, 127
Minkin, Lewis 18–19
Miners' Federation of Great Britain 97
Miners' Strike
   (1926) 31, 42, 88, 113–114
   (1984-5) 112–116, 127, 159, 174
minimum wage 145
Ministry of Technology 69–70
Mitchell, Austin 92, 121
Monk, Loraine 126
Morrell, Frances 116
Morrison, Herbert 36
Morris, William 34, 37, 66, 98, 117, 163
Mortimer, Jim 113
Mowlam, Mo 111
Mullin, Chris 145, 147

National Enterprise Board 86
National Government (1931) 42, 67, 160
National Health Service 111, 148, 171
National Plan 68–69

Index

National Union of Agricultural and Allied Workers 93
National Union of Dyers, Bleachers and Textile Workers 21–22, 73
National Union of Mineworkers (NUM) 21–22, 42, 47, 100, 112, 114, 116
National Union of Public Employees 22
New Britain, The 65
New Economy conference 171
New Fabian Essays 20, 32
New Hope for Britain, The 85, 91–92, 96, 101, 103
New Industrial Strength for Britain 119
New Labour
  academic analysis of 2–4, 16, 134–135
  compared to post-2010 Labour 175
  concessionary approach of 146–147, 149
  critique of 'Old Labour' 3–4, 109, 127, 134, 141, 150–151
  and failure to reorient the party of 150–152
  in government 143–150
  and opportunities offered by attack on Clause IV 3, 138, 141, 150–151
  and party's centennial anniversaries 146–148, 151
  presented as a return to the party's communitarian roots 143
  retrospective references to 157–163, 168, 170
  situated in broader historical context 120, 185, 190–191
  and 'values' 139
New Labour, New Life for Britain 3
New Left Review 49
New Liberalism 134–135, 142, 151
New Skills for Britain 119
New Socialist 115
New Statesman, The 45, 66–67, 69, 71, 73, 76, 89, 113, 147, 162
Nexus 141
nostalgia-identity, concept of 5–7, 9–13, 41, 52, 65–66, 77, 87, 97, 99–100, 102, 111–112, 118, 124–125, 127, 135, 139–140, 145, 150–151, 159, 161, 165, 168, 172, 175, 185–190, 192

Observer, The 95
O'Connor, Feargus 144
O'Hagan, Joe 70
One Member One Vote (OMOV) 125, 136–137
Orme, Stan 69

Osborne Judgement 71
Owen, Robert 66, 89, 97–98, 117–118, 135, 143, 163

Pallister, David 91
Parker, Geoffrey 61
Parry, Robert 117
Peasants' Revolt 89–90, 113, 118
Peel, Jack 73
Penny, Laurie 163
People's History Museum 169
Peterloo 31, 89, 115
Phillips, Morgan 41, 44
Philpot, Robert 163
picket line 13, 115
pioneers 31–32, 35, 39, 42–43, 47, 49, 51, 66–67, 71, 96–97, 99, 123, 135, 146, 148, 151, 160, 164, 166–167, 170–171, 174
Plebs 34
Policy Exchange 160
political rhetoric and nostalgia, relationship between 11–12
Potter, Dennis 42–43
Powell, Jonathan 3
Prescott, John 137, 139, 142, 145
Progress 162–164, 170
public ownership 19, 30–52, 62–63, 67–68, 85–86, 87–92, 96, 100–102, 123, 134–136, 138–141, 188

Ragged Trousered Philanthropists, The 135, 161
railways 9–11, 21, 73, 135
Record 33
Red Flag 39–40, 43, 49, 111, 138, 141, 145, 147, 149
Red Labour 165, 173, 176
red rose symbol replacing red flag 120–121
Referendum on membership of European Economic Community (1975) 86, 93–94
Reid, Jimmy 159
Reid, John 114
Revisionism 20, 30–40, 42, 46, 49, 51–52, 61–62, 189
Rhondda Socialists 97
Riddell, Mary 163
Robens, Alfred 89
Rochdale Pioneers 171
rules and norms 12–13, 18–19
Ruskin, John 66
Russian Revolution (1917) 140
Rutherford, Jonathan 161, 166

Salter, Alfred 37
Sankey Commission 97, 101
Sapper, Alan 95
Sawyer, Tom 118, 122, 124
Scargill, Arthur 113–114, 123, 138
Scottish independence referendum 167–168
Scottish national anthem 12
Scottish National Party 168
Second World War 5, 65–66, 93
Sellars, Ben 165
Shadow Communications Agency 120, 122
Shaw, George Bernard , 66
Shelley, Percy Bysshe 89, 126
shipyards and dockworkers 88, 97, 161, 168
Shore, Peter 75, 110, 121
Short, Clare 148–149
Short, Edward 68
Signposts for the Sixties 50
Skinner, Dennis 135–136
Smith, John 109, 127, 135–137
Smith, Owen 164, 173–175
Snowden, Philip 42, 75, 89
Social Democratic Party (SDP) 89
Socialist Campaign Group News 140, 144
Socialist Commentary 33, 40–41, 45, 61, 68, 70–71, 90
Socialist Conference (1987) 123
Socialist Union 33–34
Social Justice and Economic Efficiency 122–123
Socioeconomic change 3–4, 16, 20, 31–32, 36, 38, 46, 61, 64, 70–74, 78, 91, 97–100, 110, 117–118, 122–123, 125, 150, 175, 187–188, 191–192
Spencer Union 113
spontaneous and expressive nostalgia, concept of 10–11, 13, 124, 143, 145, 176, 188–189
State of the Party, The 47
Stears, Marc 161–162
steel
 industry 21, 31, 67–68, 87–88, 91, 93–94, 172
 renationalisation of 67–68
 workers 22, 97
Stanley, Edward 165
Stanley, Tim 172
Straw, Jack 116, 136

struggles of the 1920s and 1930s 38–40, 42, 48, 61–63, 70–71, 73, 77, 90, 92, 111–112, 114–115, 123, 126, 137, 140, 168, 172, 186
suffragettes 169
Sunday Times, The 126, 136
Sutcliffe, Thomas 146
Sylvester, Rachel 174
syndicalism 96

Taff Vale 71
Tawney, Richard Henry 90, 117, 171
'Tax bombshell' 127
technological change, hostility to 64, 66–67, 78, 163
textile
 industry 21, 61, 63, 73, 93, 164,
 workers 21–22, 73, 171
Textile Factory Workers' Association 22
Thatcher, Margaret 6, 91, 103, 115, 134
This is the Labour Party 41
Thomas, James 42, 75
Thorne, Will 48
Times, The 1, 3, 31–34, 43, 63, 67, 94, 163, 174
Todd, Ron 124
Tolpuddle Martyrs 31, 62, 71, 76, 93, 115, 118, 150
Tolpuddle Martyrs' Festival 2, 116, 150
Trade Disputes Act 71
trade unions 3–4, 10, 13, 18–19, 21–22, 33, 39–40, 42, 45–50, 62, 64, 68–71, 73, 75–78, 89–91, 93–94, 97–100, 112–115, 117, 124, 126, 136, 139, 150, 159, 164, 172–173
Trades Union Congress (TUC) 18, 70, 75, 77, 88, 113, 115
 annual Congress (1960) 47–48
 annual Congress (1963) 62
 annual Congress (1964) 64
 annual Congress (1965) 68–69
 annual Congress (1966) 70
 annual Congress (1967) 73, 75
 annual Congress (1968) 76
 annual Congress (1969) 77
 annual Congress (1970) 93
 annual Congress (1971) 93, 99
 annual Congress (1982) 95
 annual Congress (1983) 92
 annual Congress (1984) 114
 annual Congress (2013) 165
 Centenary Pageant 75–76
 centennial Congress (1968) 75

Index

Trades Union Congress – Labour Party Liaison Committee 100
Transport and General Workers' Union 33, 39, 45–46, 49, 69, 124
Tressell, Robert 161
Tribune 33, 37–38, 40, 42–44, 49, 63, 66, 68–69, 74, 76–77, 89–90, 94, 97, 99, 115–116, 123–124, 148–149, 160, 162, 165
Twentieth Century Socialism 33–34
Tyler, Wat 89–90

unilateral nuclear disarmament 49
Union of Communication Workers 139
Union of Democratic Mineworkers 113
Union of Shop, Distributive and Allied Workers 22
Unite the Union 173
University of Cambridge's Department of Applied Economics 94

visual representations and nostalgia 12

Walden, Brian 73
Webb, Beatrice 35, 39, 89, 140
Webb, Sidney 35, 39, 41, 89, 139–140
Wertheimer, Egon 13–14, 18
White, Eirene 48
Whitty, Larry 122, 139
Why Vote Labour? 143
Wilkinson, Ellen 111
Willis, Norman 115
Willman, John 122

Wilson, Harold
  academic analysis of 60–61, 69, 77
  becomes Labour leader 61
  and comparisons to Gaitskell 77
  and devaluation (1967) 74
  and 'first industrial revolution' 72–73
  and General Election (1964) 64–65
  and General Election (1970) 85
  and incomes policy 69–71, 76
  mobilising party members 66
  and modernisation 60–63, 65, 68–69, 71, 77, 188, 190
  and NEC meeting discussing Clause IV (1960) 44
  and response to further pit closures 72, 78
  retrospective references to leadership of 122, 141, 145
  and 'spirit of Dunkirk' 65
  and trade union reform 75–78
  and 'white heat' speech 60–64, 68, 190
Wintour, Patrick 164
Wise, Audrey 99
Woodburn, Arthur 63
Workers' Control Bulletin 97, 99
Wright, Lord 75
Wright, Tony 143
World Cup Final (1966) 6
Wyatt, Woodrow 89

Young European Left 93
Young, Hugo 112, 117, 135
Young Socialists 88

EU authorised representative for GPSR:
Easy Access System Europe, Mustamäe tee 50,
10621 Tallinn, Estonia
gpsr.requests@easproject.com

www.ingramcontent.com/pod-product-compliance
Lightning Source LLC
Chambersburg PA
CBHW070238240426

43673CB00044B/1838